BRIAN J. YOUNG is a member of the Department of History at McGill University.

The history of the north-shore railways provides a case study in the complexities of industrial development in nineteenth-century Quebec. Constructed in the fifteen years following Confederation, the North Shore and the Montreal Colonization Railways reinforced Quebec's integration into a transcontinental unit. Yet bankruptcy of both companies in 1875 forced the provincial government to assume ownership of the railways and to shoulder a financial burden that kept the province preoccupied, weak, and subservient to Ottawa.

Diverse political, clerical, and business interests united to construct the railways and to manoeuvre them from private companies into a public venture and ultimately into the Canadian Pacific system.

The two railways brought new concentrations of capital and power that cut across French and English ethnic lines and sharpened regional rivalries. Along the south shore of the St. Lawrence both French- and English-speaking inhabitants protested against the province's commitments to its north-shore railways. By the late 1870s Quebec City's English community was lobbying hard against the growing power of their English-speaking counterparts in Montreal.

The north-shore railways plagued a generation of Quebec politicians, and their construction bared incompatible regional aspirations. By 1885 years of negotiation, scandal, and political blackmail culminated in the incorporation of the two north-shore railways into the Canadian Pacific system. As this study so clearly demonstrates, Quebec paid a high price in making its contribution to linking Canada by steel *a mari usque ad mare*.

BRIAN J. YOUNG

Promoters and Politicians:
The North-Shore Railways in
the History of Quebec, 1854-85

UNIVERSITY OF TORONTO PRESS
Toronto Buffalo London

ISBN 978-0-8020-5377-0 (cloth)
ISBN 978-1-4875-8687-4 (paper)

Canadian Cataloguing in Publication Data

Young, Brian J., 1940-
    Promoters and politicians

    Bibliography: p.
    Includes index.
    ISBN 978-0-8020-5377-0 (bound). – ISBN 978-1-4875-8687-4 (pbk.)

    1. North Shore Railway (Quebec). 2. Montreal Colonization Railway.
    3. Quebec, Montreal, Ottawa and Occidental Railway. I. Title.

HE 2810.N 56Y 58   385'.09714   C 77-001552-2

I would rather meet a patent-rights man, or a book-pedlar, or a lightning-rod professor, or any other sort of man, than a man who has railway on the brain, and who comes to ask me for a subsidy.

Provincial Treasurer of Quebec
December 1875

Contents

Preface

During the turbulent years of the Laurendeau-Dunton Commission, the flag debate, Trudeaumania, and the FLQ, I was teaching in an Ottawa high school only a snowball's throw from the Parliament Buildings. Puzzled by Canada's insoluble problems, I returned to Queen's University. There I rekindled questions about Canadian society which had lain dormant since the 1962-3 University of Toronto seminars of Ramsay Cook and John Saywell. At Queen's I had the good fortune to combine Donald Swainson's approach to the politics and entrepreneurs of Ontario with Frederick W. Gibson's demanding seminars on French Canada.

Like most young academics I have received generous financial assistance. An Ontario Graduate Fellowship and a Canada Council grant helped in the early stages, and later research support was provided by the William H. Donner Foundation through the Canadian Studies Program at the University of Vermont. The Public Archives of Canada, the Douglas Library and Archives of Queen's University, Les Archives de la Province de Québec, and the government documents section of La Bibliothèque Nationale de Québec were particularly helpful as research centres.

The book has been published with the help of a grant from the Social Science Federation of Canada, using funds provided by the Canada Council, and a grant to University of Toronto Press from the Andrew W. Mellon Foundation.

This book is dedicated to Dale Leary-Young - who knows why.

Clear Lake, Muskoka
August 1976

Introduction

Between 1854 and 1885 the North Shore Railway and the Montreal Colonization Railway dominated railway development along the north shores of the St Lawrence and Ottawa rivers. Chartered in 1853, the North Shore Railway ultimately joined Quebec City and Montreal. The Montreal Colonization Railway was given a charter in 1869 to link Montreal to Ottawa and points west. Before 1867 railways were peripheral factors in Quebec's economic life. After Confederation railway mania swept the province, and Roman Catholic clerics, municipalities, competing business groups, and politicians took sides on the issue of north-shore railway development. Constructed in the fifteen years after Confederation, the two railways reinforced the province's integration into a transcontinental economic unit. The bankruptcy of both companies in 1875 forced the provincial government to assume ownership of the two railways and to unite them into the Quebec, Montreal, Ottawa and Occidental Railway. Financial difficulties resulting from its railway expenditures kept the province preoccupied, weak, and subservient to Ottawa.

Diverse political, clerical, and business interests came together to construct the railways and to manoeuvre them from private companies into a public venture and ultimately into the Canadian Pacific system. Merchants, bankers, shippers, contractors, political leaders, and clergymen could all agree - for varying reasons - on the importance of the railway. Construction of the railway was in the private or political interests of leaders like Joseph Cauchon, Hector Langevin, Curé Labelle, Hugh Allan, and Louis-Adélard Sénécal; each promoted it as being in the public interest. This union of public and private interests - a traditional tool of railway builders - was particularly useful in Quebec where railways could be promoted as 'colonization' projects or 'national' enterprises. The most vocal opposition to the north-shore railway development came from the backers of competing railways. French Canadians, attracted by the potential for profits and economic growth, joined enthusiastically in the scramble to link their villages to the larger centres of Montreal and Quebec City. Entrepreneurs were received with respect by local élites and, over a generation, the north-shore populace came to accept railways as synonymous with progress, industrialization, and colonization. Railway builders capitalized on these feelings by giving their railways regional or colonization names and by naming local priests, politicians, and merchants to their boards of directors. Construction of the North Shore and Montreal Colonization railways also emphasized the growing dominance of Montreal. Railways became steel spokes binding the periphery of the province to the hub of Montreal. This concentration of power in Montreal inevitably aroused regional sensitivities, especially from Quebec City, its aging downstream rival.

The two north-shore railways brought new concentrations of capital and power that cut across French and English ethnic lines. In Montreal the Grand Trunk and Canadian Pacific rivalry helps explain much of that city's tangled history in the 1870s and 1880s. Along the south shore of the St Lawrence both French- and English-speaking inhabitants protested against the province's commitments to its north-shore railways. By the late 1870s, Quebec City's English community was lobbying hard against the growing power of their English-speaking counterparts in Montreal. The participation of French-Canadian entrepreneurs in the construction and administration of the two railways was equally complex. Hector Langevin and Joseph Cauchon had much in common with regional politicians from other North-American communities. French Canadians like Louis-Adélard Sénécal and Joseph-Adolphe Chapleau were able to form political-entrepreneurial partnerships that exploited Quebec's railway fever with great success. On the other hand, some French-Canadian lawyers and priests were simply 'front men' for English-speaking entrepreneurs like Hugh Allan.

Railway construction always had important political implications, and the north-shore railways plagued a generation of Quebec politicians including Charles-Eugène Boucher de Boucherville, Joseph-Adolphe Chapleau, Henri Joly, and Hector Langevin. After Confederation the Conservative party in Quebec faced recurring crises – *le programme catholique*, Cartier's defeat and death, the Tanneries scandal, the subservience of the provincial party to John A. Macdonald, the issue of clerical interference, the university question. In baring incompatible regional aspirations in Quebec, the north-shore railways accentuated Conservative difficulties. Chapleau's sale of the railways in 1882 brought matters to a climax. In July 1882, he escaped to Macdonald's cabinet and left the provincial battlefield to the ultramontanes and Honoré Mercier's Liberals. By 1885 years of negotiation, scandal, and political blackmail had culminated in the incorporation of the two north-shore railways into the Canadian Pacific system.

Promoters and Politicians is not a history of post-Confederation Quebec. Jean Hamelin and Yves Roby (*Histoire économique du Québec: 1851-1896*) give an economic overview of the province; Andrée Désilets (*Hector-Louis Langevin: un père de la confédération canadienne*) and Marcel Hamelin (*Les premières années du parlementarisme québécois: 1867-1878*) treat the tangled political arena. Nor is it an attempt in the Fogel tradition to analyse systematically the social and economic impact of railways on Quebec society. This may now be possible by examining the records of the railway recently acquired by the National Archives of Quebec. Rather, this book demonstrates the degree of state interference in Quebec's economic life and the contribution of railways to the province's political instability. This approach is in contrast to the central role often given to ultramontanism, church-state relations, and Rouge-Conservative ideological battles. The theme makes the province's sale of the railway the logical climax. After 1882 the scene shifts from Quebec to Ottawa caucus rooms and the boardrooms of the Grand Trunk and Canadian Pacific. That story, although summarized in the final chapter, is yet to be told.

Maps

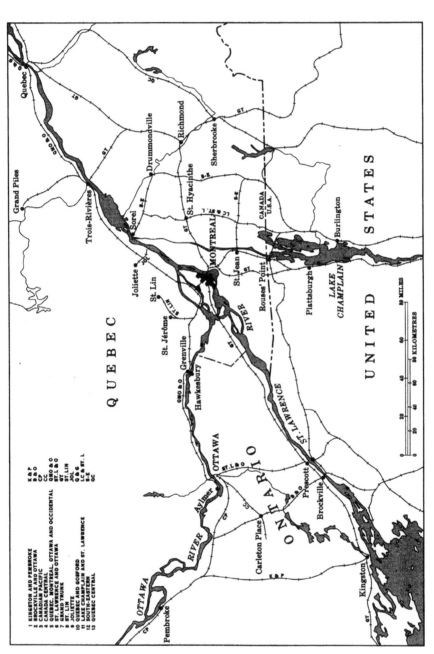

Map A Railways in the Montreal area, 1882. From *Belden Illustrated Atlas of the Dominion of Canada* (Toronto 1881) and Collingwood Schreiber, *Railways of Canada* (Ottawa 1882)

1 KINGSTON AND PEMBROKE
2 BROCKVILLE AND OTTAWA
3 CANADIAN PACIFIC
4 CANADA CENTRAL
5 QUEBEC, MONTREAL, OTTAWA AND OCCIDENTAL
6 ST. LAWRENCE AND OTTAWA
7 GRAND TRUNK
8 ST. LIN
9 JOLIETTE
10 QUEBEC AND GOSFORD
11 LAKE CHAMPLAIN AND ST. LAWRENCE
12 SOUTH-EASTERN
13 QUEBEC CENTRAL

K & P
B & O
C P
C C
QMO & O
ST. L & O
GT
ST. LIN
JOL
Q & G
LCC ST. L
S-E
QC

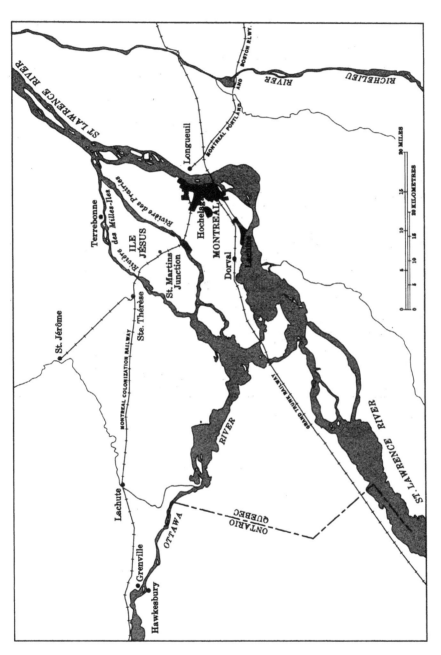

Map B Montreal Colonization Railway: Hochelaga to Ottawa River and branch line to St. Jérôme, 1880

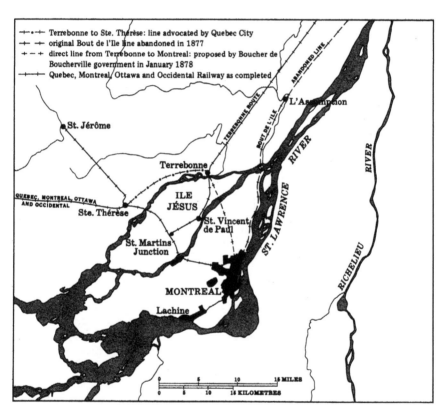

Map C Rival routes into Montreal

PROMOTERS AND POLITICIANS

1

The first charter and the search for capital

In the mid nineteenth century, railway entrepreneurs were rising to positions of dominance throughout North America. By 1860 railway mileage in the United States had increased to five times that of 1849; during the 1850s over 22,000 miles of track were laid. Time of travel between New York and Chicago was reduced from three weeks to three days.[1] Railways created new patterns of business and brought power to rising communities like Chicago. They stimulated innovations in finance, management, labour relations, and government regulation. Their social and political impact was just as important. Communities that had cherished their independence discovered that their futures were determined by decisions made in distant boardrooms, by engineering reports, and by the availability of foreign capital.

The power and gilded pockets of the railway entrepreneur enabled him to manipulate politicians, and as early as the 1850s the stage was being set for what Gabriel Kolko has called 'political capitalism' - 'the utilization of political outlets to attain rationalization in the economy.'[2] Faced by a consensus among its leaders in favour of economic expansion, the public accepted long-term tax burdens to pay for railway development. Before 1873 American state and federal governments granted $350 million plus millions of acres of land to American railroads.[3] Municipalities, panicked into competing with neighbouring communities for a route or terminus, added substantially to the public contribution to railways. The attitudes of French Canadians to railways were similar to those of other North Americans, and their politicians eagerly joined the railway sweepstakes.

By the 1850s the tone of Canadian politics was changing. The trauma caused by the 1837 rebellions, the Durham Report, and the Union Act had subsided, and the LaFontaine–Baldwin era, with its cooperation and battles for important principles, was drawing to a close. In the Upper Province, the Grits, aggressive and hostile to French Canadians, were demanding social and economic measures suited to their particular regional needs. Scrappy young communities like Toronto were contesting the hegemony of Kingston, Montreal, and Quebec City.

For their part, French Canadians were less prone to the self-pity, soul-searching, and idealism of the Papineau years. By the early 1840s, most French-Canadian politicians had put the dreams of 1837 behind them and had turned to more limited goals. Personality, patronage, and regional interests dominated their politics. Under the tutelage of L.H. LaFontaine, Francis Hincks, and A.N. Morin, young, working politicians like George-Etienne Cartier, Hector Langevin, and Joseph Cauchon saw that the imperfect political solution hammered out in the 1840s provided a means by which French-Canadian bourgeois could prosper. By the 1850s middle-aged former patriotes like Cartier had long since abandoned the rhetoric of rebellion in favour of a vigorous defence of the status quo. Acting like respectable conservatives, Lower-Canadian leaders praised the British constitution and willingly accepted the decade's innumerable compromises and coalitions. Nationalism, colonization, and catholicism were still heady, uniting symbols that could never be ignored; the failure of the Rouges to muster significant public support was continuing testimony to this reality. But whatever their rhetoric, French-Canadian politicians devoted much of their energies to protecting the economic interests of their constituents. Charged with regionalism and with class, urban, and ethnic rivalries, Lower-Canadian politics was a complicated business, and only on the gravest of national occasions could a united front be presented. Montrealers took daily swipes at their Quebec City competitors, residents on the south shore of the St. Lawrence complained about government expenditures on the north shore, and the rural populace attacked the growing dominance of urban centres. Nor could the province's English-speaking population be ignored by any politician who cherished power. Important in Quebec City, Montreal, and the Eastern Townships, the English insisted on their separate institutions, their independent way of life, and their commercial hegemony.

Despite these internal divisions, there was a general consensus throughout Canada in the 1850s on the importance of railway development. Leaders with such varying viewpoints as George Brown, Joseph Cauchon, A.A. Dorion, and the archbishop of Quebec all joined in tribute to the potential of the iron ribbon. French-Canadian politicians, entrepreneurs, and clerics generally shared this enthusiasm and equated railways with progress: to oppose them was reactionary. In their brochures and speeches, railway promoters often compared railways to the arteries of the human body. Capital became blood, and essential nourishment was to be provided by government subsidies. Any slowdown in the flow of blood, nourishment, or subsidies meant decay for the body.[4]

This consensus on the value of railways and the need for public financial support was reflected in Canada's railway legislation. The Legislative Assembly's Railway Committee dispensed charters willingly, if usually to friends of the government. Under the Guarantee Act of 1849, the government could guarantee 6 per cent interest on half the cost of any railway over seventy-five miles in length. Although this guarantee was soon restricted to specific trunk lines, the principle of government assistance to railways was firmly established. At the same time, the British government seemed ready to grant an imperial guarantee to certain railways. As well, the Municipal Loan Act of 1852 made it possible for municipalities to finance railways. With this vigorous public support, railway mileage in Canada increased from 66 miles in 1850 to 1700 miles by 1860.[5]

The North Shore Railway was conceived as Quebec City's contribution to the anticipated railway bonanza. In 1850 Quebec City had steamboat and stage connections with Montreal. Passengers bound for Montreal by stage left Quebec City at 5:00 AM and reached Three Rivers, the half-way point, after fourteen bumpy hours on the 'royal route.' With an early start the following day, the coach arrived in Montreal in the evening. The North Shore Railway could drastically improve these arduous land communications. Linking communities along the north shore of the St. Lawrence between Quebec City and Montreal with feeder lines into the St. Maurice and Ottawa valleys, the railway would bolster the sagging economic fortunes of Quebec City, enlarge her hinterland, and draw western commerce to her port.

These railway aspirations were dependent on Quebec City's successful competition with Montreal. To reach Quebec City, western trade had to pass Montreal's doorstep. However, ambitious Montrealers like the Molsons, James Ferrier, and John Young had been among the first Canadians to sense the importance of railways. They promoted lines to New York, Portland, Toronto, and Ottawa and talked of a bridge over the St. Lawrence at Montreal. Soap and candle producers, tobacco factories, planing and grist mills, tanneries, brickyards, warehousing facilities, shipyards, biscuit and cotton manufacturers, rolling mills, steam-engine plants, and nail industries gave Montreal a commercial and industrial strength which Quebec City could not match.[6] The deepening of the St. Lawrence ship channel to fourteen feet and the growth of steam power added to this concentration of power in Montreal. Her port specialized in grain, British manufactured goods, and West Indian products.[7] Ocean-steamer tonnage in Montreal increased from 5545 tons in 1854 to 62,912 tons in 1862. This economic activity was reflected in population growth: the city doubled between 1825 and 1844, and again by 1870.

The North Shore Railway's difficulties in the 1850s and 1860s can in part be attributed to Quebec City's growing subservience to Montreal. Although Montreal faced more important commercial threats – from Boston and New York, the Ogdensburg Railway and the Erie Canal – Montrealers never neglected their Laurentian or lower St. Lawrence hinterland. By 1861 Montreal had a population of 90,323. In the decade between 1851 and 1861 Quebec City had grown at a much slower pace from 42,052 to 51,109.[8] In contrast to Montreal's broadening commercial and manufacturing base, Quebec City was dependent on ship-building and the square-timber trade. Neither industry was oriented to railways. In addition, England's abolition of Baltic timber duties, the rising American demand for sawn lumber, the increasing competition of north-south trade routes, and the Reciprocity Treaty of 1854 permitting free entry of lumber into the United States were endangering the square-timber trade. The city's minor industries faced strong competition from Montreal. Quebec City's forty-four tanneries imported three-quarters of their hides from Ontario and the West, and after tanning they were returned to markets in Montreal. Of the thirty-one bakeries in the city in 1870, only two had more than four employees. The three soap and candle manufacturers depended on tallow shipped from Montreal, and the two largest breweries bought western barley since local barley was considered inferior.[9] One Maine newspaper dismissed the railway potential of Quebec City: 'in reference to a Railroad to Quebec, it was never seriously entertained by any person at all conversant with the Canadas. Quebec has for many years ceased to be a place of any considerable business, ... and though a place of great attractions for its military fortifications and historical incidents, its junctive position in the midst of a mountainous region, renders it comparatively forbidding as a place of residence, and with the exception of its lumber trade, its business is still on the decrease. Nine tenths at least of all the travel to, and from Quebec is by the way of Montreal.'[10]

The proximity of the proposed railway to the St. Lawrence River was another major weakness. The North Shore Railway would run parallel to the river, often within sight of its shipping competition. Deepening of the ship channel between Quebec City and Montreal in the 1850s permitted larger ocean vessels to sail directly to Montreal. This contrasted to the area west of Montreal where the necessity of canals and indirect water routes made railways more competitive. Nor did the north-shore counties show signs of imminent prosperity. Assomption, Berthier, Montcalm, St. Maurice, Champlain, and Portneuf counties were developed only along their St. Lawrence fringe. Except for river valleys, the back country remained the domain of the woodcutter and trapper. In 1851 the counties' main non-agricultural endeavours were small tanneries and a few family-operated carding, saw, or grist mills. Capital investment was limited, and few industries utilized steam power; the two foundries in St. Maurice county employed a total of four men. The annual produce in 1861 of Champlain county's two pot and pearl ash factories totalled $431. Portneuf was a typical north-shore county. In 1851 it had fifteen grist mills, ten carding mills, thirty-five saw mills, and two tanneries.[11] Three Rivers, the only major town between Quebec City and Montreal, was ridiculed by the Montreal *Gazette* as a 'slough of despond.'

In addition to Quebec City's weakening commercial position and the questionable economic potential of the north-shore countryside, the North Shore Railway faced powerful opposition from the Grand Trunk Railway. When completed in 1860 the Grand Trunk extended from Sarnia, Ontario, through Montreal and the Eastern Townships to Portland, Maine. Far from the main line, Quebec City was served by a spur from the Eastern Townships' village of Richmond. A rail trip from Quebec City to Montreal in 1854 took twenty-one hours and entailed a ferry crossing to the Grand Trunk station in Lévis and a change of trains at Richmond (see map A). The Grand Trunk continued to expand its south-shore operations and by 1860 had extended its line from Lévis to Rivière du Loup. Nor did it ignore north-shore trade. There were rumours of a Grand Trunk line up the St. Maurice Valley, and in December 1858 a dock was completed in Three

Rivers to facilitate trade between the north shore and the Grand Trunk spur at Arthabaska.

Committed to Montreal, Portland, and the expansion of its south-shore traffic, the Grand Trunk opposed construction of a competing line that would draw western trade along the north shore to Quebec City. The Grand Trunk had powerful banking and newspaper friends and the ear of the Canadian government: Canada's financial representatives in London doubled as agents for the Grand Trunk. With the solvency of a number of institutions, including the government, dependent upon its success, the Grand Trunk played a decisive role in delaying construction of the North Shore Railway. In 1858 one frustrated North Shore promoter concluded that 'formerly the Government was in the Grand Trunk Company, but now the Grand Trunk Company was in the Government.'[12]

Within Quebec City the Grand Trunk had powerful support. Six of its original directors - William Price, George Pemberton, James Bell Forsyth, William Rhodes, George Beswick, and Henry Le Mesurier - were prominent Quebec City businessmen. Forsyth was probably typical. A leading timber broker, he had strong family ties to banking and shipping circles in Kingston, Montreal, and London. He sold property in Lévis to the Grand Trunk and anticipated that the railway would increase the value of his south-shore holdings in Megantic County. In 1858 the Quebec City Board of Trade, on which both Forsyth and his partner had served as president, petitioned the British Parliament for financial aid in extending the Grand Trunk to the Pacific. Two years later Forsyth felt obliged to reassure North Shore Railway officials that, while his opposition to the railway was well known, he would not denigrate the railway to his London banking friends.[13]

In their battle against the Grand Trunk and its Montreal allies, the North Shore promoters could not match the political power of Cartier, Alexander Galt, and Etienne-Pascal Taché. If all else failed, Grand Trunk supporters in the Assembly drowned out their critics with what one reporter described as 'sneezing, kicking of desks, and a variety of zoological imitations.'[14] Nor could Quebec City ally with other metropolitan centres. The Toronto *Globe* for instance, had no intention of sacrificing Upper Canada to what it called 'the demands of French Canadians.'[15]

Despite these obstacles Quebec City entrepreneurs fought for decades to promote their city as a railway centre. Initially, they favoured a railway to the Maritimes. As early as 1836 New Brunswick incorporated a railway which would join St. Andrews to Quebec City; promoters in Saint John and Halifax produced a number of plans for railways to the St. Lawrence. Fifteen years later Quebec City's hopes were still high. City fathers petitioned for an imperial subsidy for a railway to the Maritimes and commissioned plans for a 3400 foot suspension-bridge across the St. Lawrence. However, by 1850 Quebec City railway promoters were competing fiercely among themselves. Some continued to advocate a link to the Maritimes, others were Grand Trunk supporters, while a third group pressed for a line along the north shore of the St. Lawrence. The latter promoters downplayed trade with the Maritimes and emphasized Quebec City's potential as the entrepôt between the West and Europe. Amid speculation that Quebec City would become the eastern terminus of a transcontinental trunk line, a public meeting was called for 9 March 1852.

At this rally for the North Shore Railway, both French and English speakers adopted the vigorous language of the North American railway entrepreneur. The seigneur of Lotbinière was typical. Refuting suggestions that a municipal subsidy might endanger the public treasury, J.H. Joly pointed out that Quebec City was 'already last in the race' and challenged his audience to 'cite a single city of the importance of Quebec in the United States, in France, or in England that has not already assured itself of a railroad.' Comparing railways to the sustaining blood of the human body, the seigneur predicted that 'wherever those iron arteries do not carry life there will be decay.'[16] Another speaker emphasized that his St. Maurice constituents 'felt so keenly their position - "Laggards, while all the rest of the world was advancing" ' - that they would undoubtedly subscribe $30,000 to the railway. Finally, Joseph Cauchon told the audience that they would be 'dishonoured' if they remained 'supinely idle while every one around them was moving.'

The meeting named a committee of seventy-five to organize the company and to secure a charter. Virtually every parish between Montreal and Quebec City was represented, usually by a local politician. Ominously, Montreal was not represented on the committee, and *La Minerve*, Montreal's most important French-language Conservative paper, suggested that the promoters intended to by-pass Montreal and to build directly to Georgian Bay: 'Les habitants de Montréal ne peuvent pas raisonnablement être appelés à coopérer dans la confection d'un embranchement dans lequel ils n'ont aucun intérêt et qui ne peut leur apporter aucun profit.'[17] With thirty-three representatives,

Quebec City dominated the organizational committee. Important businessmen like Weston Hunt, James Gibb, Jeffery Hale, and Mayor Narcisse Belleau sat on the committee as did four members of the Legislative Assembly, Joseph Cauchon, Eugène Chinic, Ulric-Joseph Tessier, and George O'Kill Stuart. Three Rivers also caught railway fever. Responding to editorials entitled 'Une Question de Vie ou de Mort' and 'To Be or Not To Be,' participants at a rally formed a railway committee and adopted unanimous resolutions in favour of the North Shore Railway and a railway in the St. Maurice Valley.[18]

Two young Quebec City politicians, Hector Langevin and Joseph Cauchon, dominated the North Shore Railway in the 1850s. Langevin, who was secretary-treasurer of the railway, had followed one of the classic routes for a French-Canadian bourgeois: studies at the Petit Seminaire, entry into the prestigious law offices of A.N. Morin and George-Etienne Cartier, and private English courses in Kingston. His brother, Jean, was curé of Beauport and later bishop of Rimouski. Another brother, Edmond, became vicar-general to the archbishop of Quebec. Langevin built up his political base by serving as an alderman and mayor of Quebec City and president of both the Institut Canadien and the St. Jean Baptiste Society. Steadfastly conservative, he rejected Papineau: 'l'homme est évidemment craqué.'[19] Joseph Cauchon, first president of the railway, was a more abrasive individual. Although trained as a lawyer, he was primarily a journalist and politician. Small and near-sighted, Cauchon was a fierce debater who had the gift of arousing strong passions: 'When Cauchon is meek / He is weak, weak, weak / When noisy and blunt / He is grunt, grunt, grunt; / When he tries to look big / He is pig, pig, pig ... '[20] Like Langevin, Cauchon opposed the annexation movement of 1849 and accused Papineau of leading French Canada to genocide: 'il y a des hommes qui sont puissants à détruire, mais qui n'ont jamais rien élevé sur les ruines qu'ils ont faites ... Mais il y a quelque chose de plus pour le législateur que de crier aux injustices du passé: il y a le besoin de l'avenir ... '[21]

Sold on railways and economic expansion, Cauchon and Langevin pushed the Quebec City committee to obtain a charter, raise capital, and find a contractor. Commissioned to survey the route between Quebec City and Montreal, Edward Stavely found few obstacles to construction. Bridges, particularly the crossing of the St. Maurice River at Three Rivers, were the major cost factors. The Stavely survey was vague on revenues, total construction costs, and financing. In 1852 J.H. Joly, basing his estimate on the general supposition that railways generated ten shillings of business for every person in the territory served, predicted annual revenues of £125,000. Two years later, Cauchon escalated this estimate to £313,000. The earliest construction estimates varied from £3000 to £4000 a mile for a total cost of between £450,000 and £600,000.[22] By 1856 estimates had risen to £8000 a mile. Initially, the promoters proposed raising half of their capital under the Guarantee Act of 1849 and the balance by a £100,000 subsidy from Quebec City, municipal and county contributions of £90,000, and individual subscriptions of £35,000.

If the financing and costs remained nebulous, the promises were not. Officials lauded the resources, mills, tanneries, timber depots, and manufacturing potential of the north shore. One company brochure commented on the stone quarry, shipyard, and pail manufacturer at Pointe-aux-Trembles, the iron mine and paper plant on the Portneuf River, and the mills, pail-maker, and foundry in the village of Industry. Nor was the commercial potential of Quebec City left unsung. Cauchon predicted that the square-timber trade, ship-building, fishing, and local water-power resources could bring prosperity to the old city. All that was needed was a railway. Local taxpayers were assured that their city would 'become the depot of the riches of the West, and one of the greatest seaport towns in the world ... ' Nor should the citizenry be concerned with heavy public investment in the railway since, in the language of one resolution, 'on this young continent credit may to so great an extent be substituted for money.'[23]

Swept along by this enthusiasm, Quebec City taxpayers voted a £100,000 municipal subsidy to the North Shore Railway even before the railway was chartered. A public meeting on 8 July 1852 approved the subsidy and urged city council to donate any city property which might serve as a site for the terminus. In April 1853 the North Shore Railway received its charter from the Legislative Assembly.[24] The company was empowered to construct a railway from Quebec City to Montreal or to a point on any railway leading west from Montreal. Up to 96,000 shares, each with a face value of 6 pounds, 6 shillings could be issued. Municipalities, ecclesiastical organizations, and other corporate bodies could subscribe up to £100,000. When £125,000 had been subscribed by at least thirty separate parties, a general meeting could be called and a nine-member board of directors elected. The major restriction of the charter was that the railway could not enter Montreal without that city's approval.

II

Long before the railway era, public funds played a central role in the development of Canada's transportation systems. Governments had financed canals, channel-deepening projects, colonization roads, and harbour improvements. Liberal charters, lucrative mail contracts, and direct cash subsidies were accepted parts of Canada's political and economic life. As entrepreneurs made the transition from wind to steam and then to the iron horse, politicians kept pace with revised forms of government aid. By the 1850s land or cash grants, monopolies, and government guarantees were essential elements in railway financing.

Montrealers had always been among the leading beneficiaries of these state-sponsored enterprises.[25] With its political strength, commercial diversity, and well-established trade patterns Montreal was able to hamper its metropolitan rival from obtaining government subsidies for the North Shore Railway. Initially, the Quebec City promoters had planned to finance half of their railway under the Guarantee Act of 1849. However, the government's growing financial commitments to the Grand Trunk and that railway's influential friends blocked any extension of the government guarantee to the North Shore Railway. In 1856, after three years of frustration, the promoters turned to another common form of railway subsidy – the land grant.

In theory, the North Shore Railway was in a highly favourable position to receive a land grant since its president, Joseph Cauchon, was a member of the cabinet and commissioner of crown lands. Cauchon originally planned to grant his railway crown lands in the St. Maurice Valley. However, Upper and Lower Canadian differences, the pervasive influence of the Grand Trunk, and the delicate political situation in the mid 1850s hindered such blatant favouritism towards the minister's railway. To circumvent these difficulties Cauchon devised a 'national' enterprise, the Lake Huron, Ottawa and Quebec Junction Railway Company. Following the St. Lawrence and Ottawa Rivers and then branching west to Lake Huron, this railway was envisaged as an amalgamation of five existing companies which held charters for various portions of the route – the North Shore Railway, the Vaudreuil Railway, the Montreal and Bytown Railway, the Bytown and Pembroke Railway, and the Brockville and Ottawa Railway.[26] Under its charter this new company could raise £6500 for each mile of the railway between the Ottawa River and Lake Huron. This imprecise description of cost had to be used since the route was unsurveyed. Nor was it clear where the terminus on Lake Huron would be located. The participating companies would each raise a portion of the capital for the section between the Ottawa River and Lake Huron proportionate to their share of the route between Quebec City and Bytown. By this method of calculation the North Shore Railway was responsible for 45 per cent of the new company's capital.

Never more than a paper project to satisfy various regional and railway interests, this complex charter was contrived to obtain four million acres of crown land west of the Ottawa River. At first Cauchon planned to grant one-third of these lands outright to the North Shore Railway. However, this plan was blocked by Premier Taché, a Grand Trunk director.[27] The charter, as finally approved, permitted the North Shore Railway to appropriate 45 per cent of the land grant but only on a pro-rated basis as the railway was built. This stipulation was important since, in theory at least, it prevented the company from stripping the land grant of its timber until the railway was actually constructed. Although the charter emphasized settlement prospects in the Canadian shield, Cauchon admitted privately that the soil's fertility was secondary. Profits would result from the sale of the grant's white and red pine.[28]

Cauchon's wheeling and dealing, his conversion to railway construction west of Montreal, and his participation in a cabinet dominated by Montrealers and Grand Trunk promoters made him suspect to his Quebec City colleagues. Napoléon Casault accused him of being in concern 'avec les autres ministres pour se moquer de nous.' After the caucus of 26 April 1856, François Evanturel, another regional MLA, announced that he could no longer stand the cabinet's duplicity. Describing himself as a 'loose-fish' he declared his intention to vote against the government.[29] Evanturel and Casault labelled Cauchon's railway bill as 'ridicule,' 'une farce,' and 'une blague.' Casault feared that the North Shore Railway would be a feeder-line for the Grand Trunk and that western trade would be transported to the United States via the bridge under construction at Montreal: 'nous avons été joués par Cauchon,' he concluded, 'et honteusement traités par lui et tout le ministère.'

Cauchon's bill faced opposition from another quarter. Upper Canadians realized that his proposed railway was a direct threat to Toronto, Kingston, and other Lake Ontario communities. They were alarmed by the charter's statement that the new railway would secure 'the travel and traffic of the Great West' and direct it down the Ottawa Valley. Privately, Cauchon agreed that he intended to divert western trade that went to Toronto via the Georgian Bay port of Collingwood.[30] During the debate John Sandfield Macdonald of Cornwall objected to granting public lands to private companies. Citing the conflict of interest inherent in the minister's proposal to grant land to his own railway, Macdonald warned that 'the history of the North Shore would be a repetition of the history of the Grand Trunk.' George Brown represented another Upper Canadian viewpoint. Charging that the Grand Trunk and North Shore companies had worked out a deal, he reiterated his familiar theme that the government was being maintained in power by the support of French Canadians: granting 25,000 acres a mile, according to Brown, was 'nothing but bribery of members.'[31]

These regional pressures accentuated the government's railway problems in 1856. The Grand Trunk, unable to pay interest on its bonds, was back at the government's doorstep for a $2 million subsidy. To keep its members in line, the government scheduled third reading of Cauchon's railway bill two days after the Grand Trunk bill. Under these conditions only five of the fourteen north-shore members dared to vote against the Grand Trunk subsidy and a few days later, accepting half a loaf as better than none, all but one north-shore member voted in favour of the Cauchon bill.[32]

While Cauchon fought for subsidies, other North Shore officials settled the construction contract. Tenders were received from François Baby, William Sykes, Joseph Archer, Thomas Walker, C.W. Starnes, and the company of Ostell and Scott. François Baby submitted the lowest bid and on 8 April 1856 a contract was signed.[33] Baby would construct the entire railway from Quebec City to Montreal, purchase the right-of-way, and provide stations, fencing, bridges, rolling stock, telegraph lines, and wharves. He would meet the expenses of North Shore officials, pay the interest on the debentures of the company and Quebec City, and employ 2500 men within four months. Construction would begin simultaneously in Quebec City, Three Rivers, and Portneuf and would be completed within three years.

The contractor estimated his costs at £8000 a mile. This was comparable to £6500 a mile paid to the Brassey Company for constructing the Grand Trunk line between Lévis and Richmond and £8000 a mile for the line from Lévis to Rivière du Loup. As part payment the North Shore Company transferred its Quebec City debentures to the contractor and agreed to ask the city for a second subsidy of £100,000.

The balance of the contract would be paid in North Shore debentures which were to be issued in £30,000 instalments as work was completed.[34]

Since the Quebec City debentures were payable only on a pro-rated basis as the railway was built, Baby had to sell the North Shore debentures to raise initial construction capital. This was difficult in the face of the reputation of Canadian railway stocks, the opposition of the Grand Trunk, the depressed economic condition of the north-shore region, and strong world competition for railway capital. With Baby unable to raise capital but obliged to pay the North Shore Company's expenses, relations between the contractor and the company president quickly deteriorated. Cauchon and another official had already travelled to England and both the secretary-treasurer and the company's London agent received salaries. In October 1856 Baby asked to be relieved of either the contract or his obligation to pay the company's expenses. He contested the legality of his contract by arguing that the project had been changed by the formation of the Lake Huron, Ottawa and Quebec Junction Railway. Cauchon insisted that the contractor honour his commitment and made the always-useful charge that Baby had come 'under the influence of the Grand Trunk.'[35] Baby retaliated by refusing to correspond with Cauchon. Since the railway's reputation would have been discredited if its contractor defaulted, Cauchon was forced to accept a compromise. In November 1856 the railway's two paid employees were released and Baby agreed to pay incidental expenses for an unpaid secretary.[36]

The dismal pattern set in 1856 continued for years. Despite the granting of a contract, construction did not begin. The major investments in the railway were municipal subsidies of £100,000 by Quebec City, $200,000 by St. Maurice County, and $50,000 from Three Rivers. However, these subscriptions were payable only on a pro-rated basis as the railway was built.[37] Virtually none of the $120,000 in individual subscriptions was paid up. Nor had Cauchon's scheme for the Lake Huron, Ottawa and Quebec Junction Railway been an asset, since the capital of all five companies had to be subscribed and 10 per cent deposited in a bank before construction could begin. The opposition of the Grand Trunk continued. In September 1856 Cauchon discovered that the North Shore Railway's surveyor in the Ottawa Valley was actually in the employ of the Grand Trunk. On another occasion the North Shore's contractor had to deny rumours that he was a Grand Trunk shareholder.[38]

In the winter of 1857 the promoters made a fresh start. Although no longer paid as secretary-treasurer, Langevin drummed up support for the railway in Quebec City. As an alderman in 1857 and as mayor from 1858 to 1861 he called for a larger municipal subsidy with more relaxed terms. In February 1857 a public meeting approved a tripling of the municipal subsidy to £300,000. North Shore Railway enthusiasts dominated the meeting. Resolutions were proposed by Charles Alleyn, who became president of the railway in 1859, and three company directors, François Evanturel, Georges Simard, and William Rhodes. Eighteen months later city council sweetened the terms again. In approving the increase it agreed to advance $50,000 to commence construction and to finance a delegation to England.[39]

Langevin also encouraged clerical support for the North Shore Railway. In February 1857 he founded a newspaper, *Le Courrier du Canada*, which his biographer described as 'l'organe québécois du clergé bas canadien.'[40] During Langevin's short tenure as editor, *Le Courrier du Canada* vigorously promoted the North Shore Railway, urged a tripling of Quebec City's subsidy, and reminded its readers that local prosperity depended on railway construction. Indeed, the North Shore Railway had received strong clerical support from the outset. While some priests were skeptical of modern technology, the hierarchy in Quebec City welcomed the railway. The Seminary of Quebec had promised to invest £300 and the archbishop £400.[41] Much of this support was due to the influence of the Langevin family. Even before the railway was chartered, Hector wrote to his brother Edmond, secretary of the Archdiocese, asking him to thank the archbishop for investing in the railway and urging that the enterprise be recommended to all clergy. Five days later, Vicar-General Cazeau wrote the religious communities under the archbishop's jurisdiction and encouraged them to invest in the North Shore Railway:

Le sousigné ... déclare qu'il approuvera volontiers la détermination que celles-ci pouvaient prendre de contribuer à la construction du dit chemin de fer. Ce projet intéresse à un haut point les Corporations qui possèdent des propriétés tant dans la ville de Québec que sur le parcours de la voie ferrée, et leur souscription libérale en cette circonstance les rendra extrêmement populaires dans l'opinion publique. C'est dans ce sens que Nos Seigneurs l'Archevêque de Québec et l'Evêque de TLOA s'en sont expliqués avant leur départ. Les Dames Religieuses savent peut-être aussi que Mgr. a pris pour £100 d'actions.[42]

At the same time, other North Shore officials sought better terms in the provincial capital. With the demise of the Lake Huron, Ottawa and Quebec Junction Railway project, they revived claims for a 1,400,000-acre grant in the St. Maurice Valley. These demands embarrassed the Taché government since the Grand Trunk was lobbying for a larger subsidy. When Taché refused to accede immediately to this north-shore pressure, Cauchon found himself allied with Rouges like John Young and A.A. Dorion in defending Quebec City and the north-shore region. On 28 April 1857 Cauchon threatened to withdraw his support for the Grand Trunk bill unless aid to the North Shore Railway was guaranteed.[43] Taché responded by accepting Cauchon's resignation from the cabinet. Angered at his sudden dismissal Cauchon charged that the Grand Trunk had an influence on the ministry 'which has something strange and fatal for the general interests of the country.' Accusing Taché of long-term hostility to the north-shore region, he blamed the prime minister for Lower Canada's inability to obtain 'justice.'[44] This infighting on the government benches delighted the opposition. George Brown opposed any further grants to Quebec's north-shore but avoided entering what he described as 'entirely a family scene.'[45]

Despite Cauchon's dismissal as commissioner of crown lands, the government could not afford to alienate its north-shore supporters. During the debate on the Grand Trunk bill, both Cartier and Taché praised the North Shore Railway. Taché was particularly effusive, assuring 'toute l'assistance compatible avec la garde fidèle et religieuse du dépôt sacré du domaine public ... '[46] As in 1856 the government ultimately gave in. The St. Maurice Railway and Navigation Company was chartered with a land grant of 1,500,000 acres. Introducing the bill, Charles Alleyn explained that North Shore officials had been 'invited by the Government to consider some other scheme, which might be more feasible' than the Quebec to Lake Huron railway project.[47] John A. Macdonald was even more emphatic. The land grant to the St. Maurice Railway and Navigation Company was a contribution to the North Shore Railway, he told the assembly, and he 'was most anxious that the North Shore Company should obtain possession of this land, and it would be the fault of that company itself if it did not amalgamate with this Company.'[48] Opposition members saw the 1,500,000 acres as a payoff for north-shore support for the Grand Trunk bill. George Brown accused the government of pushing the charter through the assembly late at night without proper debate. He complained that 'among the directors of this new Company, he found the names of Charles Alleyn, George O'Kill Stuart, G.H. Simard, Hon. Joseph Cauchon, and others. Surely these were not the members of the House.' Despite Brown's charge that the whole matter 'bore a very strange aspect' the bill passed by a majority of fifty-four to fourteen.[49]

To obtain the 1,500,000 acres of crown land in the St. Maurice Valley, the new company had to construct a twenty-eight mile railway between Three Rivers and Grand Piles and operate a steamboat on the St. Maurice River above Grand Piles (see map A).[50] As with the abortive Quebec to Lake Huron project of the previous session, the St. Maurice Railway and Navigation Company was simply a front by which lands could be granted to the North Shore Railway. With the approval of two-thirds of the North Shore Railway shareholders, the two companies could be united. The amalgamation could be effected 'without any action or assent' on the part of the newly chartered company. This provision was unnecessary since directors of the North Shore Railway dominated the new company. Andrew Stuart, Joseph Hamel, Jean-Baptiste Renaud, Charles Alleyn, Joseph Cauchon, François Evanturel, Eugène Chinic, Napoléon Casault, Georges H. Simard, George Simpson, and Jacques-Olivier Bureau had directorships in both companies. François Baby, contractor for the North Shore Railway, was a director of the St. Maurice Company and his son Michael was a director of the North Shore Railway. Of those directors not associated with the North Shore Railway, Joseph-Edouard Turcotte, Louis Desaulniers, Antoine Polette, Joseph Thibaudeau, and George O'Kill Stuart were local politicians. Aimé Desilets of Three Rivers and Olivier Robitaille and Joseph Morrin, both of Quebec City, were the only directors in the new company with no direct connection to the North Shore Railway. In June 1858 the two companies were amalgamated into the North Shore Railway and St. Maurice Navigation Company.

Although armed with a new charter, an impressive land grant and an increased subsidy from Quebec City the railway still had to raise working capital. Despite one New York inquiry, there was little expectation of attracting American investors. Before 1875, American capital accounted for only 5 per cent of the foreign capital invested in Canada.[51] This was partly due to the fact that the maximum Canadian interest rate of 6 per cent was lower than prevailing American rates.[52] Like other colonial and American railroads, the North Shore

Railway had to compete for British capital. Since it was an uphill task to demonstrate the traffic and profit potential of the North Shore Railway, London bankers often concentrated on obtaining the company's land grants, preferably without building the railway.

In London the railway faced the perennial opposition of the Grand Trunk. Baring Brothers and Glyn, Mills and Company – the two most important sources of British capital for Canada – were both deeply committed to the Grand Trunk. Although it preferred municipal securities to railway issues, Barings had a credit-rating system in North America to evaluate a railway's capital, location, management, and profit potential. Baring's Canadian business peaked in 1852.[53] By the late 1850s when the North Shore Railway was seeking funds, Barings was not supporting new North American railway issues. The company did act as financial agent for Quebec City in 1853 and 1855. In February 1857 Quebec City sent bonds worth £50,000 to the company. Barings bought one-half of the issue and sold the balance.

Glyn's, 'the railway bank,' relied on Alexander Galt and Thomas Gibbs Ridout for its Canadian financial information. Galt was minister of finance and a former Grand Trunk director and Ridout was cashier of the Bank of Upper Canada which had advanced credit to the Grand Trunk. The North Shore Railway's position was further weakened in 1858 when Galt, George-Etienne Cartier, and John Ross, president of the Grand Trunk, went to London for discussions with England's financial and political élite. At the same time, the declining value of Grand Trunk stock had a damaging effect on other Canadian railway issues. In 1860 the Glyn and Baring houses' liability on their Grand Trunk holdings was more than £600,000.[54]

With the deck stacked against them, the North Shore promoters found themselves increasingly subordinated to directives from their British bankers. The hierarchy of colonial economic power extended from London to Montreal and only ultimately to Quebec City. This lack of a strong metropolitan base was a disadvantage for the North Shore entrepreneurs. The railway's first agent in London was Eden Colvile. A former Hudson's Bay officer in Canada, Colvile introduced the North Shore directors to the London banking firm of Heywood and Company who were already acting for the Illinois Railway Company. Heywood officials were skeptical of the Canadian promoters and insisted on sending their own representatives to examine the railway's potential. They showed particular interest in the charter for the Lake Huron, Ottawa and Quebec Junction Railway. To the North

Shore promoters this company was a paper project by which their railway could obtain crown lands west of the Ottawa River. However, their London bankers suggested dropping the North Shore Railway and simply building west from Montreal into the area of the land grants. Piqued by this proposal, Cauchon pointed out that his carefully contrived charter had only been achieved after an 'incredible' struggle and could not be changed at the company's whim.[55] As an alternative, a Heywood official proposed that one million acres of the grant be divided immediately among shareholders who had paid for one-half of their shares. This too was contrary to the charter since lands could be released by the government only as the railway was constructed. The bankers continued to angle for better terms. Noting that the railway's London account was not adequate remuneration, one banker wrote that his brother welcomed construction contracts. Patiently, North Shore officials explained that the contract had already been let to François Baby.

In November 1856 Colvile was released as the company's agent and a year later Baby left for England to sell the North Shore debentures on his own. Before leaving he promised company officials that construction would begin promptly on his return.[56] In London Baby met Sir William Napier, J.P. Kennard, and Thomas Brassey. However, his trip coincided with the financial crisis of 1857. There was a sharp contraction in the London money market and railroad stocks plunged.

As before, London investors showed more interest in the company's land grant than in actually building the railway: 'Without the lands the Scheme would be worthless here. There is already a railway communication between Montreal and Quebec [the Grand Trunk]. A second route is doubtless desirable on the North Shore of the St. Lawrence, but without the Land, the operation would not be looked at in London.'[57] Insisting on specific technical information, they suggested that the government permit the immediate selection of lands on a tax-free basis. Surveys should be conducted at public expense. They wanted the government to give one title for the complete land grant; this would facilitate its subdivision.[58] One London official proposed that the railway's capital needs of £1,500,000 be divided into shares worth £1,000,000 and debentures with a value of £500,000. Each £100 share would entitle the holder to 100 acres of land. The North Shore's 6 per cent debentures would have first lien on the railroad and on 500,000 acres of land specifically appropriated as backing for the debentures.[59] In the end, blaming 'stagnation in all business,' the bankers refused to float the issue on the London market. Baby, after months of negotiation, returned to Canada empty handed.

This pattern persisted in the following years. With a stagnant market the bankers delayed introducing the stock while constantly demanding better terms. Replies from Canada showed that North Shore officials were desperate. 'We shall do all in our power,' Michael Baby wrote to Sir William Napier, 'to meet your views with reference to the removing of all restrictions from a Company whose money is destined to improve the country.'[60] Responding to suggestions from London that the company's lands be emphasized, Langevin petitioned Parliament in July 1858 to change the railway's name to the North Shore and St. Maurice Navigation and Land Company. In November 1858 François Baby, exasperated with the latest demands, wrote to Napier that local municipalities could not be expected to postpone their dividends in favour of private shareholders. 'As subscribers of stock,' he insisted, 'they must be treated like all other subscribers neither better nor worse':

However, to be frank with you, if the bill as it now stands comprising in the scheme the character of a Land Company as well, with the plans and estimates with the official assurance that the Government will make the survey of the lands, with an order in Council authorizing the Company to select the 1,500,000 acres and with $1,300,000 of stock subscribed by the City of Quebec, you do not think the scheme can be put on the London market with every prospect of success it is useless that I should go to England, I can obtain nothing more for the undertaking, therefore please answer me with the least possible delay.[61]

Despite the contractor's discouragement, Langevin and Napoléon Casault set out for England early in 1859 in yet another attempt to raise capital. To reassure their new agents, Kennard and Company, the charter was amended to permit the company's head office to be transferred from Quebec City to London. The bankers were still not satisfied. In addition to concessions already granted, Langevin agreed that Quebec City's £300,000 subscription would receive no interest for ten years and that the city would renounce its share of the company's land grant.

Langevin's concessions aroused hostility. Quebec City had advanced £13,500 to the railway and in May 1859 petitioners asked city council to stop further grants until the contract's terms were met. However, Langevin - in his dual capacity as railway vice-president and mayor -

was able to overcome this opposition, and a public meeting on 12 September 1859 approved the conditions he had accepted in London.[62] Langevin was now certain the stock would at last be issued to the public. He forwarded deeds, the power-of-attorney, a copy of Quebec City's revised subsidy, and offered to come to England at the bankers' convenience. Despite Langevin's enthusiasm the bankers remained evasive. They wanted clarification of the land grant and construction contract. Warning Langevin that the scheme 'requires much deliberation,' Kennard noted that there were 'many more steps to be taken.'[63] He expressed 'some apprehension lest you and your friends should suppose that we have in any way however slightly misled you to the ripeness of the scheme, and the ripeness of our disposition to announce it under our responsibility.' Langevin persisted and answered questions concerning traffic, the potential of the St. Maurice lands, the Quebec City by-law, and the attitude of the government. Kennard remained unconvinced that there was 'an adequate inducement to us.'

Langevin's failure to raise capital caused dissension among the North Shore directors. In June 1860 Langevin suggested that the project be scaled down and financed locally. Construction of the Grand Piles branch line and the section between Quebec City and Three Rivers would entitle the company to the government land grant and the Quebec City subsidy - the only substantial financing the railway had received. The board of directors rejected these proposals along with contracts Langevin had granted for the construction of the Grand Piles branch line. One director, Georges H. Simard, demanded publication of Langevin's correspondence with the London bankers. He further insisted that construction not begin until financing for the whole line from Quebec City to Montreal was assured and that Quebec City's £300,000 subscription be paid only on a pro-rated basis.[64]

By 1860 the North Shore prospects were bleak. The directors were squabbling, the railway had failed to attract British capital, and - despite its six-year history - the company had not laid a single rail. To further complicate matters, ambitious Ottawa and Montreal entrepreneurs were eying the Ottawa Valley turf. In 1861 the Canada Central Railway was chartered to build from Montreal to Lake Huron via Ottawa, Arnprior, and Pembroke.[65] This new railway would direct Ottawa Valley trade into the Montreal and Grand Trunk orbit; Quebec City would be peripheral. Although re-chartered in 1861 and 1866, the North Shore Railway and St. Maurice Navigation and Land Company ceased active operations in 1861.

2

Formation of the Montreal Colonization Railway

I

The years before Confederation had been discouraging for Canadian railway promoters. In 1867 the province of Quebec had only 575 miles of iron track, of which 507 miles were part of the Grand Trunk system. The balance consisted of 43 miles on the Stanstead, Shefford and Chambly Railway, 12 miles on the St. Lawrence and Industry Railway, and 12 miles between Carillon and Grenville.[1] The American Civil War and Canada's political instability had increased London's skepticism of Canadian railway issues. The crash of the Bank of Upper Canada in 1866 and the Commercial Bank in 1867 confirmed the view of many that the Canadian economy was 'unstable, impecunious and profligate.'[2] At the same time, American entrepreneurs were penetrating areas traditionally dominated by Lower Canada. In particular, the Bytown and Prescott Railway was diverting the Ottawa Valley timber trade from the St. Lawrence route to the emerging lumber entrepôt of Burlington, Vermont.[3]

Confederation prompted a revival of optimism and expansionism. The continuing American demand for lumber, Canada's improving credit position, and the acquisition of the West helped rekindle the commercial spirit. Railway development was the clearest expression of this new mood. The Montreal *Gazette* asserted that railways had no 'evil effects' on allegiance, the course of trade, or immigration, and 'the more lines of railway we can have, the better.'[4] As in the 1850s, French Canadians were as anxious as other Canadians to mortgage themselves to railways. One observer found French Canadians more enthusiastic over railways than their English-speaking counterparts: 'In fact the two races seem to have, for once, changed characters and it is now the Anglo-Canadian who has become the fossil that is to obstruct by his inertia the progress of Quebec. We have suffered long enough from such social trilobites with their antiquated ideas of commerce.'[5] Sydney Bellingham, a Quebec politician and opponent of the more expansive railway schemes, felt that French Canadians were being misled by their leaders: 'No one was expected to subscribe stock for these railways. As a rule the French-Canadian farmers, who constituted four-fifths of the electoral class, never subscribed for or read a newspaper, save the Curé or the doctor, or the notary; and no one ever entertained the idea that if the colony borrowed money the farmers would some day find themselves taxed, and their farms mortgaged.'[6]

The attitude of French Canadians to economic development was more crucial after 1867 since crown lands, municipalities, and railways within provincial boundaries became responsibilities of the province under the British North America Act. This gave the North Shore Railway interests a new opportunity to find support. However, as in the Union period, their success depended on Quebec City's ability to assert its political and economic hegemony. But Confederation had not dampened the ambitions of Montreal; the new federal structure simply forced her entrepreneurs to look to the provincial capital for the settlement of many commercial issues. Montrealers moved quickly to establish working relationships with the new government of P.-J.-O. Chauveau. Since powerful entrepreneurs such as Hugh Allan already had the respect of the French-Canadian ecclesiastical and political élite, it was, in one sense, 'business as usual.' The businessmen and French-Canadian political leaders had no difficulty in establishing common goals. Economic growth was quite compatible with faith and nationalism. Railway expansion promoted colonization: the industrialization of Montreal encouraged the repatriation of French Canadians from the United States: English-speaking entrepreneurs provided jobs for the surplus rural population while not interfering with French-Canadian mores or traditional power structures. On divisive ethnic or language issues, both politician and entrepreneur could agree that the real villains were George Brown and his Ontario allies. This comfortable union of entrepreneur and politician resulted in years of generous railway legislation. Within fifteen years of Confederation both Quebec City and Montreal had rail links to the Ottawa Valley and the west.

A notable characteristic of the provincial government was its subservience to Ottawa. Chosen by the Conservative hierarchy, Premier Chauveau accepted instructions from Macdonald, Cartier, and Langevin. Macdonald did not hesitate to disallow or rewrite provincial acts: 'I have read Chauveau's bill with not a little astonishment. It gives the local legislature infinitely greater power than we have here or the Lords or Commons have in England. The bill will not do at all but you need not say anything to him about it. I will draft a Bill which I think will hold water and do all that is necessary and will give it to you when you come up.'[7] The prime minister was blunt with Chauveau: 'By the way the disallowance of your privileges of Parliament Act will come out in the next Gazette with that of the Province of Ontario. Cartier and Langevin both thought this would be better than your repealing it.'[8] Ottawa's influence was reinforced by the double mandate which permitted politicians to sit simultaneously in both the federal and provincial houses. While minister of militia in Macdonald's cabinet, Cartier had a seat in the Quebec Assembly and was a member of the province's Railway Committee. Among the Quebec Conservatives who exercised the double mandate in 1867 were Langevin, Cauchon, Chauveau, Christopher Dunkin, George Irvine, and John Jones Ross.

Chauveau's subservience helped Macdonald's business friends. Hugh Allan regularly used federal channels to affect provincial legislation. Langevin acted as Macdonald's liaison with the Quebec government and his telegrams reflected Allan's power: 'Allan has telegraphed wishing the act chapter forty-seven [re: navigation in the St. Lawrence] repealed. The Quebec government have promised me it shall be done.' And two days later: 'Government here say that if Hugh Allan on name of promoters of chapter forty seven petitions for repeal of the same they shall repeal the act. They are communicating with Allan to that effect.'[9]

However, it was not only outside pressures from Ottawa and English-speaking Montrealers that prompted the province's liberal railway and commercial legislation. The Quebec Legislative Assembly was packed with local entrepreneurs, promoters, lawyers, and contractors. The Assembly's Railway Committee in 1871 included such friends of railway expansion as Cauchon, Langevin, Cartier, George Irvine, and Louis Beaubien. In 1869 the Quebec Railway Act limited the liability of shareholders and permitted railways to borrow at interest rates up to 8 per cent. It encouraged municipalities to invest in railways and authorized them to name an ex-officio director if they subscribed over $20,000. Railway companies were obligated to let contracts by tender and to relinquish their charters if construction was not completed within ten years.[10]

The province used both financial guarantees and land subsidies to encourage railway construction. Railways with wooden tracks were subsidized by the Colonization Railway Aid Act of 1869 which guaranteed 3 per cent of construction costs, up to $5000 a mile. In effect, this was a twenty-year government guarantee for approximately one-half of a railway's interest charges.[11] One of the four colonization railways named in this act was the Montreal Colonization Railway. Nor were the government's north-shore friends neglected. A wooden railway constructed up the St. Maurice Valley from Three Rivers would receive a 6 per cent government guarantee instead of the 3 per cent given to other colonization railways.

Despite these incentives, railway construction in Quebec was negligible, and in 1870 the government raised its ante to include land subsidies: 3,208,500 acres of crown lands were set aside to promote railway construction along the north shore of the St. Lawrence and Ottawa rivers. The lands came from four blocks - 1,827,400 acres in Pontiac county, 319,440 acres in Portneuf and Quebec counties, 371,200 acres in Montcalm county, and 685,466 acres in the counties of Champlain and Chicoutimi along the east bank of the St. Maurice River.[12] Two million acres were to be given to the North Shore Railway on a pro-rated basis as the railway was built. The Montreal Colonization Railway would receive 10,000 acres a mile when the railway was completed from Montreal to Aylmer, a village near Ottawa on the Quebec side of the Ottawa River. Alternately the cabinet could advance 5000 acres a mile as construction progressed. The government would name one-third of the directors of both railways and reserved the right to locate the junction of the two railways. This latter clause was to haunt the government.

II

With the enthusiastic support of their provincial government, Montrealers spawned dozens of railway schemes in the years after Confederation. Newspapers like the Montreal *Gazette* fed local fears by reporting the growth of American rail systems and the ambitions of Toronto, Portland, and Quebec City.[13] With the Grand Trunk dominating the St. Lawrence, the most important alternate route to the West was the Ottawa Valley. From the Ottawa River between Ottawa and

Pembroke a railway could be built west to Lake Huron and extended north or south of Lake Superior. With this potential for western trade, any railway with a charter in the Ottawa Valley attracted attention. Montrealers feared that Ottawa Valley trade would be diverted by the Brockville and Ottawa Railway or the newly chartered Kingston and Pembroke Railway. The Grand Trunk Railway realized the importance of the Ottawa Valley trade and supported the Montreal and City of Ottawa Junction Railway.[14] This railway would serve as a spur-line joining Ottawa to Coteau Landing, a station on the main Grand Trunk line. In the anti-Grand Trunk camp the two most aggressive competitors in the Ottawa Valley were the Canada Central Railway and the Montreal Colonization Railway.

Chartered in 1861, the Canada Central was originally promoted by Ottawa entrepreneurs but by 1870 was dominated by Montrealers such as Louis Beaubien and J.J.C. Abbott. The son of an Anglican clergyman, Abbott was a prominent Montreal commercial lawyer who acted as solicitor for Hugh Allan. Involved with companies as diverse as the Bank of Montreal, the Montreal Town Manure Company, and the Intercolonial Coal Mining Company, Abbott was keenly interested in railways. He participated in the Montreal and Bytown Railway (lawyer, 1855), the Chaudière Valley Railway Company (director, 1864), the Canada Central Railway (vice-president, 1870), the North Shore and St. Maurice Navigation Company (director, 1870), the Brockville and Ottawa Railway (president, 1872), the Montreal Colonization Railway (director, October 1872), the South Eastern Railway Company (director, 1873), the Montreal, Ottawa and Western Railway (vice-president, 1875), the Ontario and Quebec Railway (director, 1875), and the Lake Champlain and St. Lawrence Junction Railway Company (director, 1880).

With Abbott as its freewheeling vice-president, the Canada Central entered into a complex series of negotiations aimed at reducing competition and wheedling subsidies from governments in Toronto, Quebec City, and Ottawa. The company faced opposition in both provinces. Ontario Premier John Sandfield Macdonald opposed the extension of the railway from the Ottawa Valley to Lake Huron. Premier Chauveau, espousing the rhetoric of colonization railways, objected to the granting of public lands to what he described as 'only a commercial and industrial enterprise' and accused the promoters of trying 'to galvanize a dead body.'[15] Despite these objections, the federal government extended the Canada Central's charter for five years, permitted it to reduce its gauge to 4 feet 8½ inches, and gave it the right to amalgamate with the Montreal Colonization Railway. By 1871 the Canada Central joined Ottawa to Carleton Place and Abbott predicted that Pembroke would be reached in 1872.[16]

While construction went ahead west of Ottawa, the route between Montreal and Ottawa had not been settled. Originally the Canada Central was to be built largely in Ontario on the south shore of the Ottawa River. However, the county of Vaudreuil offered little assistance and the Chauveau government refused to grant crown land to a railway built on the Ontario side. In Montreal *La Minerve* and the *Gazette* were pressuring the city to subsidize a Quebec route. In June 1870 the Canada Central promoters announced new plans to build at least half-way to Ottawa on the Quebec side of the Ottawa River. A decision on crossing into Ontario at Hawkesbury or continuing along the north shore to Ottawa was postponed (see map A). This delay enabled the company to pressure communities on both sides of the river. Abbott asked the counties of Prescott and Russell for a $200,000 subsidy as an inducement for crossing the Ottawa River at Hawkesbury.[17] The two Ontario counties' offer of $3000 a mile fell short of the Quebec government's subsidy of 10,000 acres a mile for a railway on the north shore. In 1871 the Canada Central announced that it had abandoned its plans to join Montreal and Ottawa. Despite cries of foul from Ontario-based directors like John Hamilton and William Rodden, the company had opted to cooperate with the Montreal Colonization Railway. This eased competition in the Ottawa Valley and permitted the Canada Central to focus on building west of Ottawa. In 1872 its charter was amended to permit extension of the railway to Sault Ste. Marie.[18]

The Montreal Colonization Railway was chartered by the Quebec government in April 1869. Earlier in the year Laurentian parishes such as St. Sauveur, St. Lin, Ste. Agathe des Monts, St. Jérôme, Ste. Adèle, and New Glasgow had petitioned for a railway that would be subsidized under the Colonization Railway Act.[19] As originally chartered the Montreal Colonization Railway would run some thirty miles from Mile End, a village on the outskirts of Montreal, to St. Jérôme, a town on the edge of the Laurentians (see map B). However, the charter was flexible. From Mile End the railway could build into central Montreal or to the east-end harbour at Hochelaga. The railway's engineer, Charles Legge, proposed two termini. Although Mile End had facilities for storing Laurentian cordwood, its height made access to the centre of Montreal difficult. Legge advised construction of a short extension to Hochelaga where lumber could be shipped across the St. Lawrence to Longueuil and thence by rail to the United States. Four possible routes were surveyed between Hochelaga and St. Jérôme. Legge favoured the longest route since it required one less bridge and had the lowest cost of $14,384 per mile.[20]

The charter was also open-ended at the St. Jérôme terminus. It permitted a northern extension from St. Jérôme to the Laurentian communities of St. Sauveur, Ste. Adèle and Ste. Agathe. Alternately, the railway could be extended westward along the base of the Laurentians to Grenville on the Ottawa River. From this point connections could be made with the Canada Central Railway at Hawkesbury or the railway could be built directly to Ottawa along the north side of the Ottawa River.[21]

The company could begin operations when $100,000 had been subscribed. The original stock issue of $500,000 could be quadrupled by a vote of the shareholders. Amalgamations with other railways were permitted and subsidies were invited from municipalities. These subsidies were due only when construction began within the municipality's boundaries.

Legge's report estimated that construction costs would be $489,654 and annual 7 per cent interest charges $34,275. The province's 3 per cent guarantee for construction costs up to $5000 a mile would give the railway $5106. Yearly traffic revenues were estimated at $140,000. Legge anticipated that the railway would carry 80,000 cords of wood at a freight rate of $1.50 a cord, 450,000 bushels of grain at two cents a bushel, and 24,000 passengers at an average fare of fifty cents.[22] Allowing 80 per cent of revenues for operating expenses, the company could devote $28,200 to its interest charges. The balance of the debt would be covered by private and municipal subscriptions.

Although purportedly a colonization railway, the company's board of directors included a familiar group of Montreal entrepreneurs.[23] One of the earliest advocates of the railway was Louis Beaubien, Conservative MLA for Hochelaga. Beaubien owned property on which the railway would pass. His father had been LaFontaine's business partner and Beaubien himself was described in the Conservative press as Hugh Allan's 'right arm.' For his 1872 election campaign he received $7000 from the Allan coffers.[24] An important member of the Montreal anti-Grand Trunk circle, Beaubien was a director of the Canada Central Railway (1870), the North Shore Railway and St. Maurice Navigation

Company (1870), the Montreal Island Railway Company, the Ontario and Quebec Railway (1872), the Canadian Pacific Railway (provisional director, 1872), and the Montreal, Ottawa and Western Railway (1875).

Another member of the first board was Joseph-Edouard-Lefebvre de Bellefeuille, a Montreal lawyer. De Bellefeuille was secretary in a number of Hugh Allan's companies and at the same time was a prominent defender of Bishop Bourget's ultramontanism. In 1874 he wrote to the bishop asking special permission to have Curé Labelle act as priest at his marriage.[25] Charles Coursol was another important French-Canadian Conservative who served on the first board. Mayor of Montreal (1871-2) and president of the St. Jean Baptiste Society (1872-6), Coursol was a director of La Banque du Peuple and later the Crédit Foncier du Bas-Canada. Other members of the board included Peter Murphy, a director of the City and District Savings Bank, and Charles Legge, the engineer-in-chief. Duncan Macdonald, one of the first directors, later became the railway's contractor.

As the Allan forces became stronger in the railway some of the original directors resigned. In 1872 Robert J. Reekie, a member of the first board, was active in a competing company, the Montreal and St. Jerome Colonization Railway. David Pelletier and Godefroy Laviolette were directors of the Montreal Colonization Railway in 1869 but not in 1871. Laviolette, the mayor of St. Jérôme, was angered when his fellow Conservative directors did not support his campaign to win the provincial nomination in Terrebonne from Joseph-Adolphe Chapleau.[26] John Young and Olivier Berthelet both appeared briefly as directors but resigned in 1871 when Hugh Allan became president. Although Berthelet was president of the railway, in its first years he played little part in running the company and served only as a useful figurehead. Elderly and sick, his primary interests were the St. Jean Baptiste Society, Catholic philanthropy, and the papal zouaves. Young was a prominent Montreal Liberal and long-time opponent of the Grand Trunk. He refused to sit in the same boardroom as Allan but did continue to support the railway. By the spring of 1872 the Montreal Colonization Railway, while retaining the appearance of a bona fide French-Canadian colonization project, was very much a Hugh Allan enterprise. Shares had been bought by only a few Montreal businessmen, most of whom were associates of Allan. J.J.C. Abbott, Louis Beaubien, Duncan Macdonald, and Allan each subscribed $20,000. De Bellefeuille took shares worth $8000 and Henry Mulholland, Edwin Atwater, Gédéon Ouimet, L.A. Leblanc, and Jean-Baptiste Beaudry each subscribed $2000. In almost all cases only 10 per cent of the subscribed stock was actually paid up.[27]

These entrepreneurs envisaged the Montreal Colonization Railway as a feeder line for their steamship interests, as a competitor for the Grand Trunk, as an eastern section of the projected railway to the Pacific, or as a source of construction contracts. The railway would channel the timber and mineral resources of the Ottawa Valley and northern Quebec to Montreal and reinforce the city's position as an entrepôt. A terminus in Hochelaga would stimulate the east-end of Montreal, increase property values, encourage land speculation, and provide jobs for constituents. In its original charter the Montreal Colonization Railway was described as a wooden railway that would benefit from the province's Colonization Railway Act. Plans called for utilization of the Foster method, a construction technique in which hardwood blocks were set on end and pinned between two strong pieces of wood.[28] While useful for transporting firewood and farmers, a wooden railway did not satisfy those Montreal promoters who envisaged the Montreal Colonization Railway as part of a larger rail network to the west. In 1870 the province permitted the railway to receive aid under the Colonization Railway Act even if it was constructed of iron.[29]

During this period the railway received strong support from the Catholic clergy of the Montreal area. Curé Antoine Labelle was the most enthusiastic clerical supporter of the Montreal Colonization Railway but many other priests gave it their blessing. A railway would open the north and help to repatriate French Canadians from New England. In many Laurentian communities local priests instigated petitions urging the provincial government to charter a colonization railway.[30]

Bishop Bourget of Montreal understood the significance of railway development. In the 1850s he had chosen the site for Montreal's new cathedral with a view to its accessibility to the railway station. Thirty years later his cathedral was strategically located between the Canadian Pacific's Windsor Station and the Grand Trunk terminus: 'En fixant mon choix pour le site de la cathédrale, sur le terrain du cimetière actuel, je n'ai en vue qu'une chose, c'est de la rendre plus accessible au clergé et au peuple. Le *terminus* du chemin de fer, qui va se trouver en face de ce terrain, ne permet pas de douter que ce ne soit là le lieu le plus commodément situé pour la résidence du premier pasteur, à cause de l'importance qu'il ne peut manquer en conséquence de gagner.'[31] In the 1850s Bourget supported construction of the North Shore Railway and congratulated Hector Langevin for his efforts to raise railway capital. Important Montreal clerics including the vicargeneral and the Sulpician superior signed a petition in 1870 favouring a $1 million subscription by the City of Montreal for a railway to Ottawa. By 1873 the Seminary in Montreal held 200 shares in the North Shore Railway.[32]

The bishop's relationship with Curé Labelle and J.-E.-L. de Bellefeuille provides further evidence of his support for railway development. A prominent Catholic layman, secretary of the Papal Zouaves, and pamphleteer of ultramontanism, de Bellefeuille often served as secretary of Hugh Allan's companies. He used his influence with the bishop to free Curé Labelle from his parish duties so that the priest could participate in the rural campaigns for railway subsidies.[33] Curé Labelle advised the bishop on political matters, and in 1872 represented Bourget in Quebec City on the Sulpician question. The struggle with the Sulpicians and the university question were the bishop's primary concerns, and the actions of Labelle in these matters did not always please him. However, the two were apparently in agreement on the railway issue. It seems doubtful that either de Bellefeuille or Labelle would have participated so actively in promotion of the Montreal Colonization Railway without the bishop's approval.

Le Nouveau Monde was another index of the attitude of the Montreal clerical hierarchy. With ecclesiastics forming at least two-thirds of its stockholders, this newspaper reflected the bishop's hostility to unions and other agents of social unrest: 'en plaçant les hommes sur la terre Dieu a donné à chacun des goûts, des penchants et des aptitudes spéciales, c'est-à-dire *une vocation.* Aux uns il attribue le goût des hautes études philosophiques, littéraires ou scientifiques; aux autres une disposition naturelle pour les arts, l'industrie, et une aptitude particulière pour un genre quelconque d'industrie. C'est ce qui détermine la formation des classes et constitue ce tout harmonieux appelé la société.'[34] An advocate of high tariffs, industrial growth, and railway development, *Le Nouveau Monde* interspersed its coverage of ultramontanism and the Guibord affair with detailed railway engineering reports and support for Hugh Allan's enterprises. Railways to the north were described as 'une oeuvre nationale.' Speculating that Montreal might become the entrepôt between Asia and Europe, *Le Nouveau Monde* gave its blessing to a million-dollar municipal subsidy to the Montreal Colonization Railway: 'Nous n'avons qu'un mot à ajouter, c'est que nous approuvons entièrement le projet et qu'il ne faut rien épargner pour le faire réussir.'[35]

Curé Labelle was the most enthusiastic clerical supporter of the Montreal Colonization Railway. Sent to St. Jérôme in 1868 he worked tirelessly to bring a railway to his parish. Shortly after the Montreal Colonization Railway was chartered, he invited one of the directors to inspect the region's water resources. Speaking in St. Jérôme, John Young assured the villagers that the railway would stop emigration and provide winter employment. The cost of transporting grain from St. Jérôme to Montreal would drop from ten cents a bushel to two cents.[36] In subsequent years the curé hosted company officials on tours of the north; he usually arranged to serve refreshments in the Collège Ste. Thérèse. An 1872 meeting between the railway directors and the St. Jérôme municipal council was held in Labelle's presbytery. That evening the parish sponsored a gala banquet. In addition to company president Hugh Allan, vice-president Louis Beaubien, and directors Peter Murphy, J.J.C. Abbott, Jean-Baptiste Beaudry, and Charles Legge, head-table guests included Curé Labelle, Attorney-General Gédéon Ouimet, Thomas White, director of the Montreal *Gazette*, and the area's federal and provincial representatives - Rodrique Masson and Joseph-Adolphe Chapleau. The banquet menu bore the inscription: 'C'est le Grand Tronc du Nord que nous voulons depuis l'Atlantique jusqu'au Pacifique et non pas seulement l'embranchement de St. Jérôme.' Reflecting the spirit of the occasion, meat was served to the Protestants while the 'less fortunate brothers' contented themselves with a Lenten meal of fish and oysters. Head-table guests addressed the gathering in French except Abbott who said that although he spoke French 'he would prefer to speak in English as a symbol of the manner in which French or English were working side by side for the success of the great enterprise in which they were engaged.'[37] Masson predicted that as a result of the railway 'the beautiful river' on which St. Jérôme was located would be 'covered with manufactures.' Thomas White was even more expansive. He speculated that with the construction of a railway to the Pacific the trade of China and Japan would flow through the village.

Always popular with the railway entrepreneurs, Curé Labelle welcomed a steady stream of Montreal visitors to his presbytery; his hospitality and his mother's cooking were well known. When Charles Legge, engineer for the Montreal Colonization Railway, suffered a mental breakdown in 1872 he was entrusted to Labelle's care before being taken to a Vermont asylum. Skilled in the machinations of Quebec politics, Labelle acted as lobbyist and intermediary for the English-speaking entrepreneurs. One Quebec editor described him as 'le bras droit de Sir Hugh.'[38] He was also prominent in the Bleu hierarchy in Terrebonne and Assomption. Area politicians like Abbott, Chapleau, Masson, and Sydney Bellingham respected Labelle's power and kept him informed on political matters. In 1873 John Young, a Liberal and former director of the Montreal Colonization Railway, asked Labelle to stay out of a local by-election. The curé's active participation in the campaign, Young warned, would hurt the railway if the Liberals won power in Ottawa or Quebec.[39]

Labelle's influence on the French-Canadian habitant was particularly useful to the railway entrepreneurs. 'Come by all means,' wrote a lumber-mill owner who wanted Labelle's help in promoting a local railway subsidy, 'as I am persuaded that our French Canadian ratepayers will be delighted to see you, and learn from your experience and knowledge of what is their duty in this matter.'[40] Labelle played a key role in the campaign to raise municipal subsidies for the Montreal Colonization Railway. Company officials planned his itinerary carefully and Labelle was told when and where to present himself: 'Voici le programme tel qu'arrangé à Ottawa avec Beaubien et Wright: sous samedi, le 5 avril, une assemblée de quelques divisions de chaque localité, au village de Bryson, à 10h A.M. Il faudra donc partir de Montréal le plus tard vendredi à 8h A.M. Vous serez des nôtres avec Dr. Bernard et Loranger. A cette assemblée nous organiserons toute la compagne. Aussi, si la permission est accordée, arrivé à Montréal le plus tard jeudi, le 3 prochain.'[41] For the campaign in Pontiac County, Labelle was freed from his parish duties by the bishop. Sharing platforms with Chapleau and Beaubien, Labelle often spoke several times a day on the railway's behalf.

At times, Labelle was frustrated by the demands of the railway promoters. 'Voilà deux fois,' he wrote to a fellow priest, 'que je veux partir pour St. Jérôme et les Directeurs de la Compagnie m'en empêchent. Même on veut m'envoyer encore à Ottawa avec M.L. Beaubien.'[42] Company officials were well aware of Labelle's importance and catered to his needs. But for his holy office he would undoubtedly have been named a director of the Montreal Colonization Railway. The company did pay his expenses and welcomed him on social occasions. Hugh Allan was particularly solicitous of Labelle and in November 1872 invited him to a ball he was giving for the governor-general: 'although I do not expect you would dance, and more especially the fast dances, you might like to see it. I expect to have about 500 people at it. Will you come?'[43] On embarrassing questions such as the railway's route, Montreal Colonization officials hedged with the curé. In April 1870 Rodrigue Masson, MP for Terrebonne, was told that the railway would not pass through St. Jérôme; the village would be served by a branch line. This was not made clear to Labelle who was assured in November 1870 by Beaubien, the railway's vice-president, that St.-Jérôme would have a terminus and would become an important Quebec industrial town. Over a year later another director wrote Labelle that the company was still undecided whether the main line would pass through St. Jérôme.[44]

Curé Labelle's most timely promotion of the Montreal Colonization Railway came during the severe winter of 1872. With city council debating a $1 million subsidy for the Montreal Colonization Railway, Labelle, flanked by railway directors Beaubien and de Bellefeuille, entered Montreal with a caravan of firewood for the city's freezing poor. With the British flag flying from the first wagon, and with 'many a poor widow's eyes wet with thanks and orphans made warm by his timely and kindly aid,' Labelle's procession moved in triumph along St. Paul Street to Place Jacques Cartier. Despite *La Minerve*'s assertion that it was an act 'tout spontané' the caravan was carefully planned to increase pressure on city council. Labelle himself confided to a fellow priest that 'je travaille jour et nuit pour gagner le million.'[45] Nor was its symbolism lost upon local journalists. Montreal needed a rail link to its northern hinterland with its firewood, its resources, its riches. At a luncheon in the Jacques Cartier Hotel, Labelle called on Montrealers to make sacrifices for the railway. Industry, the exploitation of resources, and the iron horse were essential to French Canada's future: 'Je sens que la province à besoin d'un chemin de fer dans le nord et que nous ne devons reculer devant aucun sacrifice pour l'obtenir. L'émigration nous dévore. Nos ressources restent inertes dans les entrailles de la terre. Notre bois pourrit sur le sol. Allons-nous périr au milieu de l'abondance? Non, messieurs, il nous faut l'industrie pour développer notre pays, mais nous ne pourrons l'obtenir qu'en sillonnant notre pays de chemins de fer. Qui veut la fin veut les moyens.'[46]

These attitudes of parish priests, ultramontane newspapers, and the bishop permit the extension of William Ryan's interpretation back into the 1870s. The clergy, Ryan suggests, were 'usually the intermediary between the industrialist - be he French Canadian, English, or American - and the local workers ... By and large there was realistic acceptance of both industrialization and urbanization ... '[47] Priests identified with the needs of their parishes and accepted railways and English-speaking capitalists as necessary for local prosperity. As part of their responsibilities, curés fought to stimulate local agriculture, to colonize their parishes, and to find winter employment for parishioners. An entrepreneur such as Hugh Allan who spoke French, who chose a young French-Canadian ultramontane as company secretary, and who scrupulously adhered to parish and diocesan niceties received cooperation from clerics whose parishes would benefit from his enterprises. A head-table blessing, a local campaign for the best route, donation of a church-owned gravel pit, or a priest's demand for half-fares for students and the elderly easily escalated into active participation in railway projects. 'All the curés of Beauce approve of the railway planned for Lévis, Dorchester and Beauce counties,' a priest assured Langevin in 1869: 'Tous sont prêts à se mettre à la tête de leur paroisse et à travailler ... '[48] Priests often fought for competing railways. While Curé Labelle supported the Montreal Colonization Railway, A. Brunet, a curé from the south shore of the Ottawa River, appeared before Montreal City Council asking its support for a railway through the Ontario counties of Russell and Prescott. Throughout French Canada clerics served as directors of colonization railways that might aid their communities. Priests were named in the charters of the Saguenay and Lake St. John Railway, the Rimouski and Gaspé Railway, the Iberville and Missisquoi Railway, the Philipsburg, Farnham and Yamaska Railway, the Three Rivers and North Western Railway, and the Papineau Seigniory Railway. The higher clergy and seminarians were also attracted to railways through their concern to choose the best site for a hospital or school and their interest in the value of church properties. Their vigorous participation in community life made it impossible to ignore railway development. In Quebec City the Ursuline sisters donated a terminus to the Quebec and Gosford Railway, in the St. Maurice Valley new parish and diocesan boundaries were formed in accordance with traffic flow along railway lines, and in Montreal the diocese inherited shares in the Joliette Railway. The Montreal Colonization Railway, while nominally a 'colonization' project, was part of a railway to the Pacific and brought the promise of industrialization, settlement, growth, and exploitation of resources. Montreal-area clerics understood this reality and supported the railway enthusiastically.

By 1872 the Montreal Colonization Railway was a potent combination. As a Hugh Allan enterprise, it had the support of his powerful friends in Ottawa and Quebec City, access to British and American capital sources, and the promise of integration into a transcontinental rail and transatlantic steam system. At the same time strong local support from Montreal-area politicians and clerics ensured the railway favourable local legislation, a docile labouring population, and important municipal subsidies.

3

Montreal's million

Municipal subsidies were a traditional source of public funds for railway construction. Before Confederation dozens of Canadian communities had been wooed, pressured, or blackmailed into supporting railway projects. In 1871 the Quebec municipal code authorized municipalities to assist the construction of railways, colonization projects, bridges, piers, or roads.[1] Subject to approval by local electors and the provincial cabinet, municipalities could take shares, lend money, or guarantee company loans. With her position as entrepôt of the St. Lawrence and with an administration oriented to the commercial interests, Montreal was besieged with requests from railway promoters. Foremost among these was the Montreal Colonization Railway.

Always turbulent, Montreal doubled its population between 1851 and 1871. During this period the city reinforced its position at the hub of the expanding Canadian rail and steamship network. Boatworks, iron industries, biscuit and shoe manufacturers, cotton mills, breweries, and sugar refineries were built in Hochelaga and along the Lachine Canal and harbour. In the central business district, banking and commercial interests grew apace. The Bank of Montreal, Sun Life Insurance, and the shipping and trading concerns of the Torrances and the Allans expanded greatly in the Confederation period. The commercial class used the Montreal Board of Trade, the Corn Exchange, and the Montreal Harbour Commission to defend its interests locally as well as in Ottawa and Quebec City. Civic administrations during the Confederation period were dominated by 'une équipe d'hommes d'affaires'; of the first eleven mayors, nine were members of the city's commercial élite.[2] Electoral campaigns were unsophisticated and violent. With no secret ballot, victory was usually assured to the candidate with the largest bankroll. If all else failed, gangs of canal workers or sailors could be imported as muscle. Although competing fiercely among themselves, Montreal's élite – French and English, Catholic and Protestant – cooperated to keep power out of the hands of radicals and troublemakers. Médéric Lanctôt's defeat in 1867 was witness to the power of this cooperation.

While sharing common enemies Montreal's élite was deeply divided and it is misleading to emphasize a 'Great Compromise' between St. James Street and Cathedral Street.[3] The latter was itself badly splintered by the battle between Bishop Bourget and the Sulpicians while the city's commercial history in the 1870s can be analysed best within the context of internal competition. Alliances among various railway interests are easily discernible: the north-shore clergy, the east-end entrepreneurs, and the various parts of Hugh Allan's business empire formed one group. They united against the Grand Trunk forces, the Lachine Canal business group, and representatives from the south shore of the Ottawa River. These divisions formed the core of the Pacific Railway debate, the 1872 federal election campaign in Montreal, and the struggle for a $1 million municipal subsidy to the Montreal Colonization Railway.

In 1869 the Montreal *Gazette* initiated the campaign for a municipal subsidy. It pointed out that capitalists could not be expected to build a railway to Ottawa or the forests north of Montreal without 'liberal assistance' from local and provincial governments. The *Gazette* questioned the city's proposed $1 million subsidy to the Montreal Colonization Railway, preferring an outright gift of $750,000. Its reasoning was simple: 'every dollar granted by way of bonus reduces the capital and enhances the values of the private stock held by individuals for investment.' Mayor William Workman joined the campaign. Attacking what he called 'the settled supineness of our merchants,' he warned Montrealers 'to be doing before it is too late.'[4]

In December 1869 Montreal's finance committee began meeting railway promoters to consider means of encouraging 'public works.' Within a few months city council received requests from both the Canada Central and Montreal Colonization railways, and by November 1871 it faced five such demands. The Montreal Colonization Railway was represented by Peter Murphy, Louis Beaubien, J.-E.-L. de Bellefeuille, and Hugh Allan. C.J. Brydges asked the city for $200,000 to aid Grand Trunk construction in the city: the North Shore Railway, represented by Joseph Cauchon, asked for a municipal grant of

$250,000. The Montreal and City of Ottawa Junction Railway, the Lake Coteau to Ottawa Railway, and the St. Francis and Megantic Railway, the latter represented by Alexander Galt, also wanted aid.[5]

On 7 July 1870 a public meeting was held to promote a $1 million municipal grant to the Canada Central Railway. The mayor presided, de Bellefeuille acted as secretary and speakers included Thomas Ryan, Henry Starnes, Walter Shanly, Gédéon Ouimet, John Sandfield Macdonald, Côme-Séraphin Cherrier, Louis Beaubien, Duncan Macdonald, Michael Ryan, Peter Murphy, and Henry Bulmer. The resolution for a railway subsidy to link Montreal and Ottawa was moved by Cartier. The Liberal élite, including A.A. Dorion, John Young, and Luther Holton, was present and spoke in favour of a subsidy.

The increasing cooperation between the Montreal Colonization Railway and the Canada Central, and the latter's decision to concentrate on building west of Ottawa, meant increased pressure on municipal officials. In November 1870 three Montreal Colonization officials - de Bellefeuille, Murphy, and Abbott - met with the city's finance committee.[6] In the same month a petition was presented to centre ward politicians: of 580 municipal voters in the ward, 470 favored a $1 million subsidy to the Montreal Colonization Railway. A few months later another public meeting was called. The orchestra of Saint-Pierre provided music and several Oblate fathers were present. Speakers favouring a subsidy interpreted the issue as a simple question of Quebec versus Ontario and dismissed their opponents as being pro-Ontario or tools of the Grand Trunk. Some politicians did oppose the grant. William Rodden had interests in Plantagenet, Ontario, and supported a railway along the south shore of the Ottawa River. Another alderman expressed fears for the city's finances.[7] In March 1871 a delegation from Ottawa and north-shore counties along the Ottawa River visited Montreal and added to these pressures for a large Montreal subsidy.

The Montreal Colonization directors met with city council on 8 February 1871. One city official questioned granting a subsidy without a definitive survey or fixed construction costs. J.J.C. Abbott replied that the company's estimates were based on American examples of $15,000 a mile for construction and rolling stock.[8] Half of the $3 million total would be met by a $1 million subsidy from Montreal and municipal grants totalling $500,000 from other communities along the route. Private subscriptions and the provincial government's subsidy would make up the difference.

Even before he became president of the railway in the fall of 1871, Hugh Allan's presence was felt in these negotiations. The participation as early as 1869 of his associates, Abbott, de Bellefeuille, and Beaubien, in both the Canada Central and Montreal Colonization railways is clear indication of his interest. Francis Hincks - an old hand at railway politics - felt that Allan was secretly involved in both the Pacific and Montreal Colonization railways but 'knowing that these plans were in direct conflict with the Grand Trunk Company, Allan did not reveal them to the Government.'[9] John A. Macdonald, agreed:

Sir Hugh Allan had, as is well known, a very large interest in the steamship line and in getting freights for that line. He knew, as it was well known in the country, that there was an opposition line being got up under the auspices of the Grand Trunk Railway Company to run to England, and it is well-known that he was alarmed at this, because he naturally assumed that if the rival line were connected with the Grand Trunk Railway there would be preference given to that line over his own in matters of freight from the west. Sir Hugh Allan, I think, I am not wrong in supposing that this excited him very much, and that it was the primary cause of his connecting himself with the Northern Colonization Road from Montreal westward, and encouraging the building of the northern Road between Montreal and Quebec, and the extension of the inner line between Ottawa and Toronto, so as to have another and competing line which would give his line of steamers fair play. I think I am not wrong in believing that this was the origin of his connecting himself so strongly and warmly with these lines, and these lines would not, I think, especially the Road from Ottawa to Toronto, be early undertaken unless there was a chance of the Pacific Road going on westward.[10]

If Hincks and Macdonald were correct in their assessment, Allan's participation in the Montreal Colonization Railway was not simply a means of blackmailing Cartier, as Pierre Berton has suggested. The Montreal Colonization Railway was part of a larger game-plan with higher stakes than the defeat of the ailing Cartier.[11] Fearing his Grand Trunk competition, Allan saw the importance of the government's decision that the railroad to British Columbia should be built by a private company. The Montreal Colonization Railway's favourable route to Ottawa and its support by the Quebec government as a 'colonization' project enhanced its attractiveness as an eastern link to the Pacific. While the transcontinental line was being completed, the Montreal Colonization Railway could channel Ottawa Valley and Laurentian trade to Allan's steamships in Montreal. Allan also had plans to compete with the Grand Trunk in central Ontario and funnel that trade from Ottawa to Montreal on the tracks of the Montreal Colonization Railway. In 1871 the Ontario and Quebec Railway Company received a charter to build from Ottawa to Toronto via Carleton Place, Madoc, and Peterborough. Allan was a director and held one-half of the company's stock. Construction of the Montreal Colonization Railway would also increase the value of Allan's properties in east-end Montreal and along the north shore of the Ottawa River.[12]

Allan's interests were not restricted to railways and the Montreal Ocean Steamship Company. He was a director of the Bank of Montreal (1849), the Montreal Railway Terminus Company (1861), the Merchants' Bank (1861), the Citizens Assurance Company (1861), the Montreal Telegraph Company (1872), the Canada Rolling Stock Company (1870), the Montreal Warehousing Company, the Richelieu and Ontario Navigation Company (president 1876-82), the Canada Marine Insurance Company (1868), the Montreal Credit Company (1871), and the Canada Life Assurance Company (1872). In 1873 he estimated his fortune at around $6 million, one-half of which was invested in the carrying trade.[13]

Allan had great commercial power, influence with politicians at all levels, an open wallet, and lieutenants who knew how to dispense the contents to best effect. He had contacts with sources of capital in Britain and the United States. In his own bailiwick, he had been one of the owners of the *Gazette* and had subsidized *La Minerve*. A self-confident Scot, Allan adapted quickly to steel and steam and the changing economic and political structures of mid-nineteenth-century Canada. He readily accepted the pluralism of Quebec society; the enemy was not an ethnic group but his business competition. As a young immigrant Allan had lived in Ste. Rose for two years where he had learned to speak French. His closest neighbour in that village was Curé Labelle's father.[14] Publicly, Allan assured French Canadians that they were welcome in his companies: 'I assure you, to whatever nationality you may belong, you will have full justice in everything I have to do with; I know nothing of nationality; I am desirious of getting the best men in the best places and of giving everybody fair play.'[15] He explained his technique of dealing with French Canadians in a frank letter to an American colleague:

... means must be used to influence the public, and I employed several young French lawyers to write it up for their own newspapers. I subscribed a controlling interest in the stock Montreal Colonization Railway and proceeded to subsidize the newspapers, both editors and proprietors. I went to the country through which the road would pass, and called on many of the inhabitants. I visited the priests, and made friends of them, and I employed agents to go amongst the principal people and talk it up.

I began to hold public meetings, and attended to them myself, making frequent speeches in French to them, showing them where their true interest lay.[16]

Allan assiduously cultivated the French-Canadian clergy. To the disgust of the Montreal *Gazette*, Allan occasionally leaked information to *Le Nouveau Monde* before the English-language press. In 1870 he authorized a special stop of a company steamer for the new bishop of Three Rivers, Louis-François Laflèche. This permitted the influential Laflèche to disembark on his return from Rome in his own diocese instead of ascending to Montreal.[17] Allan's favourite cleric was Curé Labelle. At a dinner held in his honour in February 1873 Allan interrupted toasts to himself to pay tribute to his head-table guest. The curé responded by describing Allan as 'a new Hercules.'[18]

Allan was well treated by Montreal's nationalist and ultramontane press. *Le National*, formed in April 1872 to support the Montreal campaign of the Parti National, was an enthusiastic advocate of commercial development. Like the Conservative press it supported Allan's Pacific railway and a $1 million municipal subsidy to the Montreal Colonization Railway. The ultramontane *Le Nouveau Monde* endorsed Allan's efforts to deepen the channel between Montreal and Quebec City, to construct a new railway bridge over the St. Lawrence, and to charter a railway to the Pacific. In particular, it supported a $1 million subsidy for his railway: 'Ceux qui veulent vous faire signer des requêtes contre *le chemin de colonisation* ne sont pas les amis de notre prospérité, bien au contraire.'[19]

Nor did Allan neglect Conservative politicians or the Conservative press. His donations – usually made through his lawyer, J.J.C. Abbott – were generous. Appearing before a royal commission, Abbott explained that Allan's substantial contributions to the Macdonald government had paid off: 'On every one of these subjects the Government had a policy which was favourable to his views, and in my opinion three times the sum would have been well spent ... '[20] Allan also bankrolled Thomas and Richard White, editors of the Montreal *Gazette*. Again, Abbott acted as intermediary:

... Mr. Abbott came that evening to report the result of a conversation with Messrs White, on the subject of giving a more vigorous support to the Northern Colonization by-law, then about being put before the people, and generally to hereinafter stand strongly by that and the Pacific Railway scheme. He stated that they (Messrs White) feared the loss of a large Grand Trunk and other patronage if they took this stand and consequently urged that they were entitled to compensation ... The result of the interview was reported to be a proposal that Sir Hugh should deduct five thousand dollars from the amount still due on the paper, and also to allow the Messrs White to enter in full possession, materially as well as editorially. Sir Hugh objected to giving so much out of his own pocket, but offered to share for the present, in proper proportion with the other Colonization Railway promoters ... immediately after we noticed that the advocacy of the Gazette was all that could be desired. [21]

With the consolidation of the Montreal Colonization's clerical, political, and press support, Allan assumed a public role. In the fall of 1871 he became president of the railway and immediately began personal negotiations with the city for a $1 million subsidy. Even though powerful entrepreneurs such as Alexander Galt had been obliged to negotiate with the city in public, Allan was granted a private meeting with city council. Following this conference, he left to seek capital in Europe. During his absence he kept up pressure by writing friendly editors that English capitalists would construct the line if the city granted the subsidy.[22]

Allan was not to obtain his million from the city's taxpayers without a bitter fight. The business community was deeply divided over the subsidy and his opponents were powerful. In the case of John Young there was personal hostility to Allan and to his generous support of the Conservative party. Other opponents were important taxpayers who objected to financing railways from the municipal purse. An 1872 petition emphasized that a railway subsidy would bring tax increases and would retard park development, water-works construction, and harbour improvements. One cynic felt that taxpayers, before granting $1 million 'ought to have some guarantee that we will get something more than a R.R. depot at Hochelaga, and a few miles of a railroad to enable amateur fishermen and others to visit the scenery of the well-known "Back River." '[23]

Objections were also raised by advocates of competing railways such as William Rodden and John Hamilton who favoured a municipal subsidy for a line along the south shore of the Ottawa River. Within

Montreal there was tension between the forces of the east and west end. The Montreal Colonization Railway with its terminus in Hochelaga would aid the manufacturers, property-owners, and harbour interests of the east end. Louis Beaubien, property-owner and MLA for Hochelaga, and Victor Hudon, a Hochelaga cotton manufacturer, had obvious reasons for supporting the railway; manufacturers along the Lachine Canal were less enthusiastic.

The struggle for a municipal subsidy for the Montreal Colonization Railway had a larger dimension that transcended municipal politics and local issues. It formed part of the transcontinental and transatlantic competition between Hugh Allan and the Grand Trunk. With its through line to Chicago, the Grand Trunk was delivering increasing quantities of western produce to east-coast shippers. In 1859 the Grand Trunk and the Allan line had concluded an agreement for the shipping of passengers and freight between Montreal and Liverpool; during the winter closing of the Montreal port, trade was carried via Portland, Maine. Although the agreement expired in 1869 and was not renewed, the two companies continued to cooperate over the next few years. However, each viewed the other with growing suspicion. In a well-publicized letter C.J. Brydges, the Grand Trunk manager, complained to Hugh and Andrew Allan that 'during the last two or three years ... your firm has not acted with anything like the harmony and unity which ought to exist ... All your arrangements have been arbitrary and dictatorial ... [24] He was particularly concerned about Allan's plan to build a competing rail network to the west. With the Grand Trunk's influence on employment, its purchases of rolling stock and supplies, its access to capital, and its myriad of relationships with businessmen and politicians, Brydges could make his opinion felt in all quarters. Luther Holton, who knew Montreal well, explained the opposition of one important shipper to the Montreal Colonization Railway by noting that, while not subordinate to the Grand Trunk, David Torrance 'like nearly everybody else in Canada ... necessarily had business relations with it.' [25] In 1869 Brydges talked about a Grand Trunk line to the Pacific, of involving the Hudson's Bay Company, and of obtaining government subsidies. He also invested in the Montreal and City of Ottawa Junction Railway, a potential competitor of the Montreal Colonization Railway. During the organization of Allan's Canadian Pacific Company in the winter of 1872 the Grand Trunk refused to take shares, despite Allan's flirtations. [26]

For his part, Allan feared the Grand Trunk's monopoly on western trade, its control over freight rates, and its opposition to his railway ambitions. Montreal Colonization supporters always identified the Grand Trunk as their most dangerous enemy. Curé Labelle charged that the Grand Trunk 'had opened war' and Louis Beaubien, vice-president of the railway, commented on 'the opposition we met from the hands of the Grand Trunk, in Quebec, in Montreal and in England, when trying to negotiate our bonds.' The Grand Trunk was accused by John Young of creating a 'bogus company,' the Montreal and St. Jérôme Colonization Railway, to block the Montreal subsidy.[27] The Toronto *Globe*, a reliable spokesman of anti-Grand Trunk sentiment, supported Allan's efforts to link Quebec City, Montreal, and southern Ontario via the North Shore Railway, the Montreal Colonization Railway, the Canada Central Railway, and the Ontario and Quebec Railway. At last, exulted the *Globe*, Canadians will be able 'to exert an influence on the managing director of the Grand Trunk Railway.' It was delighted by Allan's bickering with the Grand Trunk and by his participation in the Montreal Colonization Railway: 'What is wanted, as we showed a few weeks ago, is the shortest, practicable route from Ottawa to Quebec, in direct connection with the Ontario and trans-continental railways, making very nearly an air line to what after all is the real oceanic port of the St. Lawrence, and at the same time opening up a large portion of valuable country in our sister Province, while giving a through line, effectively competing with, and independent of the Grand Trunk.'[28]

Montreal city council received two petitions opposing a subsidy to the Montreal Colonization Railway. S.E. Molson, a director of the Bank of Montreal, Molson's Bank, and the Canada Guarantee Company, was prominent in the first petition which was circulated shortly after Allan's election as president of the railway. The Molsons had been active in the St. Lawrence and Ottawa Railway and in the Montreal and Champlain Railway, both of which were part of the Grand Trunk system by 1872. William Molson had been a director of the Grand Trunk.[29] In the winter of 1872, S.E. Molson's son-in-law, David L. Macpherson, formed the Interoceanic Railway Company in opposition to Allan's Canadian Pacific Railway Company.

Another vocal opponent of the subsidy was Sydney Bellingham, publisher of the *Daily News*. As MLA for Argenteuil, Bellingham had fought bitter election battles against Allan's lawyer, J.J.C. Abbott. According to Bellingham, Allan threatened in 1858 to re-route the projected Montreal and Bytown Railroad away from Lachute if the town's voters chose Bellingham over Abbott.[30] By 1872 Bellingham was attacking both Allan and the Grand Trunk. Bellingham's motives were less than pure since he was lobbying for his own Ottawa Valley railway and a $3 million provincial subsidy.

In April 1872 a second petition, containing an even more impressive roll-call of Allan's opposition, was presented to city council. Thomas Cramp, a partner of David Torrance, signed, as did Romeo H. Stephens, Henry Munro, William Clendenning, William Murray, Henry Lyman, John Hamilton, and Joseph Hickson, secretary of the Grand Trunk. Hamilton, a Hawkesbury mill-owner and former director of the North Shore and Canada Central railways, had been a strong supporter of a south-shore route along the Ottawa River.[31] David Torrance opposed the subsidy. President of the Bank of Montreal, Torrance was best known for his shipping interests. He was a director of the Richelieu Navigation Company, Consumers Gas (1872), the Montreal Railway Terminus Company (1861), and the Canada Guarantee Company (1872). He made his sympathies clear when he became a director of Macpherson's Interoceanic Railway Company. As a shipper, Torrance had to reckon with the power of the Grand Trunk.

With their petitions, public meetings, and diversionary tactics, opponents blocked a subsidy to the Montreal Colonization Railway in the fall of 1871. In the spring of 1872 a month of furious lobbying commenced. On 13 March city council received a pro-subsidy petition signed by representatives of both the bishop of Montreal and the Seminary of Montreal. Allan himself wrote to the council excusing his absence and giving a personal guarantee that a subsidy would be well spent.[32] Council debates became bitter. Allan's opponents forced a postponement of the bylaw vote until the railway produced a complete list of its stockholders. Other opponents wanted to force the company to sell 100,000 shares to other investors before Montreal's subsidy became due. The railway's defenders succeeded in reducing this outside investment to 50,000 shares.[33]

The formation of a competing railway company was another means of muddying the waters. The Interoceanic Railway syndicate, organized by Toronto and Grand Trunk interests, lobbied in Ottawa against the Canadian Pacific Railway.[34] In Montreal Allan's opponents unveiled a local railway scheme to challenge the Montreal Colonization Railway. Hastily organized, the Montreal and St. Jérôme Colonization Railway issued its prospectus on 21 March 1872, one day before first reading of the Montreal bylaw to grant $1 million to Allan's railway.

With the obvious intention of scuttling the subsidy, the promoters pledged to finance a railway to St. Jérôme 'upon purely commercial principles.' Without any municipal aid, their railway would be built by private capital and the province's colonization railway grants.[35]

The new company's provisional board was well-stocked with important Montreal entrepreneurs: George Stephen, Alexander Ogilvie, Alex McGibbon, John Atkinson, Maurice Cuvillier, Jacques F. Sincennes, and Charles Davidson. Henry Starnes, a prominent financier and politician, was a member of the board. According to Cartier, Starnes was one of the two most 'indispensable' Bleus in the Montreal region.[36] He was mayor of Montreal for two terms (1856-7), representative of Chateauguay in the Assembly (1857-63), legislative councilor (1867), lieutenant-colonel in the militia, Montreal harbour commissioner (1855-6, 1866-7), vice-president of the Board of Trade, and active in the St. Jean Baptiste Society. Later in 1872 Starnes served as 'bagman' in Cartier's election campaign and handled the $70,000 which Allan gave to Cartier. A prominent member of the financial community, Starnes was a director of the Richelieu Navigation Company (1872), la Banque du Peuple, the Montreal Warehousing Company (1872), Canadian Engine and Machinery Company, the Metropolitan Bank (1871), the Art Union Publishing Company (1872), and the Montreal City and District Savings Bank (1870). Although an opponent in 1872 of the $1 million subsidy to the Montreal Colonization Railway, Starnes had supported earlier municipal subsidies for railways. Nor was Starnes unalterably opposed to the Allans. He was a director of the Montreal Warehousing Corporation of which Hugh Allan was president and Abbott was solicitor. Starnes and Andrew Allan were provisional directors of the Sugar Beet Company and both were directors of the Consumers Gas Company.

The two leading promoters of the Montreal and St. Jérôme Colonization Railway, according to the *Gazette*, were Alexander Ogilvie and Robert James Reekie. Ogilvie, founder of the important flour mills of that name, had been MLA for Montreal West (1867-71) and was a director of the Richelieu Navigation Company (1872), Western Loan and Trust, Montreal Loan and Mortgage, Sun Life (1872), and New York Life (1872). Reekie had been a director of the Montreal Colonization Railway in 1869 but by 1872 was associated with the Grand Trunk interests.[37] President of the Canadian Engine and Machinery Company, Reekie was a director of the Canada Guarantee Company (1872), the Canada Rolling Stock Company (1873), the City Bank

(1874), the Accident Insurance Company (1874), Mutual Life (1872), and was a shareholder in the Bank of Montreal (1872). Like Starnes, Reekie had shared the director's table with the Allans in both the Canada Rolling Stock Company (1869) and the Canada Railway Station Company (1871).

Allan had built up his strength in Montreal over a generation. For years his name had been synonymous with progress, jobs, and economic development – to Hector Langevin, Allan was 'the representative man' of Lower Canada. This confidence was not shaken despite his shenanigans with American investors in the Canadian Pacific Railway, his blatant exploitation of colonization, and his willingness to break Cartier, Montreal's most important politician. On 3 April 1872 a $1 million subsidy to the Montreal Colonization Railway was passed by council and in early May municipal voters approved it 6459 to 117.[38] Under the terms of the bylaw, Montreal would name three directors, the city's contribution was not to exceed one-third of the railway's total cost, and the station, workshops, and terminus were to be located within the city. The subsidy would be advanced on a pro-rated basis, $25,000 when the railway was completed across the Rivière des Prairies, $25,000 on completion of the bridge over Rivière des Mille-Iles, and $750,000 at the rate of $5000 a mile for the balance of the line (see map B). There was $150,000 reserved to buy the federally owned Quebec Gate Barracks and Military Hospital as a station site. Provisions were also made for links with other railways. The Montreal Colonization was to cooperate with the Canada Central Railway for a bridge near Hull and to locate its junction with the North Shore Railway within the Montreal city limits. The city planned to finance its subsidy with twenty-five year municipal bonds and to pay the 6 per cent interest with a local real estate tax.

Passage of the bylaw did not subdue the opposition. J.H.R. Molson immediately sued the city for exceeding its powers; after months before the courts, his suit was dismissed in June 1873.[39] Since municipal bylaws were subject to provincial approval, the next round took place in hearings before the legislature's railway committee. Allan's troops arrived in force. De Bellefeuille, Abbott, Joseph Coursol, and Thomas White travelled to Quebec City to reiterate the familiar charge that the Grand Trunk was impeding Montreal's development. Provincial ratification of the bylaw in December 1872 led to an appeal to Ottawa for disallowance. In conjunction with the Canada Central Railway Allan's opponents presented a petition describing the Montreal bylaw as 'defective and vicious.'[40] As well as being a federal responsibility because of its interprovincial links, the Montreal Colonization Railway was founded upon the 'extravagant and impracticable' presumption of a new bridge over the St. Lawrence. De Bellefeuille and L.O. Loranger defended Allan and the Montreal Colonization Railway. They argued that the railway fell within provincial jurisdiction and pointed out that Quebec's ratification of the bylaw was similar to Ontario legislation. The Macdonald government did not seriously consider disallowance. Weeks before a decision was announced, Hector Langevin told Curé Labelle that he could 'dormir tranquillement.' Langevin also urged Macdonald to announce rejection of disallowance as soon as possible so that Allan's efforts to raise capital would not be hindered.[41]

Allan's search for capital was less successful. The Pacific scandal, deteriorating economic conditions after 1873, and the influence of the Grand Trunk in English banking circles made Allan and Abbott reluctant to publicize their railway's prospectus. Unable to raise capital, Allan made another attempt to cooperate with the Grand Trunk. In May 1873 reports circulated that he would abandon the Montreal Colonization Railway in return for Grand Trunk support for the Canadian Pacific Railway. This alarmed Montreal Colonization supporters, and Curé Labelle received explanatory letters from Abbott, Beaubien, de Bellefeuille, and Allan. The latter wrote that he was simply testing the sincerity of the Grand Trunk: 'I did not believe this was true [that the Grand Trunk would really give assistance] and I thought the best way to meet it was to accept of his proposal which I accordingly did but on one pretext and another he [Richard Potter, chairman of the Grand Trunk Railway] has always put it off and he is no nearer to it now than he was a month ago. The truth is that he expected I would refuse to abandon the local lines and then he would have said that I sacrificed the Pacific to them. Now he is in a corner and does not know what to do.'[42] Although some newspapers ridiculed Allan's hypocrisy and pointed out that he was deceiving either the Grand Trunk or the Montreal Colonization Railway, Curé Labelle did not lose faith. Allan, Labelle insisted, was still a staunch defender of Montreal, the north, and French Canada.[43]

The Grand Trunk's most important political ally in the struggle against Allan was George-Etienne Cartier. Afflected with Bright's disease and exhausted by the rigours of his cabinet post, Cartier was a prominent victim of this struggle between rival transportation companies. Although associated with the Grand Trunk since the 1850s,

Cartier was vulnerable to pressure from the Montreal Colonization Railway since it would directly serve his riding of Montreal-East. Cartier's home was directly across the street from the ultimate site of the railway's station. In the months before the 1872 election, Allan used his power in Montreal to break Cartier and through him tried to force Macdonald to accept his charter for the Canadian Pacific Railway. The efforts of Macdonald and Cartier to unite Allan's company with the Interoceanic syndicate were interpreted in Montreal as a sellout to Toronto. The struggle between the two competing companies and their metropolises was easily translated into ethnic terms: 'The contest has been, really, between Ontario and Quebec,' an Interoceanic official wrote Macdonald, and 'Quebec has secured the prize – Thanks to French Domination.'[44] Allan effectively isolated Cartier from his east-end political base while increasing his own credibility as defender of Montreal. Early in the year Cartier was asked to join leading clerics and entrepreneurs in signing a petition in favour of a subsidy for the Montreal Colonization Railway.[45] Le National, the Gazette, La Minerve, and Le Nouveau Monde all supported the project and pointed out its advantages for Cartier's constituents. Thomas White, editor of the Gazette, visited Cartier at home for a long conversation on the railway issue. Allan, according to his own count, won the support of twenty-seven of Cartier's forty-seven French-Canadian MPs.[46]

In May a group of Allan's friends met at his home and in the office of Jean-Louis Beaudry. They drew up an ultimatum and a few days later a delegation visited Cartier in Ottawa. His five visitors were all prominent Montreal Conservatives with a stake in the construction of the Canadian Pacific and Montreal Colonization railways: Jean-Louis Beaudry was a prominent papal zouave, mayor of Montreal (1862-6, 1877-9, 1881-4), harbour commissioner (1862-4, 1865-6), director of the Jacques Cartier Bank, member of the Quebec Legislative Council, and a director of the Pacific Railway (1872); Charles Leblanc had $2000 invested in the Montreal Colonization Railway; Victor Hudon, owner of the Hudon Cotton Mills and federal candidate for Hochelaga in 1872, was a provisional director of the Pacific Railway (1872); Joseph-Adolphe Chapleau, the young but already influential Conservative, was MLA for Terrebonne through which the railway would pass; Charles-Séraphin Rodier, contractor, merchant, and manufacturer, was mayor of Montreal (1858-61), harbour commissioner (1840-50, 1859-62), vice-president of the Jacques Cartier Bank (1871), and a provisional director of the Pacific Railway (1872).

Cartier buckled under this pressure. In June 1872 he denied that his Grand Trunk interests prejudiced him and publicly supported the municipal subsidy. The issue became confused in the weeks before the election but Allan was convinced he had brought Cartier to terms. On 12 June he wrote to his American backers that he had 'the pledge' of Cartier.[47] Three Montreal Colonization directors – Allan, Louis Beaubien, and Peter Murphy – participated in Cartier's nomination meeting, and when his election committee was formed, supporters of the Montreal Colonization and Pacific Railway were again prominent. Allan's channelling of $85,000 to Cartier's election campaign was striking evidence that Cartier had come to terms.[48]

While Allan and his lawyers worked to obtain optimal conditions for the company in Montreal and Ottawa, Montreal Colonization officials faced embarrassing local questions. The shortest and most profitable route to the proposed Nipissing terminus of the Pacific Railway was increasingly incompatible with colonization in the Laurentians and upper Ottawa Valley. The village of St. Jérôme typified this conflict. Engineering and commercial factors dictated that St. Jérôme be bypassed by a more direct route up the Ottawa Valley. However, important supporters such as Godefroy Laviolette and Curé Labelle had enthusiastically promoted the railway in the belief that one of its primary functions was to stimulate the St. Jérôme region. The resignation of sympathetic directors such as John Young had added weight to rumours that the village would be bypassed and joined to the main line by a wooden spur.[49] Company officials delayed announcing their decision on the route to St. Jérôme as long as possible. In August 1872 the parish of St. Jérôme voted a $10,000 subsidy and the village of St. Jérôme subscribed $15,000. However, the financial inducements of St. Jérôme, the power of its curé, and the rhetoric of the colonization movement were no match for the realities of transcontinental commerce. In 1873 St. Jérôme was told that it would be linked to the main line by a twelve-mile spur.

Other small communities subscribed liberally. Ottawa County ratified a $200,000 subsidy and Ste. Thérèse granted $12,000. St. Andrews appended certain conditions. If the railway passed within one mile of its Episcopal church, the parish would subscribe $25,000; if the distance was between one and two miles the grant was reduced to $20,000. The $25,000 subsidy of St. Jérusalem d'Argenteuil was only to be granted if the main line passed within one-half mile of the Lachute courthouse.[50] Pontiac County received special attention from Montreal Colonization officials, especially after December 1872 when the provincial land grant of 10,000 acres a mile was extended into the county. In lobbying throughout Pontiac, de Bellefeuille, Curé Labelle, and Beaubien pointed out that the railway might by-pass the county by crossing into Ontario at Ottawa. After a three-hour meeting on 12 March 1873, the Pontiac Council approved a $150,000 subsidy.[51]

In the spring of 1873 twenty tenders were received for construction of the Montreal Colonization Railway, and on 24 July 1873 a contract was signed with Duncan Macdonald. According to the railway's engineer, Macdonald's offer was at least $83,000 cheaper than its nearest competitor. The contractor was to purchase an eighty-foot right of way and to build an iron railway equal in quality to the Great Western Railway. Work was to begin by 1 September 1873 and to be completed within two years. Based on a rate of $29,750 per mile the contractor was to be paid $4,224,500. Payment would consist of $800,000 in Montreal municipal bonds, other municipal bonds worth at least $240,000, and the balance in the company's 7 per cent first-mortgage bonds at a rate of 75 per cent of their face value. The contract included a holdback clause to ensure completion of the line: 10 per cent of every payment to a total of $100,000 would be retained until the entire line was built. All work was subject to inspection by the company engineer and the company could dismiss any employee guilty of neglect or improper conduct. The contractor was to discourage the sale of alcohol on construction sites. In cases of dispute the contractor and company would each name one arbitrator who would in turn name a third arbitrator.[52]

Within twenty-four hours of the signing of the contract, survey parties were in the field. Symbolically, the first ground was broken on 1 September 1873 on land owned by the railway's vice-president.

4

Subsidies and contracts

I

Although years from completion, the Montreal Colonization Railway had several factors in its favour. Blending colonization and economic development, it benefited from both the French-Canadian colonization movement and the ambitions of the Montreal entrepreneurs. It would open the Ottawa Valley and might become the main line between Montreal and the proposed Lake Nipissing terminus of the Pacific Railway. Its proximity to the provincial boundary enabled it to lobby for federal support and its Montreal terminus was located in Canada's financial and commercial core. While the railway had strong opponents, its president was the powerful Hugh Allan. Construction was retarded by economic conditions, the lack of capital, the Pacific scandal, the demise of the Macdonald Conservatives, and the instability of provincial politics, rather than by weakness on the railway's part.

The North Shore Railway had less potential. It had to compete with a navigable section of the St. Lawrence and with the Grand Trunk's south-shore line to Quebec City. Connecting Montreal and Quebec City, the North Shore Railway would not penetrate the Laurentian Shield. This made it difficult to exploit as a colonization railway. If an interior, colonization route was chosen, the railway would lose its commercial viability as well as the subsidies of communities along the river. In addition, the railway had its terminus in a metropolis that was slipping in relation to Montreal. Quebec City still had her grace, her churches, and the provincial seat. However, as a commercial centre the ancient capital was declining: 'The people are extremely poor, there is no work, no shipbuilding, labor in the four or five factories at

Quebec is extremely cheap.'[1] The North Shore Railway – with limited commercial potential, blocked from the west by Montreal, and ignored by capitalists – had to rely on public subsidies. Except for the investments of municipalities and religious institutions, the railway's paid-up stock in 1870 was $177.[2] Only when the railway's raison d'être was reversed and it became focused on Montreal was it able to marshall the political and economic strength necessary for construction.

Nor was the political situation encouraging. Cartier's death in 1873 left a vacuum in which the tensions between Quebec City and Montreal Conservatives remained unresolved. This had serious implications for a railway which proposed to join the two competing cities by means of government grants. The weakness of Quebec City in the administrations of both John A. Macdonald and Alexander Mackenzie did not help the railway. Hector Langevin, despite his Quebec City roots and his record as a North Shore promoter, could not favour the railway unduly since he was trying to assume Cartier's mantle for the whole province. Nor did Joseph Cauchon's accession to power in Ottawa aid the railway since, by the time he joined the Mackenzie administration, he had been ousted from the North Shore boardroom. Neither Macdonald nor Mackenzie was prepared to stimulate Quebec City and its railway at the expense of other central Canadian interests. This situation was accentuated by the subservience of provincial politicians to their federal counterparts. Finally, ultramontanism, *le programme catholique*, the struggle for Cartier's succession, the formation of the Parti National, the Tanneries scandal, and the university question, all disrupted the political stability desired by railway builders.

In the summer of 1870 the North Shore Company was revived. A small shareholders' meeting elected as directors John Hamilton, J.J.C. Abbott, Louis Beaubien, William McDougall, John Jones Ross, Joseph Cauchon, Thomas McGreevy, Col. William Rhodes, Jean-Baptiste Renaud, Georges-H. Simard, Jean-Docile Brousseau, and Willis Russell. Hamilton, Abbott, and Beaubien were Montrealers and clearly identified with the Canada Central Railway. McDougall and Ross represented north-shore counties. McDougall was MP for Three Rivers and a provisional director of the Pacific Railway in 1872; Ross was MP for Champlain and was later premier of the province. McGreevy was an important Quebec City entrepreneur. MP for Quebec-West, he served on the boards of La Banque Nationale (1863), the St. Lawrence Tow-Boat Company (1872), the Union Bank (1870), the Lévis and Kennebec Railway (1872), the Gulf Port Steam Navigation Company (1871), and the Pacific Railway (1872). In 1874 he became contractor for the North Shore Railway. Rhodes and Simard were well-known Quebec City businessmen. Rhodes was a director of the Grand Trunk (1853), the Quebec Warehousing Company (1859), and the Union Bank (1872). Simard was MP for Quebec-Centre, vice-president of the Quebec Notre Dame Savings Bank, and a director of the Interoceanic Company (1872). Renaud, an active French-Canadian railway entrepreneur, was associated with the Joliette Railway, the Pacific Railway (1872), the St. Eustache Railway (1882), the Lévis and Kennebec Railway (1872), the Stadacona Assurance Company (1874), and the Union Bank (1872). MP for Portneuf, Brousseau was secretary of La Banque Nationale (1861) and a founder of *Le Courrier du Canada*. Willis Russell was active in various mining enterprises and was proprietor of two well-known Quebec City hotels, Russell's Hotel and the St. Louis Hotel.

This new board of directors soon reflected the province's economic and political tensions. Competition between Quebec City and Montreal quickly penetrated into the North Shore boardroom. It flared up in September 1870 over Cauchon's choice of a secretary-treasurer. After 'some plain talk' from Abbott and J.M. Winchell, Cauchon yielded. Six weeks later two Montreal directors, Beaubien and Abbott, walked out of a meeting between company officials and the provincial government.[3] Although Cauchon's abrasiveness aggravated the situation, the main issue was the junction-point between the North Shore Railway and the railway from Montreal to the Ottawa Valley - be it the Montreal Colonization Railway or the Canada Central. A North Shore Railway pamphlet expressed Quebec City's ambitions:

A glance at the map will show that from those States, Minnesota, and others adjoining, it is almost a straight line to Montreal and Quebec. With a bridge across the Straits, freight and passengers can be carried from Duluth to Quebec, without shifting cars, on a 4 feet 8½ inch gauge railway, 300 miles shorter than by any other possible road from the head of Lake Superior to New York or Boston. This fact will have an important bearing on your enterprise, because cars can thus be brought from Michigan, Wisconsin and Minnesota, without requiring change or breaking bulk to Quebec, a Sea Port 480 miles nearer Liverpool than New York, a Port too, accessible from Sea for ships like the 'Great Eastern' without obstructions of any kind.[4]

Although not a member of the revitalized North Shore board, Hector Langevin seemed to support a Quebec City terminus for the Pacific railway. After alluding to British Columbia and its giant timber stands, Langevin concluded that Quebec City 'must from its position, be its real terminus.'[5] Joseph Cauchon was Quebec City's most outspoken defender on the board and he consistently opposed Montrealers 'who thought they were the whole of the Province of Quebec - a party who desired to ignore the lower sections of the Province, and rule them out from having any voice or share in the matter.'[6] Cauchon argued for a junction north of Montreal in the vicinity of Ste. Thérèse; Montreal would be served by a branch line (see map C).

The Montreal directors were adamant that the railways unite in Montreal where western goods could be transferred to Hugh Allan's steamers. Louis Beaubien, director of the North Shore, Canada Central, and Montreal Colonization Railways, put the Montreal viewpoint succinctly: 'While wishing every success for the Quebec enterprise it must be understood that they would not go to meet that railway; it must come to them ... and as one of the proprietors in Montreal he wished it to be understood that he would do nothing towards any scheme that would take the trade of Montreal past its doors.'[7]

The ambitions of the two cities were incompatible. Quebec City wanted direct access to the Ottawa Valley and western trade. Montreal was determined to expand her hinterland and to block any diversion of trade from her port. In the winter of 1871 these tensions surfaced again. Writing to Langevin, Beaubien blamed Cauchon for the North Shore's problems. A few weeks later Beaubien reported to Montreal city council that there had been a 'jealousy' resulting in 'an entire separation' of the North Shore and Montreal Colonization Railways.[8] The climax occurred in March when a Montreal delegation met provincial officials. Soon after, Cauchon backed off and accepted a junction in Montreal provided that the city grant a subsidy to the North Shore Railway. The *Gazette* reported that the provincial government had fixed a junction in Montreal's east end. Allan's accession to the presidency of the Montreal Colonization Railway in the fall of 1871 was interpreted by the *Globe* as final evidence that Quebec City, 'sluggish and unenterprising,' had lost its bid to become the entrepôt of western trade.[9]

By 1872 the division between Quebec City and Montreal within the North Shore Railway was complete. Beaubien, Abbott, and Hamilton had all resigned as directors and the newly elected board contained no Montreal representatives. Two Quebec City directors of the North Shore Railway, Cauchon and G.H. Simard, appeared in the

Toronto-based Interoceanic Railway rather than Hugh Allan's Canadian Pacific Railway. Angered by the infighting, Cauchon told Curé Labelle that Hugh Allan's supporters were 'une masse de petits grelots, sonnant à étourdir mais ne donnant toujours que du son.'[10]

Despite these internal problems the North Shore Company was revitalized in the fall of 1870. Offices were opened on the second floor of Quebec City's Union Hotel and a new register of shareholders was established. The Quebec City firm of Andrews, Caron, and Andrews was named as the railway's lawyers and General Silas Seymour as acting engineer-in-chief. Previously associated with the state of New York and the Union Pacific Railway, Seymour completed a survey by the end of 1871.

Almost as its first order of business the railway began to press for an increased subsidy from Quebec City. As in the 1850s, construction of the North Shore Railway was made synonymous with the city's prosperity: the railway was 'the only thing that can save Quebec.'[10] The promoters warned that their railway would not operate at a profit and would never be built for commercial reasons alone: 'We doubt whether the country through which it is to pass is any better than that on the South shore, and certainly the traffic returns of the Quebec section of the Grand Trunk was not such as to make it very probable that, for many years to come at any rate, the dividends on the North Shore road will be worth attaching great importance to.'[12]

In September 1870 the company named three directors, Cauchon, Thomas McGreevy, and Jean-Baptiste Renaud, to negotiate with the city's finance committee. The railway faced local opposition from what Cauchon's newspaper called 'le ring de la rue Saint-Pierre.'[13] Some wholesalers worried that local retailers would deal directly with Montreal and a few taxpayers expressed concern about annual interest charges of $70,000 on a $1 million municipal subsidy. A priest noted that the Seminary of Quebec's share of this tax would be $8000. *Le Journal de Québec* responded with editorials attacking the city's 'triste position' and 'incroyable inertie'; the North Shore Railway was essential not only for prosperity 'mais encore à l'existence de Québec, comme ville commerciale.'[14] Public meetings were organized, and Cauchon, Colonel Rhodes, Willis Russell, and Jean-Baptiste Renaud made the rounds. Prominent Conservatives like Adolphe Caron and Hector Langevin added their prestige to the campaign. In their speeches the promoters blended the promise of industrialism with plain-and-simple blackmail. The railway, Cauchon predicted, would transform the St.

Roch section of the city in the same manner as the Grand Trunk had changed Montreal's Point St. Charles. If Quebec City's subsidy was not increased, the railway would be abandoned.[15]

On 4 October 1870 Quebec City Council voted a $1 million subsidy, and two months later the provincial government approved the grant. The railway's main office was to be in Quebec City and the subsidy would be paid on a pro-rated basis. Until construction was completed the company or its contractor would pay the 7 per cent interest on the city's bonds. In addition, the railway had to raise $1 million from other sources before any municipal bonds would be issued.[16]

The campaign for a subsidy in Three Rivers followed the same pattern. For years Three Rivers had been desperate for a railway. In 1853 and 1859 it had offered subsidies to the North Shore Railway and 1856 it had subsidized the Grand Trunk. Most of this money was used to build the Grand Trunk dock in Three Rivers. Goods were ferried across the St. Lawrence to the Grand Trunk spur at Doucet's Landing (see map A). None of this activity had brought prosperity to Three Rivers. In 1870 the town had two wholesalers, two banks, and a population of 8267.[17] Trifluvians attributed this stagnation to the political power of Montreal and Quebec City and threatened to support the Liberal opposition if a seat in the provincial cabinet was not accorded to the region. The *Gazette* had another explanation. Three Rivers' condition was due 'to the want of a back country, and can never take its proper stand among the progressive centres of the Province unless assisted by railway enterprize and the innumerable benefits which always flow from it. It is in fact, another version of the old story, - Aide toi et le ciel t'aidera. The Provincial Jupiter had been sufficiently invoked. The Trifluvians should now put their own shoulders to the wheel. In no other way will they ever emerge from the Slough of Despond into which they had fallen.'[18]

The campaign in Three Rivers was typical: public meetings, support from the local élite, vigorous participation by company directors, and dire predictions for the town's future if a subsidy was refused. Opponents of the subsidy argued that railways brought high taxes and ruin rather than progress. One perceptive critic attacked the railway as a centralizing force that would further weaken the town. These negative voices were easily overwhelmed by the promoters who organized a public meeting in the Court House. Among the speakers were four members of Parliament, three members of the provincial house, editors of two local newspapers, and the mayor. Cauchon reminded the audience of the relationship between railways and property values. Railways, he contended, were one important reason for the great difference in property values in Three Rivers and centres such as Montreal, Paris, and London.[19] A company office was opened by William McDougall, a prominent local businessman, MP for Three Rivers, and North Shore director. At a special meeting on 8 September 1870 town council revoked its earlier North Shore subsidies and voted $100,000 to the railway. Shortly afterwards, council's action was ratified by municipal voters. The subsidy's most important stipulations were that the railway pass through Three Rivers and that the town's 6 per cent debentures be issued on a pro-rated basis.[20]

Until 1871 the North Shore's most enthusiastic local booster was *Le Journal des Trois-Rivières*. Despite its ultramontanism, this newspaper was an unfailing proponent of industrialism and local development. Between editorials praising the Zouaves, it promoted the Intercolonial Railway, rural banks, and a local shoe industry. The North Shore Railway was a favourite project, and when the town finally subscribed $100,000, *Le Journal des Trois-Rivières* declared itself happy and proud.[21]

II

The revitalization of the North Shore Railway after 1870 and its espousal by north-shore municipalities meant an increase in political pressures. While balancing north- and south-shore interests, Montreal and Quebec City, the English and French-speaking communities and the Grand Trunk and North Shore forces, the provincial government had to charter new railways, establish programs of cash and land grants, approve municipal subsidies, and draft the province's railway laws. The Chauveau administration was notoriously weak and Hector Langevin and the Ottawa Bleus played a major role in provincial decisions. Rumours were as abundant as railway promoters in the corridors outside Ottawa and Quebec City caucus and committee rooms. Gossips speculated that Chauveau wanted his son named as lawyer for the North Shore Railway; others insisted that the premier could not stand up to Cauchon. North Shore supporters floated rumours that Chauveau was 'sustained secretly' by the Grand Trunk.[22]

Buffeted by competing railway interests, the Chauveau government tried to formulate a transportation policy. Under its 1866 charter, the North Shore Railway had until 1 January 1872 to complete the line under the terms laid down in the acts of 1853, 1854, 1858, and 1861. In 1869 the province permitted the North Shore Company to separate its proposed branch line up the St. Maurice Valley into a distinct unit. This enabled the short spur between Three Rivers and Grand Piles to benefit from a 6 per cent guarantee under the province's Colonization Railway Aid Act. However, both the separation and construction came to naught. By 1870 the government was under mounting pressure to grant crown lands to the province's floundering railway companies. From the north shore the Chauveau administration faced a strong lobby led by the Montreal backers of the Canada Central and Montreal Colonization Railway and the Quebec City promoters of the North Shore Railway. The latter two groups wanted an extension of their charters with the same privileges and land grants they had received before Confederation. The Liberal opposition did not vigorously attack the principle of land grants, perhaps because the Liberal leader, Henri-Gustave Joly, was seeking government approval to extend his own railway, the Quebec and Gosford Railway.[23] At the same time a dozen smaller railways were clamouring for charters, concessions, and land grants. Each had its regional supporters and spokesmen within the Conservative party. The Grand Trunk lobby was ever-present. James Ferrier, Canadian chairman of the Grand Trunk and a member of the Quebec Legislative Council, led his company's forces in Quebec City. His opposition to the North Shore Company, he assured a journalist, was not based on hostility to the railway, but on fears that government involvement would lead to direct taxes.[24] This was a popular argument with politicians from south-shore and eastern township ridings. Premier Chauveau, whose law firm at one time acted for the North Shore Railway, was not impressed with this argument and pointed out the government's generosity to south-shore railways. Sydney Bellingham, MLA for Argenteuil, had plans of his own for a railway from Quebec City to the Ottawa Valley and added to the confusion by accusing the cabinet of a 'fearful blunder' in 'dispossessing themselves of the contract of the North Shore and Northern Colonization railways - Cauchon had not strength until he became president of a road with a subsidy and Allan could not have gathered a clique on the back of the M.C. [Montreal Colonization Railway] and badly damaged Sir George in the Eastern division - I warned Chauveau at the time not to part with power but hold the land to give out the contract - municipalities would then have voted with confidence ... '[25]

The cabinet finally proposed a union of the North Shore and Montreal Colonization railways; the government would grant 3,000,000 acres and name one-third of the directors.[26] Supporters of the two railways immediately caucused and asked for a land grant of 12,000 acres a mile with no government directors. The final compromise gave the North Shore Railway a new charter, the right to a $6 million stock issue, and 2,000,000 acres of crown lands on the Ottawa, Batiscan, St. Pierre, and St. Maurice rivers.

Between 1870 and 1873 the North Shore's fortunes were tied to Joseph Cauchon. Until his removal from the board of directors in May 1873, his personality and the gyrations of his career damaged the company. His struggle with the ultramontane clergy over the *programme catholique*, his involvement in the Beauport Asylum scandal, his willingness to challenge the English-speaking minority, his participation in the Toronto-based Interoceanic Railway, and his needling of Premier Chauveau on educational policy all had serious implications for the railway of which he was president.

By 1871 Cauchon's standing as a Bleu was deteriorating. A year later he resigned his provincial seat and began attacking the Conservatives and the Pacific scandal in his newspaper. For a while Cauchon and Langevin - colleagues for twenty years - maintained their relationship. Although not a North Shore director after 1870 Langevin was often consulted and one entrepreneur thanked him for his moderating influence on Cauchon. However, by 1873 Langevin had joined the bishops of Three Rivers and Montreal, the Bleu establishment, and Hugh Allan and the Montreal entrepreneurs in the ranks of Cauchon's opposition; in 1874 he described Cauchon's conduct as 'treacherous.'[27] The English-speaking community had no love for the abrasive Cauchon. Alexander Galt may have been repaying an old debt when he blocked Cauchon from becoming the province's first premier in 1867. Quebec City's English-speaking entrepreneurs complained regularly about Cauchon's wheeling and dealing, his 'corruption and political intrigue,' and his 'Star chamber policy.'[28] When a prominent Board of Trade official protested against Cauchon's attacks, a Quebec City businessman reassured him that when he 'was a little older he would learn that to be abused by Mr. Cauchon was equivalent to a high compliment.'[29]

Although disliked by many of the province's élite, Cauchon and his railway received consistent support from Quebec City clerics. While Bishop Laflèche of Three Rivers remained silent and the ultramontanist *Le Journal des Trois-Rivières* turned against him after 1871, the

Quebec City hierarchy enthusiastically backed the North Shore project. Like Bishop Bourget in Montreal, the archbishop of Quebec realized the significance of railways for his constituents. Although ultramontanism and the university question had strained relations among the bishops, there were important communications concerning railways. Archbishop Taschereau wanted the diocesan structure to conform to the traffic flow created by new railways. Since construction of the Piles Railway would orient the St. Maurice Valley towards Three Rivers, Taschereau asked Laflèche to incorporate the St. Maurice region into his diocese. In September 1871 the archbishop supported the North Shore Railway in a letter to the curés of Portneuf.[30] Writing only a few days before the county's vote on a $100,000 subsidy, the archbishop stated that the church favoured material prosperity and should not be indifferent to 'cette grande entreprise.' He urged his priests to enlighten their parishioners to the advantages of this 'oeuvre de patriotisme.' Quebec City clerics showed their support by investing in the railway. In May 1873, 124 shares in the North Shore Railway were held by the Archbishopric, 200 shares by the Sulpician Seminary, 48 shares by the Seminary of Quebec, and 40 shares by the Ursulines of Quebec.[31]

With the backing of the archbishop and armed with substantial commitments from the provincial government, Quebec City, and Three Rivers, Cauchon turned to the smaller north-shore communities. To the traditional pressures that railway entrepreneurs could apply to communities through which their railway might – or might not pass – he added twenty-five years experience in the more picayune aspects of Lower Canadian politics. Throughout 1871 and 1872 he campaigned in the counties of Montcalm, Joliette, Berthier, Maskinongé, St. Maurice, Champlain, and Portneuf – wherever encouragement was needed for a sizeable local subsidy. In St. Sauveur, accompanied by the mayor, he spoke on the church steps after mass. He sought an interview with Curé Labelle to seek better cooperation between the North Shore and Montreal Colonization Railways. While the town of Joliette was debating a subsidy, Cauchon made the rounds with two directors, Willis Russell and John Jones Ross. Do not hesitate to spend what is necessary, he told one supporter, 'la compagnie vous le remettra de suite ou vous enverra par avance.'[32] Cauchon, Ross, and William McDougall spent two weeks in Berthier County and apparently made conflicting promises as to the railway's route. According to opposition reports Cauchon agreed that the railway would pass through the villages of St. Cuthbert, Ste. Elizabeth, and Berthier. *Le Nouveau Monde* and *Le Messager de Sorel* pointed out that it would be difficult to reconcile these three promises.[33] In addition, company officials signed a notarized statement exempting two villages from contributing to the Berthier subsidy if the railway did not pass by them. Other parishes were promised branch lines.

A Cauchon campaign was never dull. The railway reportedly organized a gang of toughs in Ste. Anne de la Pérade to threaten its opponents. In St. Maurice parish the mayor disregarded legitimate requests for a second day to vote on the county's subsidy. The public vote in Portneuf county to ratify its $100,000 subsidy caught *Le Nouveau Monde*'s attention. Hostile to Cauchon and the North Shore Railway, it described the mayor's address to the public meeting: ' "Votez-vous la ratification du règlement du conseil du comté pour le chemin de fer du nord? Non, non, non," fut le cri des masses et quelques voix isolées crièrent, oui. Et sans désemparer, les maires, les les directeurs et émissaires de la compagnie du chemin de fer déclarèrent: "Vous venez de voter unanimement la ratification du règlement du conseil du comté pour le chemin de fer du nord ... " '[34]

Subsidy votes in north-shore communities were complex decisions that might be affected by economic issues, railway politics, local personalities, or even ultramontanism. The campaign in Champlain County was typical. Located on the east side of the St. Maurice River, the county was dominated by Three Rivers. In 1870 the ultramontanist *Journal des Trois-Rivières* had supported the North Shore Railway. A year later Cauchon and the newspaper's editor, Magloire McLeod, clashed over *le programme catholique* and shortly afterwards *Le Journal des Trois-Rivières* began attacking Cauchon's railway. McLeod questioned the wisdom of allowing municipalities to append conditions to their subsidies and attacked Cauchon's various promises on the railway's route. How, McLeod demanded, could the railway traverse the centre of St. Maurice County while fulfiling its obligation to pass through Three Rivers. Depicting Cauchon as 'un traître,' 'un vil courtisan' and 'lâche flatteur,' *Le Journal des Trois-Rivières* warned that the railway would be used to transport the county's children into exile: 'Electeurs du comté de Champlain, ce vote qui vous est demandé est pour vous extrêmement grave. Vous ne pouvez pas en conscience exposer le bien, le patrimoine de vos familles, uniquement pour vous procurer le plaisir d'avoir un chemin de fer qui peut-être n'aura d'autre avantage, tel qu'on veut le construire, que de transporter vos enfants sur la terre de l'exil.'[35]

In rural counties like Champlain the attitude of local priests to a railway subsidy was crucial. Petitions circulated by priests, the proselytizing of Curé Labelle, and the lobbying of the higher clergy for their particular railway interest were an integral part of Quebec railway politics in the 1870s. In Champlain County the North Shore Railway's leading opponent was the curé of Cap de la Madeleine. Unimpressed with the wonders of the iron horse, Luc Désilets was a mystic, an ultramontanist, member of a prominent Three Rivers' family, and a part-time journalist for *Le Journal des Trois-Rivières*. Writing to a fellow priest, he described the subsidy as a trap. Few in the county wanted the railway, parishes would be heavily taxed, and church construction retarded: 'Ça sera sérieux, surtout dans les paroisses qui ont des églises à construire comme chez vous et chez nous.'[36]

Désilets explained his doubts to Bishop Laflèche. He described the railway as an insidious blend of communism and capitalism; Canadian railway laws were communistic because they gave 'l'avantage du commerce avec le bien des autres.' Warming to his task, Désilets accused the North Shore promoters of using violence, corruption, and communist laws 'pour dévorer les ignorants, et les faibles.' Soon all of Canada would be under 'les pieds cruels de ces vampires qu'on appelle spéculateurs ou capitalistes.' Since several priests and the archbishop of Quebec, 'dont nous déplorons en secret les écarts,' were being used by company officials, he asked permission to speak out against the subsidy.[37] Désilets despaired that the people would be abandoned at the same time by the provincial government – the protector of order, – and by the clergy – the guardian of justice and morality. Finally, he reminded the bishop of the poverty of the county and the financial needs of church: railway subsidies would hinder payments for the cathedral in Three Rivers.

In the week before the Champlain county vote, the company put on a final push. Whiskey, dollars, and 'une foule de speechers' circulated in the back parishes. The campaign was boisterous. Speaking after mass in Ste. Geneviève, Cauchon was shouted down with cries of 'Non, vous ne parlerez pas. Pas de Cauchon ici. Pas d'insulteur d'évêques.'[38] In response to the attacks of *Le Journal des Trois-Rivières*, the North Shore promoters distributed a pamphlet accusing Magloire McLeod of being paid $2000 by the Richelieu Company and the Grand Trunk.

On 4 September 1871 Champlain voted against a municipal subscription. Two other north-shore counties, Assomption and Joliette, also rejected a subsidy. Montcalm, Berthier, Maskinongé, St. Maurice, and Portneuf originally subscribed $100,000 each, but in every case they revoked their decision or appended the condition that all north-shore counties must subscribe. By 1872 the North Shore Railway had municipal subsidies from only Quebec City and Three Rivers.

III

The granting of a construction contract was just as politicized as the campaign for municipal subsidies. Again, regional squabbles, metro-politan competition, and political infighting kept the company in tur-moil. In 1870 an almost-forgotten construction contract for the Piles spur-line in the St. Maurice Valley was revived. Early in the 1860s, Joseph-Edouard Turcotte - prominent Three Rivers politician, entre-preneur, and friend of the bishop - had contracted to build the Piles spur. His contract, according to one interpretation, included the right to the 1,500,000 acres granted by the government to the North Shore Railway in the 1850s. Turcotte's widow ceded the contract to J.M. Winchell, and in 1870 the American contractor arrived in Three Riv-ers.[39] His plans to finance construction of the Piles branch on deben-tures based on the 1,500,000 acre crown-land grant aroused the prov-incial government. Premier Chauveau pointed out that the huge grant had been intended to aid construction of the entire line from Quebec City to Montreal.[40] Cauchon, as president of the North Shore Railway, had to mediate between the contractor and premier. Having failed to annul the contract he tried to modify it so that the company, rather than the contractor, would control the land grant. The railway could then meet the government's demands and divide the land grant pro-portionately between the North Shore and Piles branch. However, Winchell had the support of two prominent Bleus, Joseph-Adolphe Chapleau and Hector Langevin. Chapleau, in particular, took up the contractor's cause by insisting that the Turcotte heirs be protected.[41]

The contract issue became more confused in the winter of 1871. The withdrawal of the Montreal entrepreneurs from the North Shore board increased the influence of Cauchon and the Quebec City forces. Winchell complained that Cauchon planned to obtain the contract for himself or the McGreevy brothers. The real issue may have been kick-backs and patronage. One newspaper reported that Cauchon refused to renegotiate the Winchell contract because Winchell refused to guar-antee him $500,000.[42]

By August 1871 Winchell had relinquished the Turcotte contract and negotiations to construct the entire North Shore line were initiated with the Chicago Contracting Company. The principals in this group were Samuel L. Keith, Perry H. Smith, and George L. Dunlap. Initially, the North Shore Company included in its assets anticipated subsidies of $1,000,000 from the north-shore counties. Later the contract was renegotiated on the basis of subsidies of Quebec City and Three Rivers. In February 1872 Cauchon and Willis Russell met the contractors in New York and shortly afterwards the North Shore board approved a $7 million contract. The contractor would be paid $1 million in Quebec City municipal bonds and the balance in 7 per cent North Shore bonds.[43]

The contractor was to build a first-class iron railroad with a gauge of four feet, eight and a half inches, from Quebec City to Montreal as well as the Piles branch (see map A). Construction was to be completed by December 1875, and the railway's machine shops and engine houses were to be located in Quebec City, Three Rivers, and Montreal. The contractors would secure the right-of-way and supply eighteen engines, 320 passenger or freight cars, and a steamboat for the St. Maurice River. Until construction was completed the contractor was to pay the company's expenses and the interest on the North Shore and Quebec City bonds.

On 18 July 1872, despite rumours that someone had 'decamped' with $40,000 in company funds, the sod-turning ceremony was held on the grounds of the Quebec City General Hospital.[44] In attendance were the premier, Justices Caron and Taschereau, every MP from a north-shore county, civic officials, and company directors. Archbishop Taschereau attended in full ceremonials, gave the benediction from an imposing red dais and broke the ground with a pick-axe. Madame Cauchon turned the first sod with a silver spade and her husband removed it in a wheelbarrow.

Despite the fanfare, construction stopped almost immediately. Over the next year the contractors, company engineer, and various North Shore directors tried to sell the company's bonds in England. The railway's prospectus, with its emphasis on the land grant, was widely circulated, and General Silas Seymour, the company engineer, published a handsome report. These paid glowing tribute to the timber lands estimating their minimum value at $4 million. Rumours circulated, however, that these lands had long since been stripped of their timber.[45] Nor did Seymour's traffic predictions correspond to other estimates, notably those of the Grand Trunk. Both the Montreal *Gazette* and *La*

Minerve pointed out that Seymour's reports had been financed by the contractors. The interests of the province, *La Minerve* charged, were at the mercy 'd'une bande de spéculateurs étrangers.'[46]

English investors showed little enthusiasm and the collapse of the contractor's first London agents, Bowles Brothers and Company, made the North Shore bonds even more unattractive. With a tight money market, British bankers questioned the lack of local investment in the railway and expressed doubts as to the firmness of Quebec City's subscription. The Grand Trunk joined in the whispering campaign against the company. Since both Quebec City and the province had made their subsidies conditional on being allowed to name directors, prospective English buyers asked for the same privilege.[47] To add to the railway's problems, John Rose, a crucial figure for any Canadian company seeking English capital, refused to help. Formerly Canadian minister of finance and a leading London broker, Rose wrote Langevin that the North Shore bonds would not be sold until Cauchon was 'turned out.'[48] Nor would Hugh Allan lend his name to the enterprise, although he acted as trustee for the bondholders. According to one report, Allan was prepared to take over the North Shore presidency if the railway rid itself of Cauchon and the construction contract.[49] Failing to sell the North Shore bonds in London, the contractors approached German banks who asked the Bank of Montreal for an assessment. It replied that while the enterprise was sound, Cauchon was 'un jobber public.'[50]

This was the final blow for Cauchon. Alienated from the Bleus, important clerics, and the English entrepreneurial community he was persona non grata to many of his fellow directors. Montrealers had abandoned the project, and his campaign for rural subsidies had collapsed. One week before the railway's annual meeting in May 1873 a group of English merchants bought stock. Within two days $100,000 had been subscribed and Cauchon's regime broken.[51] At the annual meeting Cauchon was forced to resign as president, the company was reorganized, and a full list of shareholders published. The new board included James G. Ross, Jean-Baptiste Renaud, Elise Beaudet, Andrew Thompson, Willis Russell, Colonel W. Rhodes, Thomas McGreevy, and John Burstall.[52]

The new directors soon received a financing proposal from the contractors. After months of failure the contractors accepted the terms of a London syndicate which offered to advance $3 million to the contractors in return for North Shore bonds worth $6 million. In addition to paying only 50 per cent of the face value of the bonds, they insisted on naming four English directors who would remain in London and direct the company's finances.[53] There was also a bonus clause. The syndicate would receive an additional $1 million in company bonds if the line was in running condition by the end of 1874, another $1 million if the railway was completed by 1 September 1875, and a final $1 million if both the main line and the Piles branch were completed under the terms of the contract of 5 April 1872.

These steep terms demonstrated the railway's weak reputation. In Montreal *La Minerve* attacked the contractors and their financing: 'the contract price is excessive even for a first-class railway, which the one in question is not; the contractors have no command of capital as claimed; the road must not be built under their management, or if so, the contract should be thoroughly revised with a first-class road obtained.'[54] However, the North Shore board had little choice and in June 1873 they met in the office of John Burstall and approved the financing arrangements. A shareholders meeting on 14 June confirmed the directors' decision and soon afterwards Quebec City and the provincial government gave their approval. However, in July the project collapsed when the English syndicate withdrew its offer. Without capital, construction was impossible.

5

Collapse and government takeover

The years 1874 and 1875 were characterized by growing municipal and provincial commitments to both the North Shore and Montreal Colonization railways, culminating in their takeover by the provincial government. Unsuccessful in attracting foreign capital, the entrepreneurs pressed for increased government subsidies. However, political conditions in Quebec remained unfavourable to railway development. The Tanneries investigation tainted some of the railway's political friends as well as the contractor for the Montreal Colonization Railway.[1] Scandal left the provincial government weakened and under the control of Charles-Eugène Boucher de Boucherville, the third premier in twenty months. In Ottawa, the Pacific scandal had helped Alexander Mackenzie to power. Upper Canadian in loyalty and critical of the expansive Pacific railway scheme, Mackenzie had little sympathy for the Bleu railway entrepreneurs of Montreal and Quebec City.

The provincial government did move quickly to replace its deforested land grants. In his budget speech of January 1874, Provincial Treasurer Joseph Gibb Robertson announced plans to aid the construction of railways from Quebec City to the Upper Ottawa Valley. The North Shore Railway would receive government bonds worth $1,248,634 on a pro-rated basis and the Montreal Colonization Railway $751,366.[2] In exchange for the 5 per cent government bonds, the two companies were to give the province an equal amount of their 6 per cent bonds. Aside from their main lines, the railway would build branch lines to St. Jérôme and Grand Piles and provide steamers on the St. Maurice River. The government could name one-half of the

North Shore directors and one-third of the directors of the Montreal Colonization Railway.

The government's new commitments coincided with a change of contractors for the North Shore Railway. Unable to raise capital and having spent $63,257, the Chicago Construction Company wanted out of its contract. A few days before Robertson's announcement of the $2 million grant, Thomas McGreevy met the three American contractors in the office of George Irvine, attorney-general and government-appointed director of the North Shore Railway. Cauchon's newspaper charged that Irvine and Langevin manipulated the contractors into selling their contract to Thomas McGreevy by telling the Americans that the government would not increase its aid to the railway.[3] On 28 January 1874 McGreevy announced that he had bought the construction contract. A few days later the North Shore directors met and approved the deal. By mid-February McGreevy was en route to England to find capital.

Under the revised construction contract McGreevy agreed to extend the line from the station in Quebec City to the harbour, to increase expenditures for the right of way, and to double the contractor's contribution to the railway company's office expenses. Construction would begin immediately and be completed by 1 December 1876; all work was subject to approval by the company engineer. The contractor would be paid $7 million but relinquished the $3 million bonus clause and title to the land grant. He would be paid $1,000,000 in Quebec City debentures, $1,248,634 in provincial bonds and $4,751,366 in North Shore bonds.[4]

Although Langevin assured Macdonald that in McGreevy's hands the North Shore Railway was 'as certain as anything in this world' the contractor's mission to England met the same fate as earlier trips by company officials.[5] Despite help in England from the provincial treasurer and Quebec's immigration agent, the contractor was unable to raise capital. Provincial Treasurer Robertson reported it was impossible 'to combat' rumours of speculation by insiders and over-inflation of the value of North Shore bonds. Considering British public opinion towards Canadian railways, Robertson concluded that no private Canadian company could negotiate the sale of its bonds.[6] This forced the contractor back to local sources of financing and in June McGreevy approached Quebec City and the provincial government. Emphasizing the need to reassure British investors, he asked both governments to make cash advances before work was actually done. Lo-

cal newspapers like the Quebec *Morning Chronicle* supported Mc-
Greevy and predicted that the railway would never be built if his proposal was not accepted. In November 1874 Quebec City named an
inspection engineer and a month later it paid the railway a first installment of $112,000. By the summer of 1875 Quebec City had advanced
$143,000 to the railway.[7]

The provincial government also adjusted its terms. In November
1874 it named Joseph Gibb Robertson, Henri-Gédéon Malhiot, and
Pierre Garneau as North Shore directors to replace Gédéon Ouimet,
George Irvine, and Pierre Fortin who had resigned during the Tanneries crisis. Early in 1875 the government advanced $80,000 to the
North Shore Railway even though the work had not been inspected
by the government engineer.[8] The Liberals opposed this move and initiated a fourteen-hour debate that lasted until ten o'clock the following day. Robertson, who was at the same time a government-appointed
director of the railway and provincial treasurer, explained that the
cabinet had to accept the company's word. If the government did not
pay, construction would stop. This would make the sale of the North
Shore bonds in England even more difficult. H.G. Joly, provincial
Liberal leader, questioned this blatant violation of the contract. Describing the government's railway policy as 'mischievous,' he demanded
closer supervision especially since two engineering reports described
work on the railway as below first-class quality.[9] Company officials
replied that the railway could be built to first-class standards only if
the province increased its advances to $250,000 in 1875 and the same
in 1876.[10]

Construction progress was slow. The route between Three Rivers
and Montreal had not been finalized and the advocates of an interior
route via Joliette lobbied hard against the shorter line along the shore
(see map C). The company engineer, General Seymour, bickered with
the contractor, the government engineer, the Quebec City engineer,
and the president of the railway. Uncertainty about the railway's future was augmented by rumours that the Grand Trunk planned to
bridge the St. Lawrence near Quebec City.[11]

These factors heightened the pessimism in the North Shore boardroom. Re-elected president at the annual meeting in May 1875, Colonel Rhodes outlined the company's position. Construction was at a
standstill, a number of partially constructed bridges had been abandoned, and subcontractors were unpaid. So far, $287,000 had been
received from the provincial government and Quebec City but the line

was far from completion. In the following three months the railway was unable to meet salary expenses of $2489, engineering expenses of $8825, and further claims of $72,000.[12] On 30 July company officials held a stormy meeting. McGreevy, supported by Sir Narcisse Belleau, asked for new advances to continue construction. Government directors, Pierre Garneau and Henri-Gédéon Malhiot, proposed that the government take over the railway if the contractor could not fulfil the original agreement. Provincial Treasurer Robertson typified the government's dilemma. He realized that the collapse of the north-shore railways was politically intolerable but as a south-shore politician and executive of the Quebec Central Railway he opposed further cash advances or a government takeover.[13] City Council met in closed session to discuss its advances of $143,000. Local newspapers added to the rumours. In Quebec City both *L'Evévement* and *Le Courrier du Canada* favoured a government takeover while in Montreal the *Gazette* supported increased government subsidies. On 11 August 1875 the directors announced that they were unable to construct the road. They urged 'prompt government action' and declared themselves willing to allow the government 'to deal with the question in any way they may, in the public interests, think proper, making arrangements with the contractor as may be found necessary.'[14]

II

The Montreal Colonization Railway faced similar problems. The loyalty of its president, Hugh Allan, remained very much in doubt. His role in the Pacific scandal and his apparent willingness in 1873 to abandon his local railways in return for Grand Trunk support of the Pacific Railway had not been reassuring. In 1874 rumours multiplied concerning Allan's intentions. One newspaper reported that Allan was going to build the Canada Central; another stated that he wanted the construction contract for the North Shore Railway. Curé Labelle was told by one associate that Allan was too busy to take an active part in a railway from Ottawa to Toronto. Allan himself wrote to the curé that he might amalgamate the Montreal Colonization and Canada Central Railways.[15] The engineer for the Montreal Colonization Railway pointed out that Allan could easily suppress all the rumours: 'If Sir Hugh were the man for the emergency, he would advance half a million himself.' However, Sir Hugh was a cautious man with many loyalties; by July 1875 he had invested only $4065 in the railway.[16]

Another concern of the Montreal Colonization directors was the route to be followed between Hull and the Nipissing terminus of the Canadian Pacific Railway. The provincial subsidy as well as those of northern counties like Pontiac encouraged the railway to remain on the Quebec side of the Ottawa River. In 1874 the company engineer surveyed a Quebec route and proposed a bridge over the Ottawa River near the mouth of the Mattawa River. From that point, a track could be laid along the Mattawa to the Nipissing terminus of the Canadian Pacific Railway. Later, the railway could be extended from Lake Nipissing to Georgian Bay or Sault Ste. Marie. According to the engineer's report, construction costs would be $28,000 a mile or $33,000 a mile if steel rails were used.[17]

However, a Quebec route faced increasing competition from aggressive Ontario railways. Plans to extend the Montreal Colonization Railway past the city of Ottawa raised the ire of Canada Central officials. Asa B. Foster, contractor and vice-president of the Canada Central, was angry at being left off the Canadian Pacific board by Hugh Allan and met with Grand Trunk officials to discuss cooperation between the two lines.[18] A number of southern Ontario communities had ambitions to incorporate the Ottawa Valley into their orbit. Entrepreneurs from Kingston had plans for a railway to Pembroke. The Huron and Quebec Railway Company was chartered in March 1874 to link Lake Huron to Toronto, Peterborough, and Ottawa. Other entrepreneurs proposed a line from the Canada Central depot at Carleton Place to Parry Sound on Georgian Bay. In the Ottawa area the Montreal Colonization Railway had the support of north-shore politicians and businessmen like Alonzo Wright, W. McKay Wright, G. Bryson, John Poupore, Joseph Merrill Currier, E.B. Eddy, and John Mether. However, the Ontario forces were strong and in November 1874 Ottawa granted a $25,000 municipal bonus to the Huron and Quebec Railway. A few months later city officials discussed a $100,000 grant to the Canada Central Railway.[19]

The question of a Quebec versus a south-shore route along the Ottawa River beyond Hull also depended on the exact location of the Nipissing terminus of the Canadian Pacific Railway and the terms of federal aid for railways joining that terminus to the major population centres. While Cartier was in office the government seemed to favour a north-shore or pro-Quebec policy.[20] The Mackenzie government was much less favourable to the entrepreneurs of the Montreal Colonization Railway. In January 1874 Mackenzie outlined the government's policy of cutting back on the Pacific railway project and of developing an east-west system combining steam and rail communication: 'This will involve the construction of a short line of railway from the mouth of [the] French river, on Georgian Bay, to the south-east shore of Lake Nipissing, and a grant in aid of extensions to that point of the existing and projected lines in Quebec and Ontario.'[21] This reference to 'existing and projected lines in Quebec and Ontario' at least left the door open for the Montreal Colonization Railway and throughout 1874 its supporters lobbied hard. Mackenzie met with representatives from Pontiac County and a joint delegation from the North Shore and Montreal Colonization railways. The prime minister was cool to both groups and hinted to the Pontiac delegation that the Nipissing terminus might be moved further south. This would favour southern Ontario railways and make the Mattawa River route unfeasible.

The obvious affiliation of both railways with the Bleus hindered their negotiations with Mackenzie's Liberal government. Subsidies, land grants, and permissive railway legislation all flowed from the party in power: railways responded to the largesse of their political friends by providing jobs for their constituents, patronage, legal work, and contracts. 'I enclose you a list of all applications that we have received from the Province of Quebec,' one railway executive wrote to Hector Langevin. 'Will you mark it so that I may steer clear of all objectionable parties ... '[22] Early in December 1874 the boards of the North Shore and Montreal Colonization railways held a joint meeting to prepare for their Ottawa visit. At least four members of Boucherville's Conservative cabinet represented the North Shore Railway at this meeting. Even though government directors had to be named under the terms of the provincial grant, the presence of Bleu politicians on the railway board did not endear it to the Liberals. Within the North Shore Company well-known Bleus like Thomas McGreevy served variously as director, banker, lobbyist, or contractor. Nor did the expelling of Cauchon from the company and his subsequent appointment to the Mackenzie cabinet help matters. Although Cauchon maintained an active interest in the railway he was bitterly divided from his old Bleu colleagues.[23] The North Shore Railway delegation to Ottawa included, in addition to company officials, former Premier Chauveau, and the mayors of Quebec City, Three Rivers, and St. Sauveur.

The Montreal Colonization Railway had the same political problem. The proclivities of its president, Hugh Allan, towards the Bleus had been well documented during the Pacific scandal. Other supporters of

the railway such as J.J.C. Abbott, J.E.L. de Bellefeuille, Louis Beaubien, Curé Labelle, and Gédéon Ouimet were all well-known Bleus.
Neither Télesphore Fournier nor Félix Geoffrion, two Quebec representatives in the Mackenzie cabinet, accompanied the Pontiac delegation to see Mackenzie. Geoffrion, president of the Montreal, Chambly
and Sorel Railway, dissociated himself completely from the group,
saying that the choice of route was a matter of competition. He in
turn was dismissed by Chapleau as 'l'avocat officiel et officieux des
compagnies des chemins de fer d'Ontario.'[24]

Despite their lack of political affinity with the Mackenzie Liberals,
the north-shore railway delegation came to Ottawa well prepared. Their
engineering reports showed sharp differences in costs between the
Hull - Mattawa route and an Ottawa - Pembroke line. Although the
Mattawa route was longer, the grades were less steep. According to
company figures, the all-Ontario route favoured by Mackenzie had to
cross an extra 750 feet of height which in engineering terms was equivalent to 37.5 additional miles of railroad. The Quebec group urged
that the Canadian Pacific terminus be left at the end of Lake Nipissing
where it would be accessible to the Mattawa route. They also wanted
federal assistance for a railway joining the Nipissing terminus to the
Quebec railroads rather than additional aid for Ontario's lines. This,
they pleaded, was a question of justice for Quebec.[25]

Mackenzie, accompanied by Sandford Fleming, Fournier, Letellier
de Saint-Just, and Albert James Smith, met the delegation on 16 December 1874. The prime minister was not optimistic and reiterated his
preference for the shortest route from Georgian Bay to Montreal. Two
months later he proposed a $12,000 a mile subsidy to the Canada
Central Railway to build from Lake Nipissing to the Ottawa River.[26]
Mackenzie's railway policy brought charges from *Le Nouveau Monde*
that Ottawa had once again favoured Ontario over Quebec. Ruggles
Church, an Ottawa Valley MLA, expressed the same sentiments in the
Quebec legislature: 'The Ottawa Government treated the Canada Central Railroad with the utmost generosity, but had treated the Northern
Colonization Railroad with the spirit they treated all enterprises in
the Province of Quebec.'[27] Two Quebec City Liberal newspapers,
L'Evénement and *Le Journal de Québec*, were more sanguine. They
took delight in pointing out that Mackenzie's intention of aiding the
company with the shortest route between Lake Nipissing and Montreal was the very policy advocated by Allan, Abbott, and Beaubien
when they were allied with the Canada Central. *L'Evénement* also

ridiculed the tendency of the Montreal Colonization Railway to represent itself as the 'incarnation' of Quebec simply because the railway had Louis Beaubien as its principal director and Arthur Dansereau, editor of *La Minerve*, as its 'courtier politique.'[28]

Mackenzie's subsidy bill did contain an important provision for the north-shore entrepreneurs. The Canada Central was obligated to grant running rights to the Montreal Colonization Railway and to cooperate with Montreal Colonization officials in fixing a junction between the two lines. The federal government, the Canada Central, and the Montreal Colonization each named one engineer to examine possible bridge sites over the Ottawa River. Directors of the Montreal Colonization immediately began applying pressure for a crossing as far north as possible on the Ottawa River. Beaubien put it bluntly in a telegram: 'Let Father Labelle be prepared to notify Government - that if Pembroke not selected he will declare in press Quebec to have been ill used.'[29] In fact, Labelle's influence was not necessary since the terrain on the Ontario side of the Ottawa River made a crossing between Ottawa and Pembroke impracticable, and on 2 April the committee recommended a junction of the two lines at Pembroke. Provincial Treasurer Ruggles Church, a strong supporter of the Montreal Colonization, declared that while 'not at all satisfied with the justice or wisdom of M. Mackenzie's policy' he was willing to accept that 'half a loaf is better than no loaf.'[30]

The Montreal Colonization Railway's reputation with Montreal officials presented another problem. The struggle over the $1 million Montreal bylaw, the Molson suit, and the appeals for disallowance had left a legacy of distrust. In January 1874 the subsidy issue was reopened. The provincial government's revision of its grant to the railway gave city council an opportunity to review its subsidy bylaw. The city's $1 million subscription had been made in 1872 at a time when the railway had a provincial land grant of over a million acres. The railway's critics in Montreal were increasingly wary of the company's manipulations of the route, location of the terminus, and construction deadlines. Under the terms of its subsidy Montreal had three representatives on the Montreal Colonization board. In May 1874 the railway asked Mayor Aldis Bernard, a Montreal Colonization director, to accompany the contractor to England to help raise capital. Some aldermen opposed this mixing of civic and private responsibilities. They argued that municipal officials should not accept paid trips from a private company, especially since it implied the city's endorsement for the company's bonds. The railway countered by pointing out that the provincial treasurer was accompanying the party. Hugh Allan added his weight by publicly emphasizing the necessity of the mayor's presence in England.[31]

The railway's plan to bridge the St. Lawrence in the east end of Montreal was another source of controversy. Montreal Colonization backers insisted that an independent route to New England and an alternative to the Grand Trunk's Victoria Bridge were essential parts of a new trunk line to the Pacific.[32] John Young, a former Montreal Colonization director and long-time chairman of the Harbour Commission, was the leading promoter of the Royal Albert Bridge. The project aroused opposition from important members of the Montreal Board of Trade and the Harbour Commission. They argued that a new bridge would block traffic in the harbour, raise shipping insurance rates, and was part of a plan to destroy the port at Montreal and to move it east to Hochelaga. Both sides sent delegations to Ottawa, and in March 1875 the chartering of the bridge was postponed[33] (see map B).

Another crisis erupted over the Quebec Gate Barracks. This property, located near the Bonsecours Market, was favoured by many as terminus for the Montreal Colonization and North Shore Railways. As part of its $1 million subsidy to the Montreal Colonization Railway, Montreal bought the property from the federal government for $150,000 and turned it over to the railway.[34] However, Montreal Colonization officials said it would cost $1 million for their railway to gain access to the area. They preferred a terminus further east on a site bounded by Papineau, Colborne, St. Catherine, and Mignonne Streets. In April 1875 the railway asked the city for permission to sell the Quebec Gate Barracks whose estimated value had risen to $584,000 and to put the profits towards steel rails and iron bridges. These prospective changes in the city's agreement with the Montreal Colonization enabled the railway's opposition to demand a new plebiscite of municipal taxpayers. Petitions were signed by such notables as Peter Redpath, Alex Molson, David Torrance, Thomas Workman, Theodore Hart, Mathew H. Gault, C.J. Brydges, and George Stephen.[35] Faced with this powerful opposition, city council postponed a decision on the Quebec Gate Barracks property.

Some construction on the Montreal Colonization line was carried out in 1874 and early in 1875. The company established offices at 162 St. James Street and let subcontracts for bridges near Montreal and grading of the line to Lachute. By November 1874 one hundred tons of rails had arrived in Hochelaga and preparations were made to lay the track in the spring. However, the company faced continual difficulties. In St. Jérôme, Curé Labelle's church stood on a favourable site for the railway depot. Trying to find a compromise between the priest and the company engineer, the contractor urged Labelle to attend a board meeting: 'Your presence there for ten minutes would settle the matter as you wish it.'[36] In November 1874 police had to be called to help the railway take possession of a quarry; in Hochelaga, a lawsuit for $50,000 was brought against the company. Nor was the railway free of scandal. During the Tanneries enquiry the company's contractor was implicated in the testimony of Arthur Dansereau, editor of *La Minerve*. Examination of Dansereau's financial records brought to light a mysterious $17,000. Called to the bar of the provincial legislature in February 1875, Dansereau explained that Duncan Macdonald, contractor for the Montreal Colonization Railway, had deposited the $17,000 in his account at the Jacques Cartier Bank as 'final settlement' of a partnership for 'the building of the Montreal Colonization Railway.'[37] This payoff to the most important French-language Conservative paper in Montreal damaged the railway's reputation, although Louis Beaubien tried to dissociate the railway directors from any knowledge of the secret deal. Further embarrassment was suffered by the railway in March 1875 when Charles Legge, the company engineer, had a mental breakdown. Confined to Curé Labelle's presbytery before being sent to a Vermont asylum, Legge tried to reorganize the company. He wrote telegrams proposing Richard B. Angus as president, Sandford Fleming as engineer, and Gédéon Ouimet as attorney. Michael Ryan was promised 'a larger stick to whittle.' Labelle intercepted the telegrams and kept them from circulation but Godefroy Laviollette, former director of the railway and mayor of St. Jérôme, apparently read them and believed them. He wrote to J.E.L. de Bellefeuille, the company secretary, urging him to accept Legge's offer 'and you will make for yourself a name which will shine for all time in the annals of your country's history, besides making yourself independently wealthy.'[38]

The Montreal Colonization Railway finally collapsed in the summer of 1875 for lack of capital. Allan's failure to raise British capital in the spring of 1873 was followed by an unsuccessful trip to England by the railway's contractor. Neither was able to sell the Montreal Colonization bonds. The Grand Trunk, in the final stages of changing its gauge and with plans for its new Bonaventure station in Montreal, remained adamant in its opposition. Throughout 1874 and 1875 the Grand Trunk fought its competitor on every front. In London the Grand Trunk chairman spoke out vigorously against the Montreal Colonization. C.J. Brydges, general manager of the Grand Trunk, used the press to air his differences with Hugh Allan over freight rates. Prime Minister Mackenzie received a petition signed by 10,500 British investors charging that 'the grant of public moneys in aid of such railways [as the Montreal Colonization and North Shore] is a breach of the original understanding between the Canadian Government and the Grand Trunk Railway.'[39]

In the spring of 1875 Hugh Allan, Louis Beaubien, J.J.C. Abbott, and Harry Abbott made a final effort to sell the railway's bonds. According to Allan, negotiations in London were progressing favourably when the London *Times*, inspired by the Grand Trunk, began to attack the sale of Canadian railway bonds to British investors.[40] The *Times* saw no reason for investors to subsidize a competitor for the Grand Trunk. Describing railway enterprises in Canada as 'disastrous' and 'miserable,' the *Times* told Allan to build his railway with Canadian money: 'No amount of argument can, we should hope, lead sensible people in this country to put more money into railway projects in the Canadian Dominion, for not only is there no traffic for such railways, but supposing there were, their owners are exposed to the constant danger that the Dominion Parliament may grant a subsidy for a competitive railway to run half a mile off. In this way the Canadian Southern has been built, to the ruin of the proprietors of the Canada Great Western. If the belief in the value of schemes such as we have criticized is so profound among Canadians as we are told, we say again let them find the money at home. Millions enough have been presented to the Dominion already by this country.'[41] Although Allan published a pamphlet refuting the *Times*' charges, the damage had been done and the Montreal Colonization bonds remained unsold. As an alternative Allan tried to form a syndicate that would advance $25,000 and to induce British contractors to provide capital in return for a proportion of the contract. Again there were no takers: profit potential was low and the line was too short to be built economically. On 9 June 1875 Allan sent back word of his failure to raise capital.[42]

The company's problems were intensified by Ottawa County's refusal to honour its subsidy. In 1872 it had subscribed $200,000 to the Montreal Colonization Railway to be paid in installments of $3000 a mile as construction was completed within the county. These bonds had been used by the contractor to secure his loan at the Jacques Cartier Bank. County officials charged that the railway was insolvent and incapable of paying for the right of way: private stockholders had not subscribed adequately and the railway would never be completed by 1 December 1875. In July 1875 the issue went to the courts.[43]

Facing bankruptcy and with construction at a standstill the railway pressed for increased assistance from the province. Beaubien and Arthur Dansereau met on a daily basis to plan strategy. Dansereau and Chapleau both published articles favouring an increased subsidy.[44] In mid-June the railway asked for an immediate grant of $100,000 in return for a promise to open the railway to St. Jérôme within six or seven weeks: negotiations continued over the next four months. At the railway's annual meeting in July Allan gave an account of the company's disastrous financial condition. Private investment totalled $18,881 and only four individuals had subscribed more than $1000.[45] This was in sharp contrast to government contributions. In February 1875 the province had increased its aid to the Montreal Colonization by granting $1500 a mile for the branch line to St. Jérôme and $30,000 for a bridge over the Ottawa River in Pontiac County. By July 1875 the railway had received $459,400 from the province and $346,644 from the city of Montreal. However, the railway's total income of $824,925 had been far exceeded by its expenditures of $1,566,260.[46] Sub-contractors were unpaid and the company had borrowed heavily on its bonds. In mid-August, de Bellefeuille, Chapleau, C.-J. Coursol, Curé Labelle, and Allan met with the cabinet in Quebec City. They asked that the completion date be extended and that private shareholders be put on the same footing as municipal investors. Estimating that $2 million was needed to complete the railway, they suggested a 5 per cent government guarantee for a new $2 million issue of first-mortgage company debentures. This would replace the company's unsold bonds. The government turned down these proposals along with a later suggestion that the government purchase the company's bonds.[47]

There was yet another crisis to be faced by the provincial government as the two railways slid into bankruptcy. On 10 August 1875 the Jacques Cartier Bank announced that it could not meet its obligations. The bank was brought down by the failure of the contractor for the Montreal Colonization to meet his debts. The Jacques Cartier Bank had lent $183,995 to Duncan Macdonald and $402,033 to his construction company. Due on 15 June 1875 both loans were secured on Montreal Colonization bonds nominally worth $600,000 and Ottawa County municipal bonds with a face value of $200,000.[48] Aside from its effect on the province's financial reputation, the bank's failure involved the Boucherville administration directly since the government was the bank's leading creditor. As one government official put it, the bank's collapse 'would bring ruin and desolation to many a hearth and leave hundreds of widows and orphans without sustenance.'[49]

The loan represented the close relationship between the bank, the railway company, and its contractor. The contractor, Macdonald and Company, had its offices on the second floor of the bank's new building on Place d'Armes. J.J.C. Abbott and de Bellefeuille, two of Allan's closest associates in the railway, were both shareholders in the Jacques Cartier Bank. Victor Hudon was a director of the bank and had been a provisional director of Allan's Canadian Pacific Railway in 1872. Charles S. Rodier, vice-president of the bank, and two bank directors, John L. Cassidy and Jean-Baptiste Beaudry, were also shareholders in the Montreal Colonization.

III

The collapse of the Jacques Cartier Bank and the bankruptcy of the two railway companies made further government aid inevitable. Even Provincial Treasurer Robertson, always critical of the north-shore promoters, was not prepared to accept the political consequences of abandonment of the north-shore railways. The credit of the province, the subsidies advanced by the provincial government, Quebec City, and Montreal, and the political pressures from important businessmen all dictated that the government step in directly. Prominent Bleus such as Hector Langevin added their influence. Before the takeover the provincial treasurer wrote Langevin explaining his reluctance to make further cash advances to the railways. Admitting that he might be 'unnecessarily scrupulous and narrow,' Robertson insisted that he could not violate the laws of the province by advancing money to the North Shore Railway unless the work was actually done.[50] The minister also expressed doubts over the credibility of the contractors' expense accounts. He suggested that the contractors make some sacrifices since their contracts were inflated by $500,000. But no, they preferred to let the government 'run all the risks, they retaining their contracts and profits, and if they cannot finish the works the province must suffer and the Gov't disgraced for acting contrary to Law.'

In one sense the government's railway policy had come full circle. Since 1869 the province had made increasing commitments with its liberal railway legislation and its generous land and cash subsidies. Railway expenditures by the provincial government had escalated rapidly. The province spent $48,171 in 1871 to aid railway construction and $38,700 in 1874. In 1875 government expenditures on railways jumped to $1,013,099 of which $459,000 was granted to the Montreal Colonization and $191,306 to the North Shore.[51] To protect this investment the Boucherville government was inevitably forced to intervene. Bleu politicians were also trapped by their own rhetoric. For years they had promoted a railway from Quebec City to Ottawa as essential for the prosperity, progress, and colonization of the north-shore region. Having raised the expectations of its constituents, the government could hardly back down. The only alternative to a takeover was an accelerated subsidy program to the very promoters who had placed the government in its predicament.

Still in doubt was the method by which the province would ensure completion of the two lines. In September 1875 the government announced plans to revoke both charters, to reimburse private shareholders, and to supervise directly the construction of a unified railway from Quebec City to the upper Ottawa Valley. Negotiations with Montreal Colonization officials continued until 2 November when the shareholders ratified a settlement of $57,149. Of this amount $24,801 was to reimburse the private shareholders and the balance was to pay various salaries and debts.[52] On 22 November the North Shore shareholders met to dissolve their company which had a total private investment of $18,940. Cauchon spoke out strongly at this meeting. He agreed with the government takeover but argued against immediate dissolution of the company. Fearing the influence of Montreal on a government-appointed board of directors, he urged that the company remain active as a lobby for the rights of Quebec City.[53]

The takeover was formally announced in the speech from the throne, 8 November 1875. Government speakers contended that the province's 'material progress' depended on the two railroads and that the public funds already invested had forced the government's hand. The Liberals, greatly outnumbered in the Legislative Assembly, attacked the takeover throughout the session. Their leader, Henri-Gustave Joly, suggested that since the province had made such a 'great sacrifice' in promoting the two railways and since the two lines formed 'virtually part' of the Pacific line the federal government 'should come to our assistance.'[54] The Conservatives, in defeating Joly's amendment forty-five to fifteen, pointed out that the Liberal government in Ottawa was hostile to railways in Quebec. Louis Beaubien, a member of the north-shore delegation that had been so coolly received by Prime Minister Mackenzie, argued that the interests of Quebec railway companies would never be safeguarded by the federal Liberals. Solicitor-General Angers reminded the opposition that the Pacific terminus, promised to Montreal by Cartier, was now being located in Ontario by the Liberals. Conservative newspapers defended Boucherville's actions. Israel Tarte's *Le Canadien* called Joly's proposal 'absurde' and accused the Liberal leader of being 'ni patriotique ni honnête' in opposing construction of the two railways by the government. *La Minerve* pointed out that, of four lines projected to connect with the terminus of the Pacific Railway, only the Montreal Colonization would serve the province of Quebec.[55]

Despite their lack of numbers, the Liberals kept up the pressure. Joly and front-benchers, Pierre Bachand and Félix-Gabriel Marchand, demanded a full financial statement from the two railway companies and questioned whether the province could negotiate its bonds on favourable terms. Joly emphasized that he was not hostile to railways and reminded the assembly of his long-time support for railway construction. He also praised the Grand Trunk and urged payment of the interest due to the railway's British investors: 'Canada owes an immense debt to those who sent their money in order to build the Grand Trunk.'[56]

The Liberals had powerful support in their opposition to the takeover. The Grand Trunk and a Montreal group petitioned against any further assistance to north-shore railways. Equally embarrassing for the government was a south-shore delegation from the counties of Sherbrooke, Stanstead, and Compton. Introduced by Provincial Treasurer Robertson, the member for Sherbrooke, the group had a chilly meeting with Premier Boucherville and left without shaking his hand. The premier told them that he had announced his railway policy and that his government would resign if its program was not approved.[57] George Irvine was another important opponent. A Conservative renegade, former solicitor-general in the Chauveau cabinet, ex-government director of the North Shore Railway, and active in the Quebec Central Railway, he proposed that other railways 'receive their fair proportion' of provincial funds. He urged a slowdown in construction of the North Shore Railway and distribution of the savings of $1 million among other railways in the province. Doubting that the government would be any more successful than private companies in financing railways, he concluded that it was 'a dangerous precedent' for a government 'to build, run and manage a railroad.'[58]

Although the takeover was announced at the beginning of the session the cabinet was slow in presenting its budget. Feelings ran high at cabinet meetings as ministers thrashed over the province's escalating railway commitments. Boucherville was hesitant to enter any further into the railway sweepstakes but found it hard to resist helping the Montreal Colonization Railway. North-shore politicians like Chapleau and Ruggles Church kept up the pressure. In mid-November with the cabinet wavering over railway policy, a group of federal Conservatives including Rodrigue Masson, Thomas White, Alphonse Desjardins, and Alexandre Lacoste, were invited to Quebec City for discussions.[59] Curé Labelle spent most of the session in the capital. With other Conservatives wavering, Angers and Chapleau bore the burden of defence. In two important speeches Chapleau spoke of the 'splendours of industry and commerce' and 'the value of the iron horse as an agent of colonization, fraternization and civilization.'[60] Stating that four-fifths of the province's revenues came from the north shore, Chapleau charged that the railways on the south shore of the St. Lawrence had been overly favoured since Confederation. He attacked Grand Trunk freight rates between Montreal and Quebec City and supported the Royal Albert Bridge and the linking of Quebec and the Maritimes by an extension of the Lévis and Kennebec Railway.

Ironically, the burden of preparing the budget fell on J.G. Robertson, the provincial treasurer. Representing the south shore in the cabinet and fearing defeat in Sherbrooke, Robertson was tired, plagued by headaches, and near resignation. He finally left the cabinet in January 1876. In his budget speech Robertson expressed his frustration:

From year to year, since 1869, pressure had been brought to bear upon the Government by hon. members of this House, and by parties outside the House, interested in various railway lines, to increase the subsidies in favour of railways having grants in their favour, and to include other new lines of road in the subsidized list, and I am bound to say that the Government had given great offence to many of its friends for not complying with such demands. I do not know, Mr. Speaker, what your experience may be with reference to pressure brought to bear upon you by railway men [hear, hear – Hon. Messrs. Malhiot and Ouimet], but I find it entirely useless to discuss a railway subsidy with railway men [hear, hear from both sides of the House]; every single line of railway that ever was projected and that we have in this province, in which they are interested, is of the most extreme importance, and of more importance than any other line in the limits of the Province [hear, hear and laughter]; the interests of the Government depend more, the safety and stability of the Government depend [hear, hear] upon a grant being given to this particular line more than to all the others [laughter]; the institutions of this country generally, the interests of the Dominion and of the world depend more on a grant to one small railway than in favour of any other railway in the Province. [Hear, hear – Ald. McGauvran and laughter] I do not know what your experience is, Mr. Speaker, but I would sooner meet a patent rights man, or a book-pedlar, or a lightning-rod professor, or any other sort of man, than a man who has railway on the brain, and who comes to ask me for a subsidy [laughter on both sides of House].[61]

At a late-night meeting on Saturday, 4 December, the cabinet came to final agreement, and two days later the budget was presented. In taking over both railways the government committed itself to building a united line from Quebec City to Pontiac County via Montreal. The railway would be equal in quality to the Great Western and would have a gauge of four feet, eight inches. The government also promised to build a branch line north of Three Rivers to Grand Piles and to establish steamers on the St. Maurice River.[62] To pay for what would be called the Quebec, Montreal, Ottawa and Occidental Railway the government proposed to float thirty-year bonds worth $4,185,333. The sale of the new provincial bonds in England would be handled by the prestigious Baring Brothers. The government had already renewed the contracts of both contractors. McGreevy would be paid $27,000 a mile and was to complete the North Shore or eastern section of the united line within two years. The contractor for the western section, Duncan Macdonald, would receive $3,601,649, although this figure was later adjusted. The materials and work of both contractors would be subject to regular inspection by government engineers.[63]

As well as settling with the two companies and their contractors, the government was anxious to ensure payment of the municipal subsidies. Montreal, having advanced $569,002, was particularly testy on the subject of the uncompleted Montreal Colonization Railway. In mid-September a Montreal delegation met with provincial officials. They asked that Montreal continue to be represented on the board of directors and that the preferential position of the city's bonds be maintained. Although the government refused to grant any municipal representation on the new board, it did agree to give Montreal's bonds preference over those of other municipalities. The delegation also insisted that the railway's passenger and freight depots be located near the centre of Montreal. Again the government compromised. It refused to build tunnels or bridges at all street-crossings in Montreal but did agree that the depot would be located within Montreal city limits. The location of the junction between the eastern and western sections was temporarily resolved by the province's acceptance of Montreal's demand that the junction and the terminus of the eastern section would be within the city. Terms for payment of the balance of Montreal's $1 million subsidy were also settled. The city finally agreed to pay one-quarter of the balance when the railway was opened to Ste. Thérèse, the second quarter when the line reached Grenville, the third quarter at Papineauville, and a final payment when the railway was completed to Hull.[64]

Other municipalities lacked Montreal's bargaining power. The government obligated all municipalities which had subscribed to the North Shore and Montreal Colonization railways to pay their subscriptions to the provincial treasurer. Municipalities were not allowed to exempt themselves or to modify their subsidies on the basis that the original companies had not fulfilled their commitment. Amounts already paid to the two railways by municipalities would receive up to 5 per cent interest from the government but only when the entire line was completed and when revenues permitted. All municipal representation on the railways new board of directors was cancelled.[65]

The budget of 1875 symbolized the province's growing subservience to its north-shore railways. Between 1867 and 1874 the province had enjoyed an annual surplus. In 1875 it was to incur a deficit of $29,209 and railway problems had, for the first time, forced a provincial budget that was more than a simple statement of expenses and revenues. While police costs for the year were budgeted at $66,000, education at $233,410 and agriculture, immigration and colonization at $154,400, the government was assuming direct control of a railway that had a projected cost of $10,000,000.[66]

Since private interests had been unable to raise railway capital, the government was forced to undertake the task itself. By issuing bonds in the province's name and through the offices of Baring Brothers the government could reassure English capitalists. The government's railway obligations meant that other priorities, such as colonization, had to be cut back. From a high point of $223,844 in 1869–70, colonization expenses slipped to $129,426 in 1874–5 and to $58,771 in

1875-6. The harried provincial treasurer pointed out that the province could not afford to build both roads and railways: 'It strikes me it would be better to give money in paying interest of the debt we owe for railways than give it for common colonization roads.'[67]

The government takeover brought a thickening maze of construction contracts, patronage, and ever-mounting government debts. Decisions on the north-shore railways concerning loans, purchases, the route, personnel, or expropriations had always had political overtones; this accelerated under government ownership. A central economic and political issue in the construction of the north-shore railways was the competition between Montreal and Quebec City for the Laurentian terminus of the Canadian Pacific Railway. Quebec City's decline, the end of reciprocity, the disintegration of the square-timber trade, the growing American demand for sawn lumber, and the expansion of steam-oriented transportation systems emphasized that the province was inextricably tied to the Atlantic and North American economic mosaic. The intense opposition of the Grand Trunk to the north-shore railways and the recurring interest of Hugh Allan provide further evidence that the relatively unimportant north-shore region of the St. Lawrence and Ottawa rivers was being integrated into a larger rail grid and North Atlantic transportation pattern. The entrepreneurs' failure to raise railway capital for two decades also had its base in international factors. These economic realities had important local political implications and for the next decade the north-shore railway question was at the core of Quebec politics. Constituents evaluated the railway in terms of their own expectations rather than in the light of international conditions. Their clerical, entrepreneurial, and political leaders - urban and middle class for the most part - had raised local aspirations. They now had to produce the railway whatever the cost to the taxpayer.

6

The government railway:
a noose for Boucherville and Joly

The two private railways were united by the government into the Quebec, Montreal, Ottawa and Occidental Railway, or as it was commonly called the QMO&O. To supervise construction a three-member railway commission was established. Although in theory the commission was non-partisan, the first appointments were political and part of a cabinet reorganization in January 1876. Provincial Treasurer Robertson, dissatisfied with the government's largesse to the north shore, resigned and was replaced by Ruggles Church, member for Pontiac and a perennial friend of north-shore railway development. As part of the shuffle Henri-Gédéon Malhiot of Three Rivers left the cabinet and was named to the railway commission. Senator Eugène Chinic, father-in-law of attorney-general A.R. Angers, was appointed as Quebec City's representative. Although Walter Shanly, Louis Beaubien, and Thomas White were rumoured to be candidates, no Montrealer was named to the commission.[1] Hugh Allan's lieutenant, J.E.L. de Bellefeuille, refused to accept the secretaryship of the commission. The nomination of George Irvine as the English-speaking and south-shore commissioner was controversial. A prominent Quebec City lawyer, he had left the Ouimet cabinet during the Tanneries scandal. Associated with the south-shore Quebec Central Railway, Irvine persistently criticized extravagant spending on the north-shore railways.[2] His hostility to Joseph Cauchon was well-known and later, as lawyer for British investors in the Lévis and Kennebec Railway, he would hound L.A. Sénécal.

Commissioners were paid $3600 a year and held regular meetings in Quebec City. Aided by a staff of seven they met in the Agriculture

Department or in the offices of the now-defunct North Shore Railway. As intermediaries between the government and the contractors, the commissioners participated in complex political, financial, and technical decisions. They supervised construction and made payments to the contractors from the province's Consolidated Railway Fund. In theory, they had tight control over the two contractors, Duncan Macdonald and Thomas McGreevy. No payment of public funds was to be made until the work had been approved by the government engineer, work was to be of first-class quality, the government had a cancellation option if construction was slow, and there was a 10 per cent holdback clause. However, commission minutes make clear that, despite the expenditure in 1876 of $4,442,336 of government funds, the commissioners exercised only the loosest of controls.[3] Changing government specifications, the necessity for substantial advances to the indebted contractor for the western section, government indecisiveness over the route, and ever-present political pressures hampered the commissioners.

Supervising the contractors was a recurrent problem. Former provincial Treasurer Robertson felt that there were regular violations of the McGreevy contract and that the appointment of a railway commission had simply opened the door to 'extras.' As original estimates of materials proved inadequate, the government agreed to pay the contractors for amounts used. This led to a rapid escalation of costs: 3,000,000 yards of fill were utilized, double the contract estimate; over three times the original estimate of masonry was used.[4] According to the government engineer, the contractor would go bankrupt if these changes were not accepted. The inspection of materials purchased by the contractors was another difficulty. Goods were bought all over the world and were delivered at various points along the line. Macdonald bought steel rails in London from the Rhymney Company and the Elbow Vale, Steel, Iron and Coal Company. McGreevy bought his rails in Liverpool from the Mersey Steel and Iron Company and his rolling stock in New York and London, Ontario. Canadian Engine and Machinery Company officials complained that they had been waiting months for a government inspection of locomotives they had built for Thomas McGreevy. In July 1877 they threatened to deliver them without an inspection; one month later inspectors rejected the locomotives as poorly constructed. Paying for the contractor's purchases was another problem. In Quebec City the Bank of Montreal paid for shipments and was reimbursed by the commission.[5] In other localities lengthy delays were normal. Sorting out disputes among contractors, subcontractors, manufacturers, municipalities, and workers were daily preoccupations of the commissioners. They had to settle accusations that Duncan Macdonald was three months in arrears in paying his subcontractors. On another occasion, shippers in St. Jérôme unloaded their goods from the contractor's train when a freight rate of twenty-five to thirty cents a pound was announced. One commissioner went to St. Scholastique, a village on the western line, and warned subcontractors they were overcharging. In April 1877 the commission paid a claim of $19,142 to L.B. Boomer and Sons despite McGreevy's denial that he had any debt to the company.[6] The commissioners further complicated matters by involving themselves in deals. Charges were made that McGreevy bought supplies from Commissioner Chinic's hardware store. The commissioners also remained active in politics. Malhiot wrote to Langevin on political matters and two other commissioners signed Israel Tarte's nomination papers.[7]

While the commission grappled with the daily problems of railway construction, the government's friends busied themselves with backroom financial negotiations, construction contracts, real-estate deals, expropriation cases, and the distribution of patronage. Telegraph companies, insurance brokers, real-estate speculators, notaries, lawyers, manufacturers, and shippers all benefited from railway construction. The Merchants' Bank and the Bank of Montreal helped negotiate the provincial loan in England. La Banque Nationale acted as a transfer agent for the railway. The Union Bank and Jacques Cartier Bank both held large blocks of Montreal Colonization lands as collateral.[8] A familiar group of Conservative lawyers appeared in many of the transactions. De Bellefeuille, former secretary of the Montreal Colonization Railway, was named at a fee of $2000 plus expenses to supervise the purchase of the right of way between Montreal and Aylmer, J.J.C. Abbott's law firm acted for both contractors and in various expropriation cases. L.O. Loranger, another friend of the Montreal Colonization Railway, served as lawyer for the contractor of the western section. Joseph Alfred Mousseau, then editor of *L'Opinion Publique*, acted on occasion as lawyer for the railway commissioners. Friendly newspapers received their share of patronage. *La Minerve* and three Conservative editors, Israel Tarte, Alphonse Desjardins, and Thomas White, were paid for printing and for railway advertisements. The railway commission's Montreal office at 16 St. James Street was rented from Desjardins, proprietor of *Le Nouveau Monde*.

While times were good for manufacturers, lawyers, and journalists, conditions were less attractive on the construction sites. An opposition newspaper described McGreevy as 'le roi de Prusse' and accused him of employing brutal foremen. Labourers earned eighty cents a day and were sometimes forced to buy supplies in the contractor's store. Bread cost twenty-two cents a loaf and butter thirty cents a pound.[9] Few subcontractors had the compassion of one entrepreneur in Three Rivers who decided to pay his men in cash rather than giving chits for the company store since 'it will be much to their advantage to be paid in cash every week - it would also be a popular move': 'The people here are much pleased to see the work commenced and it will be the means of keeping many poor families from great suffering. We will increase the force of men at work next week when we get the cribwork started. We could employ double the number of men we require if there was work for them - as there is very little lumbering in the St. Maurice and the labouring men usually employed in the lumber camps are very desitute.'[10] One foreman complained to the premier: 'I work at River Rouge as forman for McCormick and Shedwick in which they had a contract from McDonald, it was the coldest winter I ever saw. In the spring the work was stop so they gave me an order for $50.00 on McDonald, in which he refuse to pay. The boardinghouse kept my trunk and cloths for my board money, so I was left without anything whatever, then I gave the order to the Hon. George Irving he said he would do all he could for me, and at the same time he said that McDonald was a hard case; only for the way I am situated, I surely would not have troubling you so much, so I beg to be excuse. I hope I will see you for many years in the same position, because your a Gentleman for the poor.'[11]

Neither the government nor its railway commission showed much concern for the plight of railway workers. The Montreal *Gazette* commented that it was a good time for contractors because labour was 'cheap and plentiful.'[12] A Liberal amendment that the government recompense workers and subcontractors unpaid by the contractors was given short shrift by former provincial Treasurer Robertson, who did not see 'why there should be so much sympathy shown for workmen, who were not obliged to work on these roads. They could leave off if they pleased. Why should a contractor be hampered by a sub-contractor's indebtedness or disputes about wages ... If men worked and were not paid, it was their affair.'[13] In 1882 section-men in Calumet and Thurso struck in protest against the reduction of their daily wages from one dollar to eighty cents. The government sent police from Quebec City to control the situation and explained that salary reductions had been made in order to keep all the men working through the winter. There was always discussion among the employers and politicians as to which nationality produced the best labourers. One government engineer was reputed to follow the principle that 'he would not employ a damned French Canadian if he could help it.'[14] Another engineer found French Canadians to be good workmen: 'The old Latin adage "Nascitus non fit" does not apply to the lower grades of Railway men at all events and a wise Manager will endeavour to *make* the men on whose services he has to depend. I had hundreds of French Canadians in my employ on the Hoosac Tunnel and I counted among them some of my very best "hands." By mixing them in with skilled *Cornish* miners they soon learned the business and in many cases came to excel their teachers: Some of my most skilled and trusted Foremen were Canadian French. For Railway employment, generally, I want no better material. They are, as a rule, contented and amenable to orders: two very essential qualities in Railway Employees.'[15]

Both contractors quarreled constantly with the government over their contracts and at one point McGreevy's records were seized by the commission. McGreevy charged that he had been delayed two years by the cabinet's indecision over the route. After the government takeover, he had been ordered not to build west of Three Rivers and to stop work on the Montreal station.[16] As a result of political pressures the number of stations on his section increased from twelve to over thirty. Work did continue in the eastern portion and in December 1877 the line between Three Rivers and Quebec City opened.

Construction of the section between Montreal and Hull was equally difficult. In 1875 Duncan MacDonald, contractor for the western section, had debts totalling $794,212. As part of the takeover agreement, the government guaranteed his $423,974 debt to the Banque Jacques Cartier and paid $473,525 to his other creditors. By June 1878 the government had spent $3,925,146 on the western section, an excess of $323,496 over Macdonald's contract.[17] Work still to be completed would cost $500,000. Attacking Macdonald's 'confusion of accounts' officials accused him of 'injuring government property' by running trains on inadequately ballasted tracks. The contractor retorted that the delays were caused by frequent government changes of its bridge specifications. In Montreal he had difficulty transporting his rolling stock from the end of the Grand Trunk line near Molson's brewery to his track at Hochelaga. The Montreal Harbour Commissioners' refusal to permit the laying of temporary track meant that barges had to be utilized.[18]

Despite these problems the section from Montreal to St. Jérôme was opened in October 1876. In a gala two-hour trip Boucherville, Chapleau, Louis Beaubien, Louis-Olivier Taillon, Gédéon Malhiot, Rodrigue Masson, Jonathan Wurtele, Jean-Louis Beaudry, L.O. Loranger, Thomas White and Henry Starnes travelled with their wives and friends to St. Jérôme where they were greeted at the presbytery by an exuberant Curé Labelle. By the end of 1877 the line from Montreal to Hull was open. Travel time was three hours and forty minutes and ferry service to Ottawa cost twenty-five cents.[19]

II

Although trains were running by the end of 1877 from Montreal to Ottawa and between Quebec City and Three Rivers, politicians, engineers, and railway officials had not agreed on the route between Montreal and Three Rivers. Original plans called for the track to be located along the St. Lawrence River with a bridge to the Island of Montreal at Bout de l'Ile. However, political pressures steadily mounted to build the railway eight or nine miles to the north through the town of Joliette (see map O). In August 1875 George Bemister, a Montreal Colonization engineer, was paid by Joliette to conduct a survey. To the surprise of few, his report favoured a route that passed through the town. The Joliette route, although six miles longer, would open up timber lands, was not subject to flooding, and would not compete with river traffic. Interested parishes circulated petitions in favour of the Joliette route. Backers of the Laurentian Railway, including the railway's vice-president, Joseph Chapleau, lobbied for the Joliette route and promoted their railway as a link between the eastern and western sections of the QMO&O.[20] Inherent in the route question was whether its traffic would have to pass through Montreal. Advocates of the direct route argued that Montreal was not justified 'in exacting from Quebec and the country at large the expensive courtesy of hauling all empty cars and inanimate merchandise twenty miles out of their way for the purpose of whistling round the curve at Hochelaga, and giving employment to an extra switchman.'[21]

Unable to resolve the route question the government railway commission referred the problem to their engineers and early in 1877 received two separate reports. P.A. Peterson, government engineer on the western section of the QMO&O, favoured the original river route via Bout de l'Ile. Alexander Light, engineer for the eastern section, surveyed four routes between the village of Maskinongé and Montreal and suggested a compromise between Joliette and Bout de l'Ile (see map C). He proposed a line from Maskinongé to the village of Terrebonne. Passing within five miles of Joliette this route would be level, less costly, and would avoid possible flooding along the river.[22] With conflicting advice from its own engineers, the commission ordered outside engineering reports. In approving Light's Terrebonne route, Walter Shanly and Sandford Fleming noted that the purpose of the railway was a more important issue than costs or engineering factors. If the intent was simply to join Quebec City and Montreal the Bout de l'Ile route along the river was obviously preferable. However, both Shanly and Fleming envisaged the QMO&O as part of a network to the Pacific. Shanly proposed that the line 'be constructed with a view to shorten the distance between Quebec and the far west, as much as possible ... '[23] Fleming agreed and argued that the terminus of the Pacific Railway should never have been located in Montreal. From a junction-point in Terrebonne, branches could have been built to both Montreal and Quebec City. This would have reduced the rail distance from Quebec City to Ottawa by seventeen miles while increasing the distance from Montreal to Ottawa by only four miles.[24]

Montrealers reacted strongly to these plans to bypass their city. Envisaging the QMO&O as a funnel to Montreal they were determined that western trade not be diverted to Quebec City. One alderman charged that the Boucherville government had always intended to bypass Montreal by joining Quebec City and Hull directly. Montreal City Council asked its attorney if the province could be forced to pay for a connection in Montreal between the QMO&O and the Grand Trunk. In December 1876 Montreal gained additional leverage when the first installment of its subsidy fell due. Delaying payment of the $163,338 city fathers pointed out that the subsidy had been granted on condition that the railway would be built from the port of Quebec City 'via Montreal' to Pontiac County. One railway commissioner supported the Montreal position. Gédéon Malhiot defended the Bout de l'Ile route as the best method of joining the old parishes and of competing with the Grand Trunk for business along the north shore.[25]

Montrealers had other complaints. Angry with the government's vacillations, a local politician described Montreal as the province's 'milch cow'; another charged that the premier had treated the city 'uncivilly' and 'cavalierly.'[26] A delegation called on the premier to ask why QMO&O contractors were not obligated to buy their manufactured goods in the province. Canadian lumber was being shipped to the United States, they complained, and returning as QMO&O freight cars. Boucherville was unsympathetic and replied that, except for quality, the government had no control over the contractors' materials.[27] Other Montrealers objected to the proposed Royal Albert Bridge which would link the QMO&O to the south shore of the St. Lawrence. Without a bridge in Montreal's east end, QMO&O southbound traffic would have to be diverted around Mount Royal and over the Grand Trunk's Victoria Bridge (see map B). Continuing their year-old campaign, the Montreal Board of Trade and a majority of the Montreal Harbour Commissioners argued that the bridge would obstruct harbour traffic and channel trade to the United States. In October, 1876 the bridge promoters were again forced to withdraw their application for a federal charter.

In March 1877 the government announced its acceptance of the Terrebonne route and the premier, frustrated by the tenacity of railway lobbyists, wrote to Curé Labelle that it was 'oiseuse' to continue discussions. Engineering reports had been only one factor in the decision. By building to Terrebonne, construction of the costly bridge onto the Island of Montreal could be delayed until the city paid its subsidy.[28] If the city remained obstinate, the government could by-pass Montreal and link the eastern and western sections of the QMO&O at Ste. Thérèse (see map C). Arthur Dansereau, proprietor of *La Minerve* and astute observer of Bleu politics, felt that the choice of Terrebonne was due to the friendship between Premier Boucherville and Rodrigue Masson, MP for Terrebonne.

The choice of Terrebonne divided Montreal Conservatives. Critics pointed out that Montreal's supposed defenders were all natives of Terrebonne – Chapleau, Louis-Olivier Taillon (MLA for Montreal-East), and Alphonse Desjardins (MP for Hochelaga).[29] They supported Boucherville while Louis Beaubien attacked the Terrebonne route. Louis Archambault, Bleu MP for l'Assomption, was upset since his county seat would be bypassed. A powerful party organizer and former confidant of Cartier, Archambault accused the government of omnipotence, of sacrificing the province, and of laughing at its best friends. 'The Government,' he observed, 'always finish by giving way for the sake of peace.'[30] Montreal city council remained adamant: the city would not pay its subsidy until the Bout de l'Ile route was adopted, the junction between the eastern and western sections was placed within the city, and the Montreal station was completed.[31]

Despite its satisfaction with the Terrebonne route, Quebec City was also recalcitrant in paying the balance of its $1 million subsidy. The city had already advanced $143,000 to the QMO&O and had committed $100,000 to the Quebec and Lake St. John Railway. Negotiations between civic officials and the cabinet were still under way when the Boucherville administration fell. City fathers wanted assurance that the principal workshops would be located in Quebec City, they wanted to settle the value of the station-site and to obtain indemnities for municipal property-owners along the rail line.[32]

With the two major municipal subsidies in limbo the province turned to the federal government. In the years immediately after Confederation, the presence in Ottawa of Cartier, Langevin, and other strong Quebec ministers had assured the attentiveness of the Macdonald administration to the railway ambitions of Montreal and Quebec City. However, the Boucherville Conservatives had little leverage with the Liberal government of Alexander Mackenzie. His Quebec ministers were weak and generally unsympathetic to the north-shore railways and their Bleu friends. As a result, 1876 and 1877 were bleak years for Quebec members seeking federal railway funds. Rodrigue Masson, Simon-Xavier Cimon, Thomas White, and Henri-Thomas Taschereau lobbied in Ottawa but never impressed Mackenzie. A petition signed by the archbishop of Quebec for aid to the Quebec and Lake St. John Railway was ignored by the prime minister. Masson expressed his frustration to Curé Labelle: 'de dégringolades en dégringolades nous sommes tombés au dernier échelon auquel nous voudrions nous accrocher mais que l'on menace de nous coucher [sic].'[33]

The failure to obtain federal financing or immediate payment of the municipal subsidies forced the province to borrow the money itself. In May 1876 the province issued thirty-year, 5 per cent bonds with a face value of $4,185,333. Hugh Allan's Merchants' Bank was named as the province's London agent and soon after, in response to a letter from Allan, provincial Treasurer Ruggles Church sailed for England on an Allan ship to help sell the bonds. Allan's companies were paid over $5000 in July and August 1876 for transportation costs and for stamps on the bonds. Although the bonds were apparently to be sold at par without commission for the Merchants' Bank, there were charges that the bank bought the bonds at a 1 per cent discount. Another rumour circulated that the bank was in difficulty and was willing to sell the bonds at a 1.5 per cent discount.[34] As before, the London *Times* and the Grand Trunk Railway opposed attempts to raise British capital for the north-shore railways. The *Times* described Quebec as a 'poor' province with few sources of revenue: 'Several of our colonies are threatening to get into serious difficulty by their overeager borrowing, and this Quebec province threatens to lead the list. We should be doing it a great injury to give it money.' The provincial Treasurer countered by assuring British investors that the railway, 'a public work of the province,' would not be a rival to the Grand Trunk.[35]

Although it had been announced that the province had realized $4,257,196 from the sale of its bonds, the real situation became clear in June 1877 when the Merchants' Bank wrote off a loss of $223,990 'from unanticipated difficulties in placing the loan on the London Stock Exchange.' In September the bank still held $500,000 of the province's bonds and a bank official reported to his home office that it would be 'impossible to place them in the market - even at 95 - in quantity.' The Bank of Montreal finally rescued the Merchants' Bank and the province's credit reputation by buying the bonds from the Merchants' Bank at 96 per cent of their face value.[36] As a temporary solution for the province's financial crisis, the Bank of Montreal also agreed to advance $500,000 immediately to the provincial government and another $500,000 when needed. The 7 per cent interest charged on these loans to the province was higher than the prevailing rates of 5 to 5.5 per cent on the English market. Some saw the rate as indicative of the province's failing credit, while others charged that the bank had been rewarded for rescuing the province. The provincial treasurer replied that on short-term loans the difference between 5.5 and 7 per cent was not great and that rates in Canada were always high at harvest time.[37]

Owning the QMO&O had rapidly escalated into an expensive and complicated business. In 1876 and 1877 railways devoured provincial revenues at an alarming rate and neither the federal government nor municipalities had expressed much sympathy. For the year ending 30 June 1877 provincial revenues, aside from the sale of bonds, were $2,433,111. In the same year the province spent $3,481,670 on railways plus $407,176 as charges on the public debt. Expenses not connected to railways were under $2 million.[38] The transition from an era of provincial surpluses to a period of annual deficits was a clear indication of the impact of railways. Between 1868 and 1874 the province had borrowed over $8 million and, according to its critics, had run up deficits of $29,209 in 1875 and $14,898 in 1876.[39] Rising interest rates and stalled bond issues reflected growing suspicions of Quebec's financial health. Nor was the QMO&O near completion. The main line between Montreal and Three Rivers had not been constructed and there were no connecting links with railways to the west.

III

By 1878 politics in Quebec had soured. The Pacific scandal, the Tanneries affair, the issue of clerical influence in elections, the competition between Quebec City and Montreal, the ongoing depression, the mounting provincial debt, and the efforts of politicians to win railway subsidies for their constituents and favours for themselves had resulted in parochialism and weakened party ties. Rising political pressures had been contained by the patrician-style leadership of both Boucherville and Joly. However, by 1878 young, volatile politicians like Honoré Mercier, Israel Tarte, and Chapleau were pressing for power. Tarte's attack on the Liberals at the outset of the session of 1878 stung the usually placid Joly. Behind the scenes Chapleau and Laurier carried on negotiations for a new party alignment while in Ottawa the Conservatives tried to prop up the Boucherville administration. In Montreal the Liberals organized mass rallies; in Quebec City provincial Treasurer Angers was burned in effigy.[40] The crisis of 1878 was precipitated by the issue of the provincial debt and the route of the QMO&O railway into Montreal. Ever-growing railway expenses had devoured provincial loans of over $8 million and in 1878 a further loan of $3 million was necessary.

At the end of 1877 the route issue had apparently been resolved in favour of Quebec City and the Terrebonne interests. The cabinet, responding to Masson's pressures and angry at Montreal's refusal to pay its subsidy, had announced its intention to build from Three Rivers to Terrebonne. From there a bypass of Montreal could be completed to Ste. Thérèse. Montreal however, had not relented and insisted it would not pay the subsidy until its conditions were met. Conservative strength in Montreal was further eroded by daily Liberal attacks from Le National and Louis Jetté as well as bitter reprisals from leading Bleus like Louis Beaubien and Louis Archambault. L.O. Taillon, Bleu MLA for Montreal-East, could only fight a rearguard action against an angry city council and protesting local businessmen. Sources of party funds in Montreal evaporated and Chapleau had to appeal to Langevin for financial help.[41] Election prospects for Montreal-area Conservatives appeared grim.

Faced with unrelenting pressure from Montreal, the Boucherville cabinet had to give way. Quebec City's vision of direct access to the west fell victim to the political strength of Montreal. Thomas White and J.A. Mousseau applied local pressure and Tupper and Macdonald sent despatches from Ottawa. Chapleau used the occasion to press the government for a direct rail line from Terrebonne to Montreal. This would give his Terrebonne constituents access to the metropolis while ensuring the railway shops and terminus to his Montreal-East friends.[42] Langevin, worried about the weakness of the Boucherville administration, had to conciliate both Montreal and Quebec City. With a federal election imminent, settlement of the route question was essential and Macdonald expressed a willingness to intervene personally. Langevin met with unhappy party officials like Louis Archambault. Afterwards, he assured Macdonald that Archambault 'will not make trouble.' Adolphe Caron, explained to Macdonald that 'the Archambault matter has been arranged. Quebec interests, to a great extent, have been sacrificed to Montreal exigencies. But we felt that the paramount interest was to save the Government [of] De Boucherville, in view of the general federal elections.'[43]

Early in 1878 the cabinet succumbed to these pressures and Attorney-General Angers outlined a revised route. He reviewed the takeover of the two north-shore railways and the transfer of municipal subsidies from the two private companies to the government. He noted that Montreal was committed to paying its subsidy as construction to Ottawa was completed and that no mention of the route to Quebec City had been made in the original agreement. Angers insisted that the decision to build to Terrebonne had been based on engineering rather than political factors. However, as a concession to Montreal the government was prepared to abandon its planned bypass to Ste. Thérèse and to build directly into Montreal from Terrebonne. Montreal would be the terminus of the Quebec to Montreal section of the QMO&O and the junction between the railway's eastern and western sections. In return, Montreal and other delinquent municipalities would have to honour their subsidies. If civic officials refused to sign their municipal bonds, the cabinet could issue them in the municipality's name and seize municipal property to pay interest on them.[44]

The compromise did little to resolve the confusion. Montrealers were not content with half a loaf. Aldermen angrily denounced the provincial government as tyrannical, cavalier, and Russian. Montreal Liberals organized two anti-government rallies in the Bonsecours Market.[45] Conservative front-benchers, Ruggles Church, L.O. Loranger, and the combative Angers, did their best to defend the government. Loranger argued that Montreal city council in opposing the compromise represented the views of speculators who had bought property along the rejected route. In the Legislative Council, John Jones Ross attacked his Bleu colleague, Louis Archambault. Montreal's major Conservative papers, *Le Nouveau Monde*, *La Minerve*, and the *Gazette*, supported the government. Although hedging on which route it favoured, the *Gazette* argued that Montreal was obligated to pay its subsidy. Despite the haggling, the ultramontane *Le Nouveau Monde* sustained its enthusiasm for railways. The province's debts, it asserted, were nothing in terms of 'les bénéfices considérables que le commerce, l'industrie et l'agriculture de la province retireront des magnifiques chemins de fer ... '[46]

The government's concession to Montreal coupled with Angers' threat to 'throttle' Montreal if it did not pay its subsidy left Conservatives even more divided. On the one hand, advocates of the Bout de l'Ile route along the St. Lawrence were not reconciled. Louis Archambault and Arthur Turcotte, an important Bleu from Three Rivers, both voted against the government bill. The compromise also roused Quebec City. The Conservative *Morning Chronicle* charged that the city had once again been sacrificed to Montreal and that Quebec City's politicians lacked 'the backbone' to obtain direct access to the west. The Liberal *L'Evénement* was contemptuous: 'Les Trains salueraient la Métropole mais passeraient outre. On lâcherait quelques wagons, on jetterait les malles sur le parapet, et on filerait à toute vapeur vers l'ouest. Un petit bonjour de la main, et adieu.'[47] The Quebec City Board of Trade, the Chamber of Commerce, the Harbour Commission, and City Council described the Montreal bypass and direct access to the west as 'vital' to the interests of Quebec City. Wealthy property-owners were reportedly prepared to pay for the link between Terrebonne and Ste. Thérèse out of their own pockets. Premier Boucherville rejected Quebec City's demands. He pointed out that the original agreement with Montreal committed the government to build from Quebec City to Pontiac County *via* Montreal and to locate the junction of the eastern and western sections of the QMO&O in Montreal.[48] Early in February sixty influential Quebec City citizens met in the legislative library to press their claims. Boucherville refused to meet the delegation and attacked the 'discourteous and offensive' language of their resolutions.[49] The government's snub of Quebec City was apparently the final straw for William Rhodes, ex-president of the North Shore Railway. Rhodes wrote to the *Morning Chronicle* that he could no longer remain 'to help these poor Quebec people to battle for their rights, and I may also add their British liberties ... The future of Quebec certainly looks "blue"!! with every prospect of a French domination, with a French cure. We all know that this means, "Dragonades" on one side, "Revolutions" on the other. The great mistake of my life was settling in Quebec.'[50]

Although they tried to exploit the route issue, Liberal strategists found it just as difficult as the Conservatives to straddle the inimical ambitions of Quebec City and Montreal. Their regional division was exposed by their refusal to accept a Bleu challenge to introduce a bill favouring the Bout de l'Ile route. Instead they demanded that the railway's ex-engineer, General Silas Seymour, testify before the public accounts committee and that the issue of municipal subsidies be referred to the courts.[51]

The railway issue and provincial politics were further inflamed by Lieutenant-Governor Letellier's dismissal of the Boucherville government on 2 March 1878. A strong Liberal, Letellier was angered at Attorney-General Angers' snubs and the cabinet's failure to keep him informed of its railway policy. He insisted that delinquent municipal subsidies were a matter for the courts rather than the legislature. Months before the final crisis he warned Premier Boucherville that millions were being granted to aid railway construction 'at a time when our finances did not appear to me to be in a condition to warrant a lavish expenditure.' According to Letellier, Boucherville admitted to him that 'rings' of railway men controlled the legislature and that railway subsidies were motivated by 'political consideration.'[52]

Boucherville's dismissal and Joly's accession to power and quick defeat added further confusion to an already complicated political situation. Weakened after a decade of rising debts, railway intrigues, scandals, economic depression, religious strife, and subordination to the federal government, the province went to the polls on 1 May 1878. Among the election issues were municipal subsidies, the railway route, railway 'rings,' the lieutenant-governor's prerogatives, and the 'corrupt, prodigal and unscrupulous' tactics of the Boucherville administration. The Liberals avoided a definite position on the railway issue and Conservative newspapers accused the Liberals of having one policy in Montreal and another in Quebec City. In Montreal-East the Liberal candidate attacked the Conservative's choice of the Terrebonne route as 'a standing danger to the prosperity, and even to the maintenance of our city.' At the same time, Quebec City Liberals accused the Conservatives of succumbing to pressures from Montreal. When cornered on the route question Félix Marchand, a south-shore Liberal minister, would only reply that the matter was under consideration.[53]

Both parties called on their railway friends for election help. An Ottawa Liberal advised a provincial colleague to postpone prosecuting a railway contractor for 'if properly handled [he] will throw all his influence in our favour and it is considerable in the counties of Hochelaga, Terrebonne, Two Mountains, Argenteuil and Ottawa.'[54] Thomas McGreevy, contractor for the eastern section of the QMO&O, had a provincial seat and was a regular contributor to the Bleu war chest. According to Chapleau, McGreevy was 'the strongest man we have in Quebec.'[55]

Despite giving them their best showing since Confederation, the election left the Liberals with only a tenuous hold on power. The Assembly was divided equally between Liberals and Conservatives and the balance of power was held by Arthur Turcotte. Member for Three Rivers, Turcotte had broken with the Conservatives over railway policy and had run as an independent. His acceptance of the speakership permitted the Liberals to survive, but the lack of a working majority handicapped Premier Joly in implementing a program. He was further weakened by the under-representation of Montreal in his cabinet. Luther Holton's refusal to accept a cabinet post left Henry Starnes, a former Bleu, as Montreal's only representative. The death of provincial Treasurer Pierre Bachand in November 1878 was another blow. His important portfolio was given to François Langelier who was attacked constantly by former treasurers Joseph Gibb Robertson and Ruggles Church. While the Liberals faltered, the Bleus recovered rapidly. Macdonald's victory in the federal election of October 1878, the continuing bitterness over the Letellier affair, and Chapleau's accession to the provincial leadership kept the Bleus at election pitch.

After the provincial election Joly immediately abolished the railway commission established by Boucherville in 1876. This economy measure followed the example of Alexander Mackenzie who had abolished its federal counterpart. Railways running within the province were placed under the control of the Department of Agriculture and Public Works, a portfolio which the premier reserved for himself. The cabinet also had to make a final choice between the Terrebonne and Bout de l'Ile routes. Joly ordered work to continue on the Terrebonne line and asked Walter Shanly to prepare yet another engineering report. In July 1878 the premier announced that he had accepted Shanly's report in favour of the Terrebonne line. This prompted Chapleau to congratulate Joly for his 'integrity' in accepting Conservative policy: 'The original cause of the downfall of the late Government was what the Premier had declared just now to be the true interest of the Province of Quebec: the route through Terrebonne.'[56]

Acceptance of the Terrebonne line did not settle the railway issue. In January 1878 the Boucherville government had agreed to build a direct line from Terrebonne to Montreal and to locate the junction of the eastern and western sections of the QMO&O within the city. During the provincial election campaign the Liberals had hedged on the question. By November 1878 the eastern section of the QMO&O had been built to St. Vincent de Paul, a village on Ile Jésus (see map C). At this point a bridge could be constructed over the Rivière des Prairies and the railway extended directly into Montreal. Alternately, the railway could be built west on Ile Jésus and join the Montreal-Hull section of the QMO&O at St. Martin's Junction. This would save the estimated $300,000 cost of a separate line to Montreal and western traffic bound for Quebec City would not have to detour into Montreal. The St. Martin's Junction connection would also facilitate construction of a spur to the Grand Trunk line at Pointe Claire in Montreal's west-end.

The issue was complex and Joly held discussions with Thomas McGreevy and government engineers. The premier originally favoured providing stage-coach service while a bridge and direct line into Montreal was being built. However, McGreevy offered to build a temporary line to St. Martin's Junction at no immediate cost to the government. Joly accepted this proposal and in return gave the contractor the rights to profits from running the eastern section of the railway until the end of 1879.[57]

In February 1879 an inaugural train celebrated the opening of the line from Quebec City to St. Martin's Junction. On board when the train left Montreal were the premier, cabinet members, and journalists. At St. Vincent de Paul officials disembarked for the presentation of a bouquet to Madame Joly. Then the party followed the local parish priest into a ravine to examine the railway trestle. At the Terrebonne bridge the train stopped for the driving of the last spike. The gala occasion ended with a torchlight parade from the Quebec City station to the premier's house.[58]

Completion of the main line did not end Joly's railway problems. A bridge over the Ottawa River and a connection with the Canada Central Railway were essential if the QMO&O was to have access to western trade. Despite the presence of Liberal governments in both Quebec City and Ottawa, negotiations were not easy. The Canada Central, still Alexander Mackenzie's preferred railway, had recently amalgamated with the Brockville and Ottawa Railway and had little enthusiasm for a junction with the QMO&O. Nor did Quebec politicians agree on a location for the junction. Most Liberals favoured a connection with the Canada Central at Ottawa and Joly began negotiations with Ottawa officials for a $60,000 municipal grant. Luther Holton muddied the waters by promoting a scheme completely separate from the QMO&O. He called for a bridge over the St. Lawrence at Coteau Landing; this would serve his constituents in south-western Quebec. Powerful Montrealers supported a bridge at Ottawa, and one engineer told Joly that without an Ottawa connection the QMO&O would remain 'a cripple, a mere local line.'[59] However, Conservatives like Masson and Langevin still preferred a federal subsidy for an extension of the QMO&O along the Quebec side of the Ottawa River to the area of Pembroke or Mattawa. This would promote development in northern Quebec as well as bringing additional patronage to the province. Langevin complained that the Liberal government had 'refused to build a mile of railway' in Quebec. Laurier angered these Conservatives by rebutting that 'it mattered very little whether the subsidized portion of the road happened to be upon the soil of Quebec or Ontario.'[60]

Macdonald's return to power late in 1878 did not help Joly. In the bitter aftermath of the Letellier affair, Macdonald had little sympathy for Joly's woes. In addition, Chapleau had accepted the provincial Bleu leadership on the condition that Macdonald support his railway policy.[61] In Ottawa both Liberals and Conservatives jockeyed for position on the Quebec railway question. J.A. Mousseau of the Conservatives blamed the 'odious' conduct of 'rich' municipalities for having blocked the 'numerous, robust, industrious population' of the north shore from 'their iron highway.' Laurier retorted by describing the

Boucherville government as having been oligarchic and 'ruled by rings, the greedy appetite of which had to be fed from the Public Treasury.' The only constructive railway legislation for Quebec to come out of this session was a charter for the bridge at Ottawa.[62]

In the provincial capital Joly faced recurring railway and financial crises. His administration continued to depend on the tie-breaking vote of Speaker Arthur Turcotte. The Turcotte family's longstanding interest in railways in Three Rivers led to charges that Joly's decision to build an expensive spur line in the town was a political payoff.[63] The purity of the Liberal administration in railway matters was questioned further in 'the nutlock affair.' In theory at least, the nutlock was a simple and cheap device to stop track vibrations from loosening the plates which joined the rails together. Without nutlocks, sectionmen periodically had to tighten the plates. A very minor innovation, nutlocks had not attracted much attention from the railway's engineers or administrators. One railway commissioner recalled that they had approached the question with 'extreme caution'; another stated that they had decided against the purchase of nutlocks.[64] However, one of the nutlock patent-holders was a determined Quebec City doctor, John M. MacKay. During 1878 MacKay hounded Liberal politicians and was a regular supplicant to the office of Premier Joly. He showed the premier a model of the nutlock and letters of recommendation from engineers. MacKay finally persuaded the premier to test them on a short section of track in Quebec City. Reaction from railway officials was critical or at best non-committal. One engineer stated that the nutlocks had not been durable but that the government had never asked for his opinion. Despite continuing pressure from the tenacious MacKay, Joly refused to install them throughout the line and in April 1879 left for a six-week visit to England. Lobbying was stepped up in the premier's absence, especially in the office of Henry Starnes, acting commissioner of agriculture and public works. Starnes and other prominent Liberals were visited by Jean-Charles Langelier, a Quebec City MPP and brother of the commissioner of crown lands. MacKay also called on the lieutenant-governor who reportedly offered to arrange the matter while Joly was away.[65]

Less than three weeks after Joly's departure, MacKay was authorized to install nutlocks throughout the whole line. Starnes later admitted that he knew nothing of the technical aspects of the nutlock but had awarded the contract on the basis of the representations of MacKay and his friends. Although the nutlocks cost less than two cents each and installation costs were between three and five dollars a mile, MacKay was to be paid fifty dollars a mile.[66] In addition, Starnes authorized a $5000 advance. Behind the whole affair were rumours of kickbacks to Honoré Mercier's by-election campaign in St. Hyacinthe. MacKay confided to one railway official that the nutlock contract was conditional on the kickback of several thousand dollars to party coffers and a prominent Liberal admitted that MacKay had donated $2000 to Liberal candidates in Montreal. The same official noted that the Conservatives had not been aggressive in the nutlock affair because the Liberals had an affadavit showing that MacKay had bribed federal Conservatives.[67]

On taking power in October 1879. Chapleau inherited the nutlock contract. Aside from MacKay's rumoured payoffs to the Liberals and the questionable usefulness of the device, Chapleau's brother had a patent on nutlocks. To complicate the issue further, MacKay was related by marriage to Arthur Dansereau, proprietor of *La Minerve* and colleague of Chapleau. As compensation for the cancellation of his contract, MacKay asked for $1800 and a government position. After negotiations he settled for a civil-service post paying $1200 a year.[68]

Land purchases for the railway were always vulnerable to political influence. Two land sales involved the reputation of the Joly government. In 1876, when the Boucherville government took control of the QMO&O, tracks had already been laid across a property known as the Gale farm. Adjacent to the station in Hochelaga, the property was suitable for the construction of workshops. However, the asking price was high and Boucherville's railway commission decided to buy only a small portion of the farm as right of way. In 1878 Joly was told by his engineers that Hochelaga would develop like the Grand Trunk yards in Point St. Charles. Arbitrators set the price of the Gale farm at $141,375 and the government, despite Joly's feeling that this was an inflated price, bought the farm.[69] More than engineering factors were involved in the sale since Henry Starnes, a member of Joly's cabinet, had invested $22,000 in the property. Although Starnes reportedly kept out of the transaction, the *Gazette* charged that the arbitrators were 'all strong partisans of the Government and intimate friends of Mr. Starnes.'[70] According to the *Gazette*'s calculations, the Boucherville government had paid four and two-thirds cents a foot for the land in 1876 while the Liberals paid over twelve cents a foot two years later. Other critics attacked the usefulness of the site since it was cut off from Montreal by the city's gas-works and stables.

The purchase of Bellerive, a property on the Montreal waterfront, also embarrassed the Joly government. Here the issue was one of judgment rather than corruption. The premier and Walter Shanly walked the area and the engineer recommended it as providing good access to the St. Lawrence. Grain elevators could be built on the site to serve western trade. In December 1878 the government bought the property for $52,992.[71] However, when the Montreal terminus was placed closer to the centre of the city, the property became useless to the railway. The Canadian Pacific Railway which later bought the government railway refused to buy the Bellerive property and it was subsequently leased to Montreal as a park.

Day-to-day supervision of the QMO&O was exasperating for Joly. By June 1878 McGreevy, the contractor for the eastern section, had been paid $3,989,992 but he still quarrelled regularly with officials over finances, bridge washouts, the quality of locomotives, and the date when the government would take possession of the railway.[72] Under the terms of his contract, Duncan Macdonald, contractor for the western section, had the right to operate the line for his own profit until construction was completed. Although trains were running from Montreal to Ottawa by the end of 1877 Macdonald retained control of the line. While in office Boucherville had refused to permit the railway commission to evict the contractor by force.[73] The Liberals, before the election in May 1878, were also reluctant to alienate the election patronage of the contractor. Four months of negotiation followed the election. The key issue was whether the government or the contractor would have possession of the railway during arbitration of the contractor's claims. By this time, the contractor had hired Joseph Doutre, the well-known Rouge lawyer. Despite the presence of Doutre and the influence of federal Liberals like Félix Geoffrion and Rodolphe Laflamme, negotiations broke down.[74]

In September 1878 Joly took action. With the aid of local sheriffs and reinforcements from the Montreal Volunteer Force, B Battery from St. Helen's Island, the 65th Rifles, the 6th Fusiliers, and the Montreal Garrison Artillery, the government cut the telegraph wires and took possession of the railway at Hochelaga. Further up the line at Ste. Thérèse, the contractor barricaded himself and the railway's rolling stock in a gravel pit. Food supplies were brought in from the village on a hand-car and employees were armed with revolvers and axes. With the threat that the contractor would dismantle the engines and hide the parts, the government moved quickly and seized the gravel pit on 2 September. Special constables were posted along the line to prevent further incidents.[75]

The forcible takeover of the western section posed new problems for the government. Ballasting was needed on the forty miles of track between Papineauville and Hull while near Hochelaga the track was 'unfinished and slovenly.' Machine shops were located five miles from the Hochelaga station and water service along the line was 'in a very lame and imperfect condition.'[76] Administration of the railway was lax. Some accounts were not certified and purchases were made without tenders. The railway's engines were changed from wood to coal-burners without consultation with important railway officials. With only ten engineers, four passenger cars, and a unspecified number of freight cars, the railway's rolling-stock was far below North American standards. Fifty-four land claims were still outstanding against the railway. An estimated $560,000 was necessary to put the line in satisfactory condition and construction of a $400,000 bridge at Ottawa was essential for access to western trade. Two station-fires, fatal accidents, constantly spiralling costs, and the artificial division of the railway into eastern and western sections were additional thorns for government officials. In September 1878 a passenger train and a freight train avoided a head-on collision by stopping ten yards apart. Free passes were another nuisance since they could be issued by personnel down to the level of railway messengers. Investigations showed passes made out to 'two persons' and 'Dan's servant girl.'[77]

Joly spent much of his time encouraging payment of the municipal subsidies. As one of his own ministers commented: 'les municipalités souscrivent très bien. Mais elles ne paient guère.'[78] Town engineers, politicians, and local businessmen besieged his office with the particular railway needs of their communities. Invariably they wanted to settle local problems before paying their subsidies. Ottawa County, Three Rivers, Quebec City, and Montreal had large, unpaid subscriptions. Ottawa County's $200,000 subsidy had fallen due when the railway was completed to Hull and the province had been forced to initiate a suit against the municipality. Three Rivers was a more delicate situation since the government's survival was based on the tie-breaking vote of the town's MLA. In 1878 Joly satisfied local officials by agreeing to build a spur line that would serve Three Rivers' harbour and commercial districts. He also succeeded in improving relations with Montreal. The bitter feuds of the Boucherville years were replaced by an atmosphere of negotiation and compromise. Construction of the line to St. Martin's Junction ended the divisive issue of the route and attention shifted to hard bargaining on the location of the Montreal station, access along the harbour front, and a junction with the Grand Trunk.[79] Joly was also able to mollify Quebec City's sensitivities. Civic leaders had been badly shaken by Boucherville's decision to build from Terrebonne to Montreal instead of connecting Quebec City to the western line at Ste. Thérèse. Joly's negotiations with the city progressed more smoothly, perhaps because Quebec City had strong representation in his cabinet. The Quebec *Morning Chronicle* praised Joly's 'courtesy' in comparison to the 'brutal and illegal tactics' of the Boucherville government.[80]

Joly was not able to disguise the province's distressing financial condition and was forced to cut back government expenses in other sectors to compensate for QMO&O expenditures. His government claimed to have saved $50,000 by the abolition of the provincial police; critics pointed out however, that credits to municipal police departments had risen. Expenses in the department of crown lands were cut and the salaries of school inspectors and superintendents reduced. Expenditures on colonization declined steadily from $223,844 in 1870 to $38,000 in 1879.[81] The province took a $3 million loan on the New York market and short-term loans of $270,000 from the Bank of Montreal and $498,125 from A.R. Cassils and Company of New York. In October 1879 the provincial treasurer estimated that the province, in addition to its long-term debts, had an immediate deficit of $131,000.[82]

Under these conditions the provincial government pressed for payment of Quebec City's $1 million subsidy. Bargaining continued throughout 1878. Michael Baby, a powerful Conservative, outlined the city's point of view to the attorney-general. He noted that the city had already contributed nearly $150,000 to the railway and had provided a $150,000 site for the terminus. Despite this contribution, the province had turned down Quebec City on 'a matter of life and death,' the connection between Terrebonne and Ste. Thérèse. As well, the workshops in Quebec City were 'a bitter joke' compared to those planned for Montreal. Baby wanted to delay payment of Quebec City's subsidy until the entire line was completed, a link to Ste. Thérèse was constructed, and the railway incorporated into the Pacific network. At that time Quebec City could be forced by the courts, rather than a partisan Liberal government, to honour its subscription.[83] Joly tried to appease civic officials. He met with the city's market and roads committee to discuss possible sites for the railway's engine houses, fuel yards, and machine-shops. Later he agreed to extend the railway to Commissioner's Wharf and the deep-water docks of the Allan and Richelieu Navigation companies. To soothe city council the province laid on a special train to Three Rivers complete with a champagne luncheon. The provincial government also repaired Dufferin Terrace 'as bait to the ancient capital, the easier to get its million.'[84] These efforts paid off in September 1878 when Quebec City Council voted to pay a $257,000 installment on its subsidy.

In contrast to the aloof Boucherville, Joly was always willing to compromise and to negotiate in person. On one occasion he hiked fourteen miles on snowshoes along the projected route and was greeted on his return by several hundred townspeople and a band. However, Joly's affability had not kept his administration out of the mire of railway politics. The nutlock affair, the Three Rivers' spur line, and the Montreal land deal showed that the Liberals, like their Conservative counterparts, rewarded their friends. Nor was Joly able to solve the province's mounting financial crisis. His precarious majority, lingering bitterness from the Letellier affair, and the hostility of the Legislative Council prevented him from dealing decisively with the province's financial and railway problems. By the summer of 1879 Joly's tenuous majority was near collapse. His determination to abolish the Legislative Council had aroused that body's Conservative majority. His railway legislation was passed by the Assembly but was delayed in the Legislative Council. After waiting two months Joly reconvened the Assembly and introduced a bill confirming the railway subsidy. Defeated on an opposition amendment Joly resigned on 31 October 1879 and bequeathed the province's railway and financial millstones to Chapleau.[85]

Chapleau and the railway: 1880-1

When Chapleau and the Conservatives took power in October 1879 the province had spent $9,226,129 on the QMO&O.[1] In return for this investment Quebec had obtained a rail line along the north shores of the St. Lawrence and Ottawa rivers from Quebec City to Hull. Although there were daily trains from Montreal to Hull and Quebec City, the QMO&O still had serious problems. The bridge at Ottawa was not completed, ballasting was needed throughout much of the western section, Quebec City, Montreal, and Three Rivers were in arrears with their subsidies, the location of the Montreal station was still under negotiation, connections with the Canada Central, Intercolonial, and Grand Trunk were incomplete, and over 125 miles of track between St. Martin's Junction and Quebec City were still in the possession of the contractor.

While the Letellier, university, and ultramontane questions lingered on, Chapleau's main preoccupations were the province's railway and financial problems. Like Joly he reserved the agriculture and public works portfolio for himself. In December 1880 he named himself to the new post of commissioner of railways and asked Walter Shanly to examine the condition of the QMO&O. The engineer's report emphasized the need to reform the railway's administration, to unite the eastern and western sections of the railway, and to establish separate traffic, accounting, rolling-stock, and workshop departments. His most important recommendation concerned the appointment of a general superintendent. This officer, with headquarters in Montreal, would manage the railway and answer directly to the minister. 'Railways,'

Shanly told Chapleau, 'can only rightly be managed by one man power and the general superintendent is king.'[2]

As general superintendent, Chapleau appointed Louis-Adélard Sénécal, his crony and business associate. The only French Canadian named to the railway's senior administration, Sénécal was a prominent railway entrepreneur. Among his railway interests were the Richelieu, Drummond and Arthabaska Railway, the Montreal, Sorel and Chambly Railroad, the Lévis and Kennebec Railway, the South Shore Railway and Tunnel Company, the Laurentian Railway, the Vaudreuil and Prescott Railway, the Cumberland Coal and Railway Company, and the Montreal City Passenger Railway. As general superintendent of the QMO&O, Sénécal received a commission of 2.5 per cent of the railway's profits; between July 1880 and 30 December 1881 he was officially paid $16,000.[3]

Under Chapleau and Sénécal the railway faced its traditional headaches. Land claims were a recurring problem. In Ottawa County arbitrators were reportedly awarding claimants $300 an acre on land worth $25 an acre. A Quebec City plaintiff was awarded damages because railway construction had lowered property values.[4] The QMO&O's rolling stock was grossly inferior to that of the Grand Trunk, Intercolonial, or Great Western railways. In 1881 the Grand Trunk had one engine for every 3.2 miles of track; the QMO&O had a total of thirty-six locomotives or one engine for every ten miles of track. To bring the railway's rolling stock up to standard, 600 cars were ordered from Montreal and Coburg manufacturers, and in Lévis William Carrier began construction of a new locomotive plant.[5] Maintenance shops were built on Crown Street in Quebec City and at Papineau Square in Montreal. Officials had difficulty forecasting the railway's freight needs. In January 1880 with almost 40,000 tons of hay awaiting shipment to the United States, ninety cars had to be hastily converted into hay wagons. Accidents were a constant danger. In June 1881 a broken axle derailed a coach in which Curé Labelle, Honoré Mercier, and Premier Chapleau were travelling. Among the lesser problems was an eight-foot fish which bit workers at the Chaudière Bridge in Ottawa. It was finally driven away by a diver who stabbed it with railway spikes. In the parish of St. Augustin, railway detectives caught 'a freak' who had been throwing stones at train windows. In 1881 right-wing Catholics tried to force the government to prohibit Sunday trains.[6]

Financial pressures mounted constantly. By 1882, $12,537,980 had been spent on the railway and another $1,140,000 was needed to pay for shops, branch lines, stations, docks, and ballasting. The railway's income remained embarrassingly low. In the financial year 1881-2, 80 per cent of the line's receipts were devoted to operating costs, leaving only $206,377 to cover the province's annual debt charges of $750,000. To add to the railway's woes both contractors sued the government. Duncan Macdonald's suit for $1,500,000 was settled in August 1882 when arbitrators awarded him $137,904. Soon after the government took possession of the eastern section in January 1880 Thomas McGreevy claimed over $1 million to cover work supplemental to his contract. The government finally paid him $150,000 and left the balance for arbitration.[7]

The location of the Montreal passenger station and workshops was still unresolved. Temporary terminal facilities had been built at Hochelaga, an isolated site on the eastern outskirts of Montreal. Contending factions in Montreal could not agree on a new location. In 1877 Papineau Square had been surveyed and speculators quickly bought up the surrounding land. This site was favoured by east-end politicians but railway officials favoured a more central location. A station at the Quebec Gate Barracks, near the Bonsecours Market, would provide easy access to the business district, the main hotels, and the harbour areas. After a year of negotiations Montreal city council agreed in January 1881 to permit the QMO&O to build an embankment along the St. Lawrence from Hochelaga to the Quebec Gate Barracks. The passenger depot would be located on this site and the workshops on the old prison grounds at Papineau Square.[8]

While Chapleau described the negotiations with Montreal as 'agreeable and satisfactory,' Quebec City remained hostile. Competition between the two cities had not abated despite the rhetoric of Montrealers that their city was 'only an extension of the harbour of Quebec' and that the two cities might obtain the grain trade 'hand in hand,'[9] The Montreal *Gazette* bluntly told Quebec City to show more 'self-exertion' in adapting from the lumber to the grain trade: 'What has caused the grain trade to be centred in Montreal is the fact that the merchants of Montreal have put their money into this particular trade. The shipments have been chiefly upon Montreal accounts, and so long as this is the case, and Quebec simply trusts to embankments and elevators, the history of the past will be the history of the future.'[10] As a Montrealer and a Conservative, Chapleau had little sympathy for the claims of Quebec City's Liberal administration. He responded to one delegation's demand for more workshops by pointing out that the

city was behind in its subsidy payments. The mayor retorted by out-
lining Quebec City's grievances. These included back taxes owed by
the province, the government's failure to pay for its station-site, the
lack of Quebec City representation in the railway's management, and
the government's delay in extending the railway to the city's harbour.[11]

Dispensing patronage was a daily task for railway administrators.
The QMO&O purchasing agent insisted to a royal commission that
Sénécal's instructions were simply to buy 'dans les meilleures conditions possibles sans aucun égard d'influence politique ou autre.'[12] More
typical was a superintendent's statement that under Sénécal's administration ' ... il faut employer plus de monde, qu'il n'est nécessaire, et
souvent il faut faire des achats de personnes, qui n'ont pas de matériel
de la même valeur que ceux que l'on doit acheter. On n'a pas le privi-
lège de faire le choix, ou prendre le meilleur marché parce que le gouvernement veut que l'on achète là de préférence à d'autres places.'[13]
Important patronage appointments were political decisions. The cabinet split over the appointment of an engineer for the western section.
Provincial Treasurer Robertson supported the reappointment of P.A.
Peterson, his associate in the Quebec Central Railway. Peterson had
the added advantage of being the half-brother of George Irvine, a former Conservative minister who pulled 'wires all over the country.'
However, John A. Macdonald supported Alexander Light for the same
post and Chapleau promised to appoint Light 'if the friends of Mr.
Peterson don't choke me before I can do it.'[14] According to the provincial treasurer, himself a railway president, the QMO&O was particularly vulnerable because people 'fancy they are the owners of the
road as it belongs to the province ... ' In one section cost overruns
from 36 per cent to 269 per cent occurred and the number of stations
increased from twelve to twenty-eight. When the Canadian Pacific
took possession of the QMO&O between Montreal and Ottawa fifty
superfluous employees were immediately dismissed.[15]

During Sénécal's tenure as general superintendent the charges of
corruption and maladministration multiplied. His very appointment
aroused intense politicking and Chapleau complained that both the
French- and English-speaking Conservatives were trying to dominate
the railway's administration. Prominent Conservatives like Joseph Gibb
Robertson and Michael Baby looked upon Sénécal's appointment as
'a disgrace to the party.' Baby feared that Chapleau had fallen under
the unsavoury influence of Arthur Dansereau, Simon-Xavier Cimon,
and Sénécal.[16] The Liberals had little affection for Sénécal. Joly des-

cribed the general superintendent as 'le type canadien du Boss Tweed' and Wilfrid Laurier attacked Sénécal in a newspaper article entitled 'The Den of Forty Thieves.' Laurier charged that as manager of the Pierreville Milling Company, Sénécal had pocketed $40,000 in company funds. George Irvine was another consistent critic of the general superintendent. He accused Sénécal of dishonesty and of exercising undue influence over the cabinet. By 1881 Irvine had initiated fifty-four suits against Sénécal on behalf of the English creditors of the Lévis and Kennebec Railway.[17]

Sénécal had a reputation for ready cash and financed Conservative candidates in 1880 and 1881; in the vote on the QMO&O sale these Conservatives returned the favour. The general superintendent reportedly gave $100,000 to Langevin's war-chest for the federal campaign of 1882. His name was persistently linked to unsavoury deals. In 1881 his cheque for $12,000 appeared in a complicated transaction for 5000 acres of government phosphate land. Although personal notes were unacceptable in crown-land sales, Sénécal's cheque was accepted by the land office. Eight days later the sale was cancelled.[18] A few weeks before his appointment as superintendent, Sénécal was involved in a $30,000 loan which the province made from La Banque du Peuple. Although the official interest rate was 5 per cent, the provincial treasurer discovered some months later that the broker, E.A. Prentice, had made the loan at 6 per cent and had covered the difference himself. With the provincial treasurer apparently unaware of the real interest rate. Sénécal was asked to lend Prentice $1500 to cover the difference in the interest rates. At a meeting in a St. James Street restaurant, Sénécal agreed to advance Prentice the money through Chapleau's confidant, Arthur Dansereau. No security was given for the loan although Sénécal reportedly asked for two-thirds of Prentice's brokerage fee on a forthcoming provincial loan of $4 million. Prentice later explained his 'fib' on the interest rate by saying that 'I did not like to have such puritans as Mr. Robertson know of it ... ' A legislative committee which investigated the loan concluded that Sénécal's only motivation had been 'a personal desire to serve the government.'[19]

Some of Sénécal's cash came from QMO&O revenues. Opponents charged that as general superintendent Sénécal tampered with the railway's books and depreciated its value by hiding revenues. This enabled his syndicate to buy the eastern section of the QMO&O for a reduced price. The haphazard accounting system, the constant juggling of construction, salary, and operating accounts, and the destruction of QMO&O records in fires in the Hochelaga Station and the legislative buildings made it difficult for critics to prove their charges. Later investigations did show that Sénécal had diverted railway funds for his private use. All QMO&O receipts were supposed to be deposited in government accounts at the Bank of Montreal or the Jacques Cartier Bank. Withdrawals from these accounts could only be made by approved cheques. To circumvent these regulations Sénécal simply tapped the railway's revenues before their deposit in the bank:

Q.   [before the Routhier Commission] What do you mean by payments in suspense?
R.   [Samuel Shackell, railway auditor] That means, for instance, Mr. Sénécal or the chief accountant might order a payment to be made in suspense for expenses, for special travelling expenses, or anything like that, to be accounted for at the end of the month, or as soon as properly authorized vouchers could be prepared for the purpose.
Q.   Were these amounts paid in suspense, large?
R.   I cannot speak of my own knowledge of that. I have observed there have been some amounts paid by the general superintendent's larger than the ordinary expenses would be. They might amount to a few thousand dollars – I don't know as they were not under my direction.
Q.   Do you remember for what purpose those amounts were required?
R.   No, I do not.
Q.   If I understand you rightly, those sums were paid by Mr. Quevillon to the superintendent himself, without being deposited in the Bank?
R.   Those amounts were paid by the cashier to the superintendent, or to whoever the superintendent ordered; it might be to the order of the superintendent, not personally to himself.
Q.   And not deposited in the Bank?
R.   Not deposited in the Bank.
Q.   Then all the receipts of the administration were not deposited in the Banks?
R.   All the receipts of the administration were not in all cases deposited, at the time of receipt; whether they were subsequently I cannot say, as at a later period I only remained as traffic auditor.[20]

Another Sénécal tactic was to enter into collusion with a contractor and to pay him for non-existent work. Ludger Roberge, a St. Hyacinthe contractor, had a ballasting contrast and since inspections were rare the general superintendent simply paid the account and then accepted the money back from the contractor. Roberge denied the charges, but did admit that he had 'loaned' Sénécal between $15,000 and $20,000.[21]

The general superintendent also benefited from the construction of two branch lines. The twelve-mile line from Lanoraie to Joliette was one of the oldest railways in the province. Unballasted, in a bad state of repair, and closed during the winter, the line's average annual earnings between 1872 and 1879 had been $4619. Its value, exclusive of rolling stock, was estimated at $44,000.[22] The Joliette Railway did have some value as a feeder for the QMO&O and if extended six miles north of Joliette would give access to a large gravel pit. Ballast was needed throughout the whole QMO&O line and this pit was supposedly the best source of gravel between Montreal and Quebec City. In May 1880, Sénécal and his railway engineers urged Chapleau to buy the Joliette Railway.

During this period Sénécal quietly bought up stock in the Joliette Railway and soon controlled the company. At a shareholders meeting in the Chevalier Hotel in Joliette on 6 December 1880 a new board of directors was chosen. Sénécal's obliging friend Ludger Roberge was elected as president, Jean-Baptiste Renaud as vice-president, and Senator Alexandre Lacoste and Sénécal as directors.[23] The new management rebuilt the railway using $7805 worth of government rails and then offered it to the province for $75,750. The Chapleau administration finally bought it for $55,195. Roberge and Renaud were paid $33,946, C.H. Panneton, secretary-treasurer of the railway, $19,948, and Lacoste $1000 for his legal services.[24] Roberge later testified that he had ceded his stock to Sénécal and Lacoste. Renaud admitted that he had invested nothing in the railway and had simply obliged Sénécal by letting him put stock in his name.

Similar manipulations were evident in the extension of the Joliette Railway and the sale of the gravel pit. Again, government materials were used in constructing the railway. Sénécal, with Chapleau's approval, was behind the deal although official ownership of the pit and the railway extension remained in the hands of his front-man, Ludger Roberge. A Conservative judge later described it as an 'imprudence' for Sénécal, as a public official, to provide government materials to his own railway: 'c'est-à-dire qu'il se fournissait à lui-même les matériaux appartenant au Gouvernement.'[25]

Sénécal used the same tactics in the construction of the Berthier branch line. In May 1880 a South-Eastern Railway official asked Sénécal if the government would consider building a short feeder-line from

Berthier Station to Berthier, a village on the St. Lawrence. From this point, ferries could transport freight to the South-Eastern line at Sorel (map A). The South-Eastern offered to rent the branch from the government by paying 8 per cent interest charges on construction costs of up to $25,000. Sénécal, as government superintendent, was again in a conflict of interest since it was in this period that the South-Eastern Railway paid him $49,000 for his stock in the Drummond and Arthabaska Railway.[26]

Sénécal urged Chapleau to construct the Berthier branch line and predicted annual revenues of $6000 to $10,000. A few months later Sénécal told Chapleau that the ever-helpful Ludger Roberge, with Sénécal as secret partner, would build the line for $25,000. Since he had construction contracts on the QMO&O main line, Roberge built the Berthier branch with materials and labour diverted from his government contract. Roberge later denied any such impropriety but was unable to show that he had ever bought any rails for the Berthier line. Sénécal explained that he and Roberge had been motivated by a desire to help the government. They had formed a dummy company, had used government materials and were simply reimbursed by the Chapleau administration for their expenses. Estimates of government payments to the partners ranged from $22,929 to $29,000.[27]

Sénécal's manoeuvring did not disturb Premier Chapleau, who described the general superintendent as 'intelligent et dévoué.' Chapleau himself was no stranger to the shadier side of Quebec railway politics. As a young politician he had invested in the Montreal Colonization Railway, served as director of the Montreal Island Railway and had been among the incorporators of the Ontario and Quebec Railway, and the St. Lawrence Bridge Company. In 1881 the premier denied receiving $14,000 from the Crédit Foncier in return for granting it a charter.[28]

Chapleau and Sénécal had been associated in the Laurentian Railway. As a young MLA, Chapleau had served as vice-president of this company which had a subsidy of $4000 a mile to build from St. Jérôme to St. Lin (map A). By 1875 his father-in-law, Charles King, had sunk $45,000 in the railway and was near bankruptcy. Sénécal invested $5000 and then withdrew. In 1878 Chapleau and his Laurentian Railway associates were accused of trying to defraud the government. However, the Conservative majority in the Assembly was able to vote down a proposed investigation of the railway; the *Gazette* summarized the affair as 'a patriotic under-taking.'[29] Later, Sénécal was able to help Chapleau's father-in-law by a series of complicated stock trades. In 1882 the line was included in the sale of the QMO&O to the Canadian Pacific Railway. Chapleau's father-in-law was paid approximately $40,000 and Sénécal received $100,000.[30]

In any case, Sénécal's indiscretions formed only a small part of Chapleau's preoccupations. Montreal's representation in the federal cabinet, rumoured coalitions with the Liberals, and the ever-present religious and nationalist issues kept provincial politics in a turmoil. Harried on all sides, Chapleau confided to Macdonald that if he abandoned provincial politics either 'the ignorant set' or 'the contemptible clique' of Conservatives would take over. The province's finances were a constant worry. Provincial loans of $3,893,333 in 1874, $4,185,333 in 1876, and $3,000,000 in 1878 had been exhausted in railway expenditures. On 1 July 1880 the province issued a fourth bond issue for $4,275,853. This brought the provincial debt to over $15,000,000 and annual debt charges to $750,000.[31] Sale of the QMO&O was one solution to this deteriorating financial condition.

II

One of the QMO&O's major liabilities was its lack of connections with other railways. To tap transcontinental trade it needed links with major railways like the Intercolonial, Canada Central, Canadian Pacific, or Grand Trunk. In 1880 the South-Eastern Railway agreed to carry QMO&O freight to the United States from its Longueuil and Sorel depots. However, crossing the St. Lawrence was a major problem. Although the Grand Trunk's Victoria Bridge had been in operation for twenty years, QMO&O traffic had to cross the St. Lawrence by ferry or by rails laid on the ice in winter. In 1880 over 500 freight cars used the ice bridge.[32] Quebec City officials were also unhappy with the QMO&O's isolation. Increasingly vociferous, the Quebec City Board of Trade demanded a link to the Grand Trunk line west of Montreal and a postponement of discussions concerning the leasing of the QMO&O.[33] They pressed Chapleau to improve connections between the Intercolonial Railway and the QMO&O terminus in Quebec City. A new dock, steam ferry, and a twelve-mile branch line from Lévis to the main line of the Intercolonial at St. Charles would give shippers two options. Intercolonial traffic from the Maritimes could continue west on the Grand Trunk or cross the St. Lawrence at Quebec City and proceed west on the QMO&O. Conversely, east-bound Canadian Pacific traffic could cross to the Intercolonial at Quebec City. In March 1881 Chapleau proposed that Quebec and Ottawa split the cost of providing this link. Negotiations became arduous when it became clear that the federal government's share would be over $500,000.[34] Langevin and Tupper met in Quebec City with Intercolonial and QMO&O officials and in January 1882 Sénécal, Chapleau, and members of his cabinet went to Ottawa for discussions. Chapleau tried to hurry Macdonald: 'am sorry that we cannot announce at opening of Session the connection with Intercolonial so much desired by our people.'[35] In his own throne speech Chapleau stated his government's intention to attract Intercolonial traffic onto the north shore and his expectation that Ottawa would establish a ferry service at Quebec City.

A new factor in these negotiations was the changed attitude of the Grand Trunk once construction of the QMO&O was completed. Traditional enemy of north-shore railway construction, the QMO&O's major opponent on the British capital market and its chief competitor for the trade of Montreal and Quebec City, the Grand Trunk now feared that the Ottawa to Quebec City line would become the eastern segment of the Canadian Pacific Railway. As early as 1878, Joseph Hickson, the Grand Trunk's tough general manager, offered the olive branch. Although complaining of the 'injustices of government ownership, Hickson wanted to avoid 'an unprofitable rivalry.' The QMO&O and Grand Trunk had mutual interests and should cooperate to avoid price-cutting: 'I further venture to suggest that it is not in the interest of the Government line that the competition for traffic between this city [Montreal] and Ottawa should be carried on as it had been since the Government Road was opened – charges have been unnecessarily reduced, and it is quite certain that unrestricted by some conciliating agreement between the Government Road and the Grand Trunk Company, this competition can only lead to the business becoming unremunerative to both interests. Such a state of things cannot ultimately benefit the public.'[36]

The Grand Trunk's new friendliness had an appeal for Chapleau, for if the province was to recoup its investment its railway had to carry western trade. A link with the Grand Trunk in Montreal or with the proposed Grand Trunk line from Toronto to Ottawa would facilitate this. Quebec City was particularly anxious for a connection with the Grand Trunk and direct communications with the west. In March 1881 the Quebec City Board of Trade urged construction of an eight-mile Montreal bypass from the QMO&O line north of Montreal to the Grand

Trunk main line. Four months later legislation was passed permitting the QMO&O to join the Grand Trunk line at Dorval.[37]

Despite these flirtations with the Grand Trunk, the emerging Canadian Pacific system was the key to the QMO&O's future. Pontiac County officials were still pushing for an extension of the QMO&O along the north shore of the Ottawa River to Pembroke. In 1880 the Pontiac Pacific Junction Railway Company was incorporated and a year later was granted a provincial subsidy of $6000 a mile. However, Chapleau had accepted Joly's decision to bridge the Ottawa River at Hull. The province let a $193,000 contract for the bridge in 1880 and passed legislation to establish an Ottawa terminus.[38]

The usefulness of the Ottawa bridge was dependent on an arrangement with the Canada Central or the Canadian Pacific. These negotiations formed part of long-term efforts to sell the government railway. Corruption, inefficiency, and runaway expenditures led three successive premiers to try to rid the province of the QMO&O. Late in 1877 Boucherville called for tenders to lease the railway. Eight offers were received. The Northern Transit Company had a familiar roster of Montrealers that included Hugh Allan, J.E.L. de Bellefeuille, Jacques Grenier, L.H. Massue, Henry Bulmer, Michel Laurent, Sévère Rivard, and Joseph-Octave Villeneuve. This syndicate proposed an annual rent of $350 a mile for the western section and $250 a mile for the eastern section, a total of $95,300. Another group of entrepreneurs which included Sénécal, Alex McDonnell, and A. Laberge offered $50,000 a year plus 15 per cent of the gross receipts. Two other syndicates proposed to pay the government 20 per cent of the railway's receipts. Duncan Macdonald made an offer of $60,000 or 25 per cent of the receipts for the western section.[39] All of these proposals were conditional on construction of a bridge at Ottawa and completion of the railway in good working order.

Before any of these tenders could be accepted, the Letellier affair brought Joly and the Liberals to power. Hindered by his lack of a working majority, the political touchiness of the sale, and the ambitions of some of his Liberal colleagues to participate in the syndicates, Joly postponed the issue. A year later he received an attractive offer from the contractor for the eastern section. Members of Thomas McGreevy's syndicate included Ezekiel Hart, Charles-Ovide Perrault, and Thomas Tiffin. The province would be paid $200,000 a year and an additional $25,000 when the all-important bridge at Ottawa was built.[40] The premier's experience in Quebec railway politics had convinced him that governments could not operate railways efficiently, and in July 1879 his cabinet voted to accept the McGreevy proposition. However, before the sale could be approved by the legislature the Liberals had fallen from power.

Chapleau's accession to power initiated two years of negotiations with Ottawa, the Canadian Pacific Railway, the Grand Trunk, and entrepreneurs in Montreal and Quebec City. Chapleau on taking office announced that his administration's major task would be the disposal of the QMO&O. He also decided to sell the railway privately rather than by public tender. Canadian Pacific officials favoured private negotiations and his engineering advisers told him that this method would avoid frivolous and embarrassing offers.[41]

In May 1880 Chapleau and the provincial treasurer went to Ottawa for discussions. Although prepared to write off $4 million on the QMO&O, the province needed immediate financial assistance. Ottawa could solve the problem by buying the QMO&O for $7 million or by including it as a subsidized portion of the Canadian Pacific Railway. Chapleau warned Macdonald that if the Grand Trunk gained control of the QMO&O the federal government and Canadian Pacific would face 'a serious obstacle and loss ... In these days of railway warfare and dangerous combinations it is not a speculative view that I am bringing to your consideration.'[42] He also revived the familiar complaint of injustice to Quebec. Ontario had been granted subsidies for the Canada Central, the Maritimes had been helped by construction of the Intercolonial, and the West by Canadian Pacific subsidies. Quebec on the other hand had 'not received justice from the Federal Government.' Macdonald played a waiting game. He refused to buy the provincial railway but did promise to use his influence on Canadian Pacific officials.

Five months later Chapleau was back on Macdonald's doorstep with a warning that 'the financial existence of the province of Quebec' depended on the sale of the railway and that a decision could not 'be long delayed without exposing our Treasury to a disaster.'[43] He told Macdonald that an offer of $6.5 million had been received from a syndicate which would direct trade for the 'next twenty years' through the American centres of St. Paul, Milwaukee, and Chicago. Chapleau raised three questions. Would Ottawa compensate Quebec if it sold its railway to the Canadian Pacific at an exhorbitant loss? Could the Canadian Pacific be imposed upon to offer more than $6.5 million? If the province kept the QMO&O, would the federal government grant a bonus equal to that granted to Ontario's Canada Central Railway?[44] Macdonald, sympathetic to Chapleau but hard-pressed by the Canadian Pacific's financial problems, delayed Chapleau by asking him to await the return to Canada of Canadian Pacific officials.

Chapleau's negotiations with Canadian Pacific officials were long and arduous. Quebec was a small part of their transcontinental system and Richard Angus, William Van Horne, and George Stephen made concessions to the province only grudgingly. They responded to Chapleau's pressures by fostering rumours that they would build a competing line from Montreal to Ottawa. Alternately, they threatened to use the Brockville and Ottawa Railway or the newly chartered Ontario and Quebec Railway to siphon off Ottawa Valley trade. Chapleau countered by mentioning offers from the Grand Trunk and the Osler interests in Toronto.[45] In January 1881 Chapleau spent two weeks in Ottawa but Canadian Pacific officials remained evasive. Angus told Chapleau that the company looked upon the QMO&O as 'the natural outlet of the Pacific Railway towards the seaboard' but refused to make any formal traffic arrangements.[46] Unwilling to rely on 'a mere expression of the good will of a Company,' Chapleau asked Macdonald and Langevin for their aid and reminded them that 'against an elaborate contract clothed with the sanction of a Parliament, the expression of good feelings from a Railway Company is very pale.'[47] The QMO&O should be considered as part of the Canadian Pacific's transcontinental system, 'of the great national work' that was going to cost $100 million. Quebec had completed the railway into the centre of Montreal, had constructed the bridge at Hull, and had purchased $500,000 worth of rolling stock. Having spent $13 million, the province was willing to sell the QMO&O for $7 million. Macdonald, harried on all sides, asked Chapleau to 'be moderate in your idea of price.'[48]

Throughout 1881 negotiations continued. Chapleau encouraged rumours that the Northern Pacific was interested in the government line and went to New York to meet American capitalists. During the provincial election campaign of November 1881 Chapleau frequently mentioned the sale of the QMO&O. Speaking on the church steps in Ste. Thérèse, he explained that the province was prepared to sell the railway at a loss since it had originally planned on a $5 million subsidy for its north-shore railways.[49] He mentioned that the province had refused an offer of $6,750,000 and noted that with the assistance of Macdonald 'to conciliate conflicting interests,' a sale to the Canadian Pacific could probably be worked out. However, Canadian Pacific officials remained indifferent and dismissed the rumoured offer of $6,750,000 as 'folle et extravagante.'[50]

8

Sale of the QMO&O

By 1881 the Conservative party in Quebec was in difficulties. It had faced a decade of crises: *le programme catholique*, the defeat of Cartier, the Tanneries scandal, the rise of ambitious Young Turks like Chapleau and Tarte, the issue of clerical influence in elections, the Letellier affair, the university question, and attempts to abolish the legislative council. Ultramontanism, regionalism, resentment of Montreal's growing dominance over the province, economic depression, continuing corruption in party ranks, and the deteriorating financial situation were also part of Boucherville's legacy to Chapleau. The new premier added to his difficulties by relying on his Montreal cronies. Sénécal's gross exploitation of the QMO&O, his trip to Europe with Chapleau in the summer of 1881 and the pair's involvement in the Crédit Foncier scandal aggravated the situation.

The party's ultramontane elders, known as the Castors, dominated the legislative council; from this stronghold Boucherville, Louis Archambault, and John Jones Ross kept Chapleau under pressure. This right-wing group drew powerful support in Quebec City from Tarte and Montrealers like Beaubien, de Bellefeuille, and Louis-Olivier Taillon. In their attacks on the railway policy and easy-going morality of Chapleau's friends, the nationalistic Castors were joined by strange bedfellows, frustrated members of the English communities of Quebec City and the Eastern Townships. This was evidenced by the political, commercial, and legal skills which the Quebec *Chronicle*, Michael Baby, Joseph Gibb Robertson, and George Irvine brought to bear on Chapleau. Their long-standing alliance with the Conservative party had been jeopardized by the railway struggle, the province's disastrous financial condition, the growing resentment of entrepreneurs outside of Montreal, and rancor over Sénécal's power in the Chapleau administration.

Faced with this disintegration within his party, Chapleau tried to build a new, moderate base when he took office in 1879. He included two Liberals, Edmund James Flynn and Etienne-Théodore Paquet, in his cabinet and began negotiations with Mercier.[1] Frustrated by the continual sniping from Castors entrenched in the Legislative Council, Chapleau apparently accepted Mercier's demand to abolish that troublesome body; as well, both leaders agreed that the QMO&O would be sold or leased. When negotiations stalled, perhaps because of Liberal antipathies to Sénécal, Chapleau called an election for December 1881. His advisers felt that in the existing unstable conditions moderate Conservatives could give a 'dernier coup' before 'un grand changement de décors et d'acteurs.'[2] Running largely on a platform of solving the railway issue Chapleau won the largest majority since Confederation.

With a strong mandate to dispose of the QMO&O, Chapleau tried to move quickly. However, months of private negotiations and political warfare had poisoned the atmosphere. Railway entrepreneurs jockeyed to form syndicates, Ottawa Conservatives sought a middle ground, and the provincial cabinet squabbled over its railway policy. While Chapleau shuttled to frequent meetings with Canadian Pacific officials in Montreal and Ottawa, his critics attacked his alliance with the Sénécal clique. The opposition demanded publication of official correspondance relating to the sale of the QMO&O and Israel Tarte asked that public tenders be called for the sale of 'la plus importante propriété que nous possédons.'[3] Chapleau refused to terminate his policy of private negotiations but did encourage the submission of offers for the QMO&O, particularly from French-Canadian entrepreneurs.

With the Canadian Pacific continuing its delaying tactics, other tenders were made for the QMO&O. Behind the propositions were two familiar entrepreneurs – Sénécal and Hugh Allan. Both Sénécal and Allan had important shipping interests. As well as dominating the Montreal Ocean Steamship Company, Allan had been president of the Richelieu and Ontario Navigation Company. In 1882 Sénécal became president of the latter company. For years Allan had promoted railways that would give him an alternative to the Grand Trunk system, which increasingly directed western trade to its own shipping company, the Dominion Line.[4]

Aside from his shipping interests, Sénécal was an obvious choice to lead a French-Canadian railway syndicate. The province's leading

French-Canadian entrepreneur, he was a trusted friend of Chapleau. In December 1881 the premier refused to accept Sénécal's resignation as general superintendent of the QMO&O. As a result, the entrepreneur's name did not appear among the early participants in what was known as the North Shore syndicate. However, Sénécal dominated the group and handled negotiations with the government.[5]

Officially, the North Shore syndicate was led by Thomas McGreevy, J. Aldéric Ouimet, and Alphonse Desjardins. Other participants included James Gibb Ross, Pierre-Vincent Valin, Nazaire Turcotte, William Carrier, Télesphore Normand, Edward C. Wurtele, John McDougall, Jean-Baptiste Mongenais, Bradley Barlow, and Thomas Wilson.[6] They offered to lease the entire line for twenty-five years at an annual rent that would rise from $415,000 in the first two years to $455,000 for the last eleven years of the contract. Their proposal included the right to buy the QMO&O during the first five years of the contract for $8.3 million. The offer was conditional on the government paying the $1 million costs of completing the line. When informed in February 1882 of the impending sale of the western section of the QMO&O to the Canadian Pacific, the syndicate withdrew its offer.[7]

Allan participated in three syndicates. One was led by J.J. Ridley of London. This group offered to pay the government's asking price of $8 million subject to the government's expenditure of up to $400,000 to complete the line, a provincial guarantee of an annual interest or dividend of $90,000, and the government's payment of a commission of $80,000 to the London brokers of Panmure, Gordon and Company.[8] At the very time the Allan–Ridley offer was being presented to the government, Robert N. Hall of Sherbrooke told Chapleau that Allan had agreed to accept the presidency of his syndicate. Allan assured the premier that he would participate with Hall only if the Ridley offer was refused. The Hall group offered to lease the railway for twenty-five years for an annual rent that would rise progressively from $427,500 to $517,000. Their proposal included the right to buy the railway for $8.5 million during the first ten years of the contract or for $9 million thereafter.[9] Both the Ridley and Hall propositions were marginal and had little chance of success in competition with the Sénécal and Canadian Pacific syndicates.

To raise the bidding Chapleau circulated the terms of Sénécal's offer. The premier's emissary, Arthur Dansereau, visited Allan, Beaubien, and John Jones Ross, minister of agriculture and public works and gave them the impression that the absence of French Canadians in their syndicates had hindered their success.[10] Shortly afterwards, Allan organized a new syndicate with Sévère Rivard, ex-mayor of Montreal and a well-known ultramontane. Other participants were L.H. Massue, M. Laurent, Andrew Allan, Hugh McLellan, Thomas D. Milbourn, Jacques Grenier, de Bellefeuille, S. St. Onge, F.X. St. Charles, and Gustave Drolet. Some members of this syndicate were ultramontanists, many were long-time associates of Allan, and all were prominent members of Montreal's political and commercial community. The Allan-Rivard group wanted to compete with the Canadian Pacific by assuring the province of 'deux chemins de fer du Pacifique au lieu d'un.'[11] Under its control the QMO&O would bring western trade via Sault Ste. Marie and Georgian Bay to Allan's steamships. The syndicate offered to lease the railway for $425,000 annually for the first five years with increments to $500,000 for the final five years of the twenty-five year contract. They could buy the railway for $8.5 million during the first decade of the contract or for $9 million thereafter. The government would be responsible for completing station and workshops in Montreal. According to Sévère Rivard, the syndicate was told that a *sine qua non* of any arrangement was the purchase for $300,000 of the St. Eustache and St. Lin branch lines in which Sénécal and the Chapleau family had interests.[12]

There were negotiations between the Sénécal and Allan-Rivard syndicates. Arthur Dansereau acted for Sénécal and Beaubien for Allan; on several occasions the two met in Dansereau's office at *La Minerve*. Sénécal visited Allan at least once to discuss a union of the two syndicates while Allan used his friend Curé Labelle as a pipeline to the provincial cabinet. Chapleau proposed a union of the two syndicates and a three-way split of the stock with one third for Allan and his English-speaking associates, one third for Sénécal's partners, and the final third for the Rivard group.[13]

While encouraging the formation of a Quebec syndicate Chapleau still favoured the integration of the QMO&O into the Canadian Pacific system. In January 1882 he went to Ottawa and told Macdonald of the other offers. Macdonald was soon acting as a mediator between Quebec and the Canadian Pacific. Chapleau asked for $8 million at an interest rate of 5 per cent. The Canadian Pacific countered with an offer of $8,750,000 paid over fifty years at an annual interest of 4 per cent; according to Chapleau, the Canadian Pacific offer would cost the province $12 million. As an alternative the Canadian Pacific offered $3 million for the western section of the QMO&O and warned

Chapleau that they could build their own line from Montreal to Ottawa for this price.[14] In September 1881 Curé Labelle and Joseph Tassé met with J.J.C. Abbott who again threatened to construct a separate line. Labelle felt the Canadian Pacific had a cavalier attitude to the province and angrily reminded Abbott that Quebec had contributed $30 million for construction of a railway to the Pacific. In return for this investment the province wanted to repatriate 600,000 French Canadians from the United States to colonization lands opened up by the railway. If the Canadian Pacific would not make concessions to Quebec 'nous serions obligés de leur faire la guerre, et une guerre à mort.'[15] Although Canadian Pacific officials continued to threaten to build a competing line to Ottawa, privately they were aware of the advantages of a monopoly: 'We could have built a line that would have given us an Ottawa connection, as well as a connection with our main line, at a very much smaller sum; but it was best to pay a larger price, rather than to build a new line, which would certainly only get a portion of the Ottawa and Montreal business; it was better to pay a higher price, and have the only line.'[16] In addition to these economic considerations, the Canadian Pacific was subject to strong political pressure. It was Macdonald, according to Chapleau, who finally forced the Canadian Pacific to raise its offer for the western section from $3 million to $4 million.[17] On 25 February 1882 the Chapleau government accepted the Canadian Pacific's offer.

The sale of the western section included rolling stock worth $450,000 and the branch line to St. Jérôme. The Canadian Pacific agreed to construct a $60,000 station in Montreal, a $100,000 branch line to unite with the Grand Trunk near Dorval, and to complete other works worth $300,000 in the Montreal area.[18] The sale included two small, private railways, the St. Eustache Railway and the Laurentian Railway. The Canadian Pacific paid $300,000 for the latter railway; Sénécal was president and Chapleau's father-in-law had important interests. Sénécal realized a profit of $100,000 from the sale and there were charges that the selling price of the QMO&O had been reduced $400,000 to cover the purchase of the two branch lines. One lawyer who saw a list of Laurentian Railway shareholders stated that Chapleau held 500 shares.[19]

The sale of the western section of the QMO&O meant new negotiations for the eastern section from St. Martin's Junction - a few miles north of Montreal - to Quebec City. Despite its disputed economic value the line had great political significance in the Quebec City region. Its importance had been increased by the Canadian Pacific's commitment to build a spur from St. Martin's Junction to the Grand Trunk line at Dorval (map B).

Once again the same cast of Conservative entrepreneurs jockeyed for position. On 21 February 1882 Chapleau met Sénécal's North Shore syndicate in the Windsor Hotel and told them that the western section would be sold to the Canadian Pacific.[20] One week later the Sénécal group submitted a bid for the eastern section. They offered $4 million at 5 per cent interest and would assume the $448,000 cost of completing the line. The government would relinquish its right to the municipal subsidies of Quebec City and Three Rivers. It would ensure traffic arrangements with the Canadian Pacific and Grand Trunk as well as access to Montreal.[21] To assure a direct link with the Intercolonial Railway, the government would pay half the cost of ferry service between Quebec City and Lévis.

Chapleau again tried to unite the Allan-Rivard syndicate with the Sénécal group. Negotiations stalled when Rivard demanded one-half of the shares. Sénécal was prepared to relinquish one-third to the Allan-Rivard syndicate; two-thirds, he insisted, would be divided between himself and the McGreevy group. On 1 March, with negotiations still continuing with the Allan-Rivard syndicate, the cabinet accepted the offer of Sénécal's North Shore Company. Three days later Sénécal's name appeared for the first time alongside McGreevy, Desjardins, and Ouimet as an official participant.[22]

Despite acceptance of the Sénécal offer, Chapleau had not abandoned a fusion of the two syndicates. When Allan's representatives - Beaubien, Curé Labelle, Sévère Rivard, and de Bellefeuille - continued to demand a 50 per cent interest in the company, Sénécal made a counter proposal. Meeting in de Bellefeuille's law offices Sénécal offered to relax his conditions if the Allan forces made an immediate cash payment of $75,000. In the silence that followed, Gustave Drollet laughingly asked Sénécal 'si ces soixante-quinze mille piastres étaient pour faire dire des messes, ou pour payer des messes qui avaient été dites auparavant.' Sénécal replied 'cela est mon affaire, vous ne le saurez pas.'[23] Chapleau later denied any knowledge of Sénécal's demand but stated that he saw nothing wrong with the general superintendent asking for a $75,000 commission: 'Où serait le mal? Ceux qui s'étaient mis à la tête d'une pareille entreprise avaient droit de demander une telle commission. Cela ne forçait pas le gouvernement à la payer ... Ce qui reste acquis, c'est que M. Sénécal n'a rien demandé au gouvernement.'[24]

When the legislature met in March 1882 the Chapleau government faced a barrage of questions on its railway manoeuvring. Fed by participants in the rejected syndicates, the opposition revealed details of the sale. Henri Joly, leader of the opposition, made three major points. He questioned whether the newly completed railway – which was just beginning to acquire its real value – had been sold at an opportune time. He opposed the division of the railway. The sale of the western section to the Canadian Pacific condemned Three Rivers and Quebec City to an 'isolement absolu.' Joly also attacked the selling price. Reviewing the fifty-one pages of official correspondence released by the government, he concluded that the Allan-Rivard offer was higher than either the Canadian Pacific or Sénécal proposals. His most bitter comments were reserved for Sénécal: 'Ce n'est pas un homme que j'attaque, c'est tout un système dont il est le symbole. Ne rétrécissons pas la question. M. Sénécal est le type canadien du Boss Tweed, de New York, et comme derrière le Boss Tweed il y avait, à New-York, une armée puissante, le Tammany Ring, derrière M. Sénécal ici, il y a aussi une armée puissante, c'est elle que j'attaque, et non pas un homme seul.'[25] Other Liberals – Joseph Shehyn, George Stephens, Ernest Gagnon, James McShane, and Félix-Gabriel Marchand – joined in the attack. Sénécal, they charged, had financed twenty Conservatives in 1881 and their votes would now guarantee approval for his purchase of the eastern section. One Conservative, John Hearn, angrily denied being bribed by Sénécal but did admit that after voting in favour of the sale to Sénécal, QMO&O officials had rented his Quebec City property as a depot. George Irvine, a persistent critic of the Chapleau regime, pointed out Sénécal's paradoxical position as public servant and purchaser of the government railway.[26]

Quebec City officials quickly registered their opposition to the division of the QMO&O. Chapleau met with Quebec City MLAs but was unable to reassure them. Montreal, they felt, was becoming the Canadian Pacific terminus while the railway to Quebec City had been raffled to the premier's friends. Quebec City newspapers were divided over the sale. Le Journal de Québec, Le Quotidien, and L'Evénement supported Chapleau; Le Canadian, Le Courrier du Canada, L'Electeur, and the Chronicle opposed the sale. The Chronicle attacked Montreal politicians who spoke out against the sale while speaking in Quebec City but were as 'dumb as oysters' when they returned to Montreal. In Montreal, La Minerve and the Gazette supported the sale. The Gazette expressed satisfaction that the 'more business-like men of the Liberal Party' approved Chapleau's policy. In Three Rivers, Le Journal *des Trois-Rivières* opposed the sale while *Le Constitutionnel* approved Chapleau's policy. *Le Constitutionnel* dismissed the opposition as simply 'les jaloux et les désappointés.'[27]

Many of the opposition's charges were confirmed by insiders. According to Israel Tarte, the Sénécal group contributed $100,000 to Conservative coffers in 1882 in return for promises that the federal government would either buy the eastern section outright or force another railway to buy it from Sénécal. Tarte also publicized Sénécal's proposal for an 'up front' payment of $75,000 as a sweetener for a coalition with the Allan forces.[28] Louis Beaubien, member of the Allan-Rivard syndicate and former Conservative Speaker, was another persistent critic of Chapleau's railway policy. He demanded the names of Sénécal's associates and pointed out that participants like William Carrier, a Lévis manufacturer, held government contracts.

Chapleau lost two members of his cabinet over the QMO&O sale. Joseph Gibb Robertson, a Sénécal critic, resigned as provincial treasurer on 18 January 1882. Although Chapleau cited personal reasons, Robertson stated that he was forced out for revealing the existence of higher offers for the QMO&O than that favoured by the cabinet.[29] His departure emphasized the growing alienation from the party of English-speaking Conservatives outside of Montreal. A few weeks later the cabinet's decision to divide the QMO&O brought the resignation of the minister of agriculture and public works. John Jones Ross, a prominent Castor and Quebec City politician, favoured the sale of the entire line to the Canadian Pacific. Ross continued his attacks on Chapleau from the legislative council and noted that members of the Sénécal syndicate were directors of the Richelieu and Ontario Navigation Company. By selling the eastern section of the QMO&O to these entrepreneurs, the government had instituted 'a dangerous monopoly.'[30] Other Conservative legislative councillors such as James Ferrier, Louis Archambault, and Godefroy Laviolette joined in the attack. Former Premier Boucherville was particularly incensed. He insisted that Chapleau should have called for public tenders and attacked the sale of the Laurentian and St. Eustache railways to the Canadian Pacific as a political pay-off. The municipal debentures of Quebec City, Three Rivers, and St. Sauveur should not, according to Boucherville, have been ceded to a private company led by Sénécal.[31]

Despite a telegram of support from most of the province's federal Conservatives, Chapleau was stung by this 'war to the knife.' He accused Langevin, Adolphe Caron, and Israel Tarte of encouraging the

Castors and dismissed his legislative council opponents as 'old women': 'it is so strange to see just the body guard of Langevin and Caron leading the battle against me: If Joly had not been an ass, he would have had a splendid opportunity of crushing forever that disgusting clique of religious pickpockets, the pest of all governments [i.e.: the Legislative Council]. But Joly will die what he was born, a good natured fool.'[32]

Tired by the infighting, attacks of bronchitis, and 'irritated nerves,' Chapleau remained in the Hotel Saint-Louis for much of the 1882 session. However, on 27 March he took his seat to introduce his railway resolutions. In a speech that lasted until 1:00 AM Chapleau tried to placate all elements of his badly splintered party. He called on old Conservative loyalties by reminding them that he was simply fulfilling Cartier's policy of making Montreal the terminus of the Pacific Railway. For its part Quebec City had 'une garantie complète.' The division of the railway and its sale to Sénécal and the Canadian Pacific would ensure fair rates, equitable traffic arrangements, and jobs in the Quebec City repair shops. Chapleau's speech even contained bait for the Castors. He denied charges that his friends had made $300,000 on the sale of the Laurentian Railway to the Canadian Pacific and assured the nationalists that, under Sénécal's management, the eastern section of the QMO&O would serve as 'une école' where young French Canadians could learn a railway career.[33]

Chapleau's opposition could not overcome the Conservative majority in the Legislative Assembly and the railway resolutions were approved by wide margins. The Liberals were distracted by Mercier's unseating of Joly as provincial leader and their amendments were defeated thirty-nine to twelve and forty-nine to nine. Second reading of the bill to sell the eastern section passed thirty-four to thirteen.[34] Chapleau's railway legislation faced stronger opposition in the Castor-dominated legislative council. Louis Panet, an elderly Conservative, was carried into the chamber by his grandson. When the key vote was called Panet did not at first respond 'but stared vacantly around for some time' despite the efforts of his colleagues to make signs with their 'fingers and elbows.'[35] Even with Panet's vote Boucherville's anti-government amendment was defeated twelve to eleven and early in the summer of 1882 the new owners took possession of the divided line. The western section of the QMO&O was incorporated into the Canadian Pacific main line while the eastern section remained in Sénécal's hands until its sale to the Grand Trunk in the fall of 1882.

II

The division and sale of the railway ended the provincial government's direct involvement with the north-shore railways. After 1882 the focus shifted to Ottawa and railway boardrooms in Montreal and London. Sénécal quickly consolidated his position. Before taking possession of the eastern section, he improved it at public expense. While still general superintendent of the provincial railway he apparently ordered repairs and rolling stock. At the same time he bought out most of his partners in the North Shore syndicate. On 2 December 1882 he signed an agreement with the Grand Trunk: 7000 out of the North Shore Company's 10,000 shares were transferred to the Grand Trunk in return for $250,000 cash and $1,000,000 of a new issue of North Shore bonds. Sénécal had the option of transferring the remaining 3000 shares of old stock for the new bonds.[36] The Grand Trunk's acquisition of the eastern section of the QMO&O was a clever ploy by the company's general manager, Joseph Hickson. Since 1879 the Grand Trunk had promoted scores of small railways in eastern Canada and the northern United States. The line to Quebec City had a particular appeal. It gave the Grand Trunk a stranglehold on north-shore trade and an important trump card for horsetrading with Ottawa and the Canadian Pacific. The Grand Trunk and Canadian Pacific were soon at odds over the complicated issue of running rights in the Montreal area and in the winter of 1884 the Grand Trunk cancelled its competition's running rights to Quebec City.[37]

The Conservatives now had to contend with renewed fury from Quebec City. Sénécal's latest manipulation gave the Grand Trunk a monopoly of rail trade into the city on both the north and south shores of the St. Lawrence and destroyed lingering hopes that Quebec City might become the Canadian Pacific terminus. Pressures on Ottawa mounted rapidly. Area newspapers, the Quebec City Board of Trade, and citizen groups in Three Rivers and Quebec City demanded that the Canadian Pacific terminus be located in Quebec City and that a new bridge be constructed over the St. Lawrence.[38]

In July 1882 Chapleau became Macdonald's secretary of state. Until the railway had been sold Montrealers had pressured Chapleau to remain as premier; after the sale Montrealers wanted their strongest politician in Ottawa.[39] Chapleau left provincial politics without having appeased or destroyed the Castors. Inspired by the railway battles of 1882 they soon eliminated the Chapleau-Sénécal group from the provincial party. In addition to pressure from the Castors, federal Conservatives had to contend with the province's desperate financial situation which was described by one former minister as 'an abyss.' As early as 1879 Chapleau had tried to obtain better terms for Quebec. If increased federal aid was not forthcoming, he warned Rodrigue Masson, 'nous irons à la banqueroute, à l'Union législative ou à l'Annexion.'[40] By 1880 debt charges accounted for 23 per cent of the province's total expenditures.

The crisis occurred in 1884 when Macdonald announced a new Canadian Pacific subsidy of $22.5 million. The situation was aggravated by the open contest for power between Chapleau and Langevin. Ottawa officials were beseiged by delegations, letters, and threats. The Seminary of Quebec contributed ten dollars to the travel expenses of a Quebec City delegation to Ottawa; one of Langevin's intimates described Sénécal as a 'vampire.'[41] In February 1884 the entire provincial cabinet, except for ailing Premier Ross, met in Ottawa with Macdonald's cabinet and Canadian Pacific officials. The Quebec delegation made several demands: an increased federal subsidy, a bridge at Quebec City, reimbursement for North Shore Railway construction costs, and the location of the Canadian Pacific's summer terminus in Quebec City.[42] On 15 February the political situation for the Conservatives deteriorated further. Boycotting the Commons' debate on the Canadian Pacific subsidy, French-Canadian Conservative MPs held a special caucus and insisted that Quebec's financial and railway demands be settled before the subsidy vote. Faced with this angry Conservative rump and near-revolt from Langevin, Macdonald succumbed. With Langevin in tow he visited the French-Canadian caucus and offered Quebec a retroactive federal subsidy of $12,000 a mile for construction of its north-shore railways between Quebec City and Ottawa as well as assurances that Quebec City would be the Canadian Pacific terminus; $1,140,000 would be granted directly to the province as a federal contribution for railway construction between Montreal and Ottawa; $960,000 was reserved to help the Canadian Pacific buy the North Shore Railway or to construct its own line to Quebec City.[43]

Macdonald's transfusion initiated a final year of negotiations between Canadian Pacific and Grand Trunk officials and politicians in Ottawa and Quebec City. Canadian Pacific executives like George Stephen, J.J.C. Abbott, and William Van Horne were masters at parlaying political pressures into increased benefits for their company. One Canadian Pacific memorandum forwarded to Macdonald concluded that a link at Quebec City with the Intercolonial 'would be of questionable value.'[44] Quebec City's demand to be incorporated into the Canadian Pacific system could be played off against other political pressures to build to the Maritimes through the Eastern Townships. While pleased with the $6000 a mile subsidy to his company, Stephen refused to make any commitment. He told Langevin that it would be 'impossible to define the precise form or conditions which will characterize the arrangements, when finally made.'[45] As well as the subsidy to Quebec City, the Canadian Pacific had been granted a subsidy of $170,000 a year for fifteen years to join Montreal and the Maritimes. With an option to build via Quebec City or the Eastern Townships, Canadian Pacific officials kept the pot boiling throughout 1884. Speaking in Portland, Maine, Stephen hinted that the company might build to the Maritimes through the United States. Much of this rhetoric was directed at inducing the federal government to pressure the Grand Trunk to sell out. George Stephen told Macdonald privately that construction by the Canadian Pacific of a second line along the north shore to Quebec City would be 'ruinous,' 'little short of madness,' and 'a criminal waste of capital.'[46]

The Grand Trunk was just as evasive. Competing fiercely with the Canadian Pacific for routes in Ontario, the Grand Trunk was quite prepared to squeeze both its rival and Ottawa over access to Quebec City. As a delaying tactic the Grand Trunk offered to grant running rights to the Canadian Pacific or to operate the North Shore Railway as a joint project. William Van Horne of the Canadian Pacific retorted that the Grand Trunk had acquired the railway for 'the sole purpose of keeping the Canadian Pacific out of Quebec.'[47] Over the next months Grand Trunk officials told Macdonald that they looked upon the North Shore Railway 'in the light of insurance' and demanded compensation if their monopoly was broken. Visiting Canada in the spring of 1885 Sir Henry Tyler, president of the Grand Trunk, accused the Canadian Pacific of having 'the rich people of Canada and the Government at their back, while we are obliged to live on our income. We must work upon commercial principles.'[48]

While the two companies jockeyed for position, Quebec City kept up the pressure, Macdonald was told the issue was a matter of 'life and death.' Langevin wrote that the Quebec City press was 'at it again' and Chapleau noted that a 'bridge craze' was developing in Quebec City.[49] The Montreal *Gazette* reported that provincial politicians were 'unanimous' that Ottawa had been unjust to Quebec City and that anyone expecting friendly relations between the two levels of government would 'experience a shock.' In May 1885, angered by the slow progress of negotiations the Quebec City Board of Trade resolved that ' ... nothing short of the immediate sole control of the north shore railway by the Canadian Pacific Railway Company will be considered as a virtual extension to Quebec.'[50] A month later it accused Macdonald of breaking his pledge to bring the Canadian Pacific to Quebec City and urged the resignation of cabinet members from Quebec City and Three Rivers.

By the summer of 1885 the Riel crisis had intervened, all sides were drained, and Macdonald was able to force a settlement. Stephen of the Canadian Pacific told the prime minister that he had had enough of 'high diplomacy,' and Hickson of the Grand Trunk feared that he was becoming a 'North Shore Maniac.'[51] The complicated transaction began in June when the Macdonald government granted the Canadian Pacific $1.5 million to aid the company in gaining access to Quebec City. If it was unable to buy the North Shore line within two months, the Canadian Pacific could use the subsidy to build an independent line to Quebec City.

In the second part of the deal the federal government used $525,000 of the Canadian Pacific subsidy to buy the North Shore Railway from the Grand Trunk and agreed to pay $82,500 still owing on properties in Quebec City and Hochelaga.[52] On 19 September 1885 the Canadian Pacific took possession of the North Shore Railway with assurances from the government that it would not lose money. If receipts from the operation of the line between Montreal and Quebec City were insufficient to pay the interest on the North Shore bonds the Canadian Pacific could draw on the $975,000 left over from the $1,500,000 subsidy.[53] With the integration of the North Shore Railway into the Canadian Pacific system Quebec City finally had its link to the west.

9

Conclusion

Originally the dream of Quebec City entrepreneurs, the north-shore railways by the 1880s had become a nightmare that brought the province to financial despair. Their history, while similar to other North American railway projects, had some particular twists. In Quebec, colonization and nationalism were attractive symbols that could be used against the federal government or to rally local support. Both French- and English-speaking entrepreneurs participated enthusiastically in the construction of the railways. In the 1850s French-Canadian leaders like Joseph Cauchon and Hector Langevin controlled the North Shore Railway, although never to the exclusion of English Canadians. Langevin wrote English perfectly and was well-versed in the niceties of high finance and politics. However, he was promoting a railway based on the declining metropolis of Quebec City and he faced heavy opposition from the Grand Trunk Railway and deteriorating conditions in world capital markets. By the early 1870s the Quebec City group was being squeezed out by rising capital needs, the transcontinental implications of the Canadian Pacific Railway, and Montreal's increasing influence as the province's commercial, shipping, and manufacturing hub.[1]

Railways accentuated this concentration of power in Montreal. English Canadians dominated the Montreal marketplace and French Canadians like Curé Labelle or Louis Beaubien were used only to provide ethnic respectability and political leverage. It was, as Hugh Allan put it, a matter of showing French Canadians 'where their true interest lay.'[2] However, when the railway was taken over by the province in 1875 French Canadians proved as adept as their English-Canadian counterparts in exploiting the iron horse mania. L.A. Sénécal and his banking, entrepreneurial, contracting, and political friends took second place to none in bleeding the public treasury.

Lack of capital was the railway's most persistent problem. Told by the London *Times* to 'find the money at home,' the promoters sought Canadian public funds.[3] By the 1870s the province's generosity to the north-shore railways had begun to take its toll of provincial politicians. Headaches, 'bad nerves,' lingering illnesses, and bouts with the bottle became regular plaints of Quebec politicians trying to settle the deteriorating railway and financial situation. Initially, provincial leaders had to grapple with the chartering of railways, regional pressures, and the establishment of the province's railway laws and subsidy programs. By 1880 provincial bankruptcy was their major concern. Factors external to the province – fluctuating capital markets, competition from expanding American cities, changing technology, and struggles between transcontinental railways – added to the complexity of the problem. Boxed into a federal structure with limited financial resources, facing over-population, emigration, and agricultural recession, Quebec's politicians suffered a high mortality rate. The short tenures of Chauveau, Ouimet, Boucherville, Joly, Chapleau, and Mousseau were symptomatic of the unstable political situation. The politicians lack of technical knowledge, the province's primitive administrative structures, and the prejudiced advice of the government's friends produced many dubious decisions. Swamped by office-seekers, confused by complex technical decisions, and worried by the province's debts, politicians were an easy mark for railway entrepreneurs.

Railway promoters adjusted quickly to changing political and economic situations. For a generation, the Grand Trunk obstructed construction of the north-shore railways. However, once they were built, the Grand Trunk moved to end rivalry since, as one official explained to the premier, competition 'cannot ultimately benefit the public.'[4] In their role as bankers, shippers, manufacturers, promoters, insurance agents, and land speculators, entrepreneurs like Allan or Sénécal could apply varied pressures on Quebec politicians. Leverage could be gained by a well-placed campaign contribution or construction contract, a telegram to Ottawa or London, the hiring of a party official as company lawyer or a special stop of a company steamer for a local bishop.

Corruption and patronage were integral parts of the railway's history. Kickbacks, falsified contracts, overlapping directorships, conflicts of interest, political pay-offs, dummy companies, inflated construction deals, lucrative expropriations, and secret takeovers all contributed to the steady drain of public funds. In the political climate of the 1870s, the provincial treasurer felt obliged to apologise for being 'unnecessarily scrupulous and narrow' in insisting that the law be respected and that public funds not be advanced unless railway construction was actually done.[5] By 1878 exploitation of the QMO&O reached a frenzy as construction companies, patent-holders, bankers, mayors, and cabinet ministers grabbed for the bonanza. A former railway director himself, Liberal Premier Henri Joly could only stand by helplessly as members of his own party bled the railway unmercifully; his administration's record demonstrated that the provincial Liberal party was as vulnerable to corruption as the Conservative. Sénécal's appointment as general superintendent of the QMO&O initiated two years of blatant Conservative exploitation. Premier Chapleau responded to charges that he and Sénécal had made thousands from their railway manipulations by pointing out that most of his critics had their own hands in the till.[6]

Construction of the north-shore railways had a devastating effect on provincial finances. In the first years after Confederation the provincial budget was an informal statement of expenses and income. This had changed by 1875. That year's budget speech included traditional items such as $3000 for the parliamentary library, $11,000 for colonization roads, $720 to repair the Gaspé Court House, $66,000 for police costs, and $233,410 for education.[7] Alongside these moderate expenditures, the province announced that it was assuming ownership of a railway with a projected cost of $10 million. The implications of the takeover were soon clear. In the budget year ending June 1877 the province spent $3,481,670 on railways and $407,176 as charges on the public debt. All other government expenditures for the year totalled under $2 million. Government expenditures to aid railway construction jumped from $48,171 in 1871 to $1,013,099 in 1875; by 1882 the province had spent $12,537,980 on the north-shore railways.[8]

In 1873 Quebec had no provincial debt. Over the next eight years the province contracted loans on the British, French, and American markets to pay for its mounting railway expenditures. Debt charges in 1880 accounted for 23 per cent of the province's total expenditures.[9] Quebec's commitment to the north-shore railways is clear from a comparison with Ontario's railway subsidies. In 1879 Ontario's aid totalled $479,064. The largest grant was $118,889 to the Credit Valley Railway. Two years later Ontario granted railways $205,528 from a total budget of $2,585,053.[10]

Quebec's increasing financial commitments forced it to assume ownership of the North Shore and Montreal Colonization railways in 1875. The takeover was a means of rescuing the government's railway friends and of maintaining the province's credit reputation. Efforts to rid the province of the QMO&O began in 1877. The railway's sale in 1882 accentuated the difficulties of the Conservative party in Quebec. Macdonald, Cartier, Langevin, and Masson had all tried to reinforce the wobbly administrations of Chauveau, Ouimet, and Boucherville.[11] The party had been shaken by the publication of the *programme catholique*, the defeat of Cartier in 1872, and the resignations following the Tanneries scandal. Cartier's death in 1873 left a vacuum in which the tensions between the Quebec City and Montreal wings of the Conservative party festered. This conflict hindered attempts to join the competing metropolises by rail. Cauchon's exit from Conservative ranks and the efforts of Masson and Chapleau to form a moderate coalition were further indications of the party's problems. By the late 1870s it was clear that Langevin and Masson had failed to keep the party together. In their bitter attacks on Chapleau's railway policy the Castors represented more than what John Saywell and Blair Neatby describe as an attempt to 'consolidate the French Canadian race and the Roman Catholic religion in the Province.'[12] Some Castors used colonization, nationalism, and the morality of Chapleau's friends as a screen for other economic and political goals. Rather than a confrontation between nationalism and materialism, the Castor-Chapleau struggle – in terms of the north-shore railways – was part of a complex power struggle that included metropolitan competition between Montreal and Quebec City, and between the north and the south shore of the St. Lawrence, the failure of Langevin's leadership, and the deep internal divisions within the province's English- and French-speaking communities. Associates of Hugh Allan like Edouard de Bellefeuille and Louis Beaubien used colonization as a political tool: Israel Tarte's ultramontanism must be balanced against his record as a pragmatic defender of Quebec City. Louis Archambault's alliance with Boucherville and the Castors can be interpreted in terms of his battle for a rail route that would serve his community. Later, he was disturbed by the railway's effect on village life and by the railway's pull of his county into the Montreal orbit.

The north-shore railways also tested the Conservative party's traditional alliance with the province's English-speaking population. Never homogeneous, this community, like the rest of the province, was deeply divided by the impact of railways. In Montreal the Grand Trunk and Canadian Pacific forces had battled for over a decade. In 1872 this struggle had been an important factor in Cartier's defeat in Mont-real-East. In Quebec City the English-speaking community belatedly realized the city's decline and fought to withstand Montreal's growing power. South-shore politicians led by James Gibb Robertson and George Irvine joined the Castors and other opposition elements in protesting against the government's generosity to the north-shore rail-ways.

Chapleau's accession to the party's leadership gave the Montreal Conservatives a temporary advantage. Angered at the 'old women' in the party's Castor wing and advised to strike before 'un grand change-ment de décors et d'acteurs,' Chapleau hurried to resolve the railway and financial issue. The sale of the QMO&O and Chapleau's subsequent departure for the Macdonald cabinet meant further Conservative blood-letting. Neither Mousseau nor the ultramontane Ross could contain the centrifugal forces within the provincial party and Chapleau's sup-port for Macdonald in the Riel crisis opened the way for Mercier's new coalition.

The north-shore railways acted as a weathervane. Their construc-tion at tremendous public expense demonstrated that Quebec - albeit pastoral, Catholic, and élitist - was interested in railways. More than half of the debates in the provincial legislature from 1875 to 1878 concerned railways.[13] The province made financial commitments to railways far beyond those granted in Ontario. While politicians in other provinces sought provincial autonomy, the investment of public funds by Quebec's politicians had the effect of tying the province into a transcontinental railway grid. Construction of the north-shore rail-ways showed the influence of entrepreneurs in the new province. There was a consensus that railways were in the public interest: the goals of the entrepreneur had become the goals of the province. Rail-way builders looked to the provincial government for favourable rail-way legislation and generous subsidies. Some public officials acted as the railways' agents in raising capital. When the two railways went bankrupt, the province nationalized them and borrowed millions in its own name to complete construction.

The north-shore railways reflected the tensions between Quebec City and Montreal. In the 1850s the North Shore Railway represented the ambitions of Quebec City to tap western trade and to revive her fading status as an entrepôt. Twenty years later, railways were rein-forcing the polarization of power in Montreal. As late as the mid

1870s, Quebec City leaders perceived the province as a unit in competition with other North American centres. They accepted the rhetoric of Montreal leaders like Andrew Robertson that the two cities were destined to go 'hand in hand with each other' and that the Montreal Harbour was 'after all, only an extension of the harbour of Quebec.'[14] In fact Montrealers paid only lip service to the concept of a community of interest with Quebec City. Throughout the 1870s Montreal fought hard to exploit the north-shore railway issue so that the city would not be left with what one newspaper called 'un petit bonjour de la main et adieu.'[15] Colonization, the dreams of Quebec City, and the linking of the villages along the north shore of the St. Lawrence became lost in the scramble to ensure Montreal's position as terminus of the railway to the Pacific. The struggle over the route of the north-shore railways drove home to Quebec City leaders the inherent antagonism between their city and Montreal.

Quebec had proven to be a vulnerable victim for railway entrepreneurs. Throughout North America, internal improvements such as roads and canals had traditionally been a community responsibility. Many American states had learned a bitter lesson in the canal-building era when the huge investment of public funds had led in many cases to unfinished canals, unexplained bankruptcies, and large public debts. Even so, American communities participated vigorously in the railway sweepstakes. To these North American tendencies, French Canada added its special enthusiasm for colonization, repatriation, and 'national works.' Chapleau for example, reminded his colleagues that in addition to the 'splendours' of industry and commerce which the railway would bring, the iron horse had great value as 'an agent of colonization, fraternization and civilization.'[16]

The enthusiastic support of railways by the Roman Catholic Church permits the application of William Ryan's interpretation to the Confederation period.[17] At all levels from archbishop to curé, the Church joined in the exhilaration for railways, industrial capitalism, and the new technology. Entrepreneurs capitalized on these susceptibilities by inviting priests into executive boardrooms, by putting French-Canadian lawyers in their front offices, and by labelling their railways as colonization projects. However, just as it demonstrated factionalism within the province's English-speaking community, the north-shore railways reflected deep divisions within the Roman Catholic Church. The archbishop of Quebec was the largest shareholder in the North Shore Railway. The Seminary of St. Sulpice, the Ursulines, and the

Seminary of Quebec also invested heavily. Bishop Bourget of Montreal contributed nothing to this railway which would bring little to his constituents. He did however give strong support through Curé Labelle to the Montreal Colonization Railway. At the local level, priests represented the views of their parishioners. This led to conflicting positions on the railway issue in the Three Rivers and Ottawa Valley regions.

While leaders in Montreal and Quebec City fought the battle of metropolitanism, the railway was bringing change to the north-shore communities. French-Canadian villagers usually welcomed the railway and discussed it in terms of jobs, the export of local products and the repatriation of their children from the United States. The iron horse may have brought the realization of some of these hopes but at the same time it had urbanizing influences similar to those in other North American communities. Steel, technology, manufactured goods, capital, and English Canadians intruded into north-shore life. Living in Montreal and Quebec City, the province's élite imposed on the countryside the urban values of technology, industrialization, and resource development. French-Canadian leaders like Joseph Cauchon and Hector Langevin played the same role as journalists, politicians, and entrepreneurs in bringing rural Quebec into the orbit of Montreal and Quebec City as George Brown did in Ontario.

It was ironic then that French-Canadian leaders seized on railways as a means of keeping French Canadians in the province, of opening the north, and of stimulating growth in the ancient capital. For railways with their capital flow, their technology, and their steel rails were levelers that tended to blur cultural and national lines. Construction of the north-shore railways and their incorporation into the Canadian Pacific system were an important part of Quebec's integration into a transcontinental state. At the same time, the province's railway debts left her suspicious, weak, and highly mortgaged. In making its contribution to tying Canada by steel *a mari usque ad mare*, Quebec paid a high price.

Notes

CHAPTER 1

1 Alfred D. Chandler, *The Railroads: the Nation's First Big Business*, 3
2 Gabriel Kolko, *The Triumph of Conservatism*, 3
3 Kolko, *Railroads and Regulation 1877-1916*, 15
4 See, for example, the speech of Francis Hincks in *Statement, Reports and Accounts of the Grand Trunk Railway in Canada*, 71
5 O.D. Skelton, *The Railway Builders*, 84
6 *Census of 1851*, 376-81
7 M. Denison, *Canada's First Bank*, vol. 1, 109
8 *Census of 1861*, vol. 1, 4
9 *Le Courrier du Canada*, 29 July 1870, 24 August 1870
10 *Eastern Angus*, 25 April 1844, clipping in Poor Papers, Portland, Maine
11 *Census of 1851*, 352; *Census of 1861*, 256; *Census of 1851*, 328
12 Quebec, *Journals of the Legislative Assembly*, 9 March 1858

13 J.B. Forsyth to H. Langevin, 9 January 1860, Box 11, Chapais Collection, APQ
14 Quebec, *Journals of the Legislative Assembly*, 20 November 1854
15 *Globe*, 28 August 1851
16 *Further Correspondence Relative to the Projected Railway From Halifax to Quebec*, 13, 15
17 *La Minerve*, 15 March 1853
18 *L'Ere Nouvelle*, 20 January, 3, 16 November 1853, 1 March 1854, clippings in Archives of Diocese of Three Rivers
19 Andrée Désilets, *Hector-Louis Langevin: un père de la confédération canadienne*, 45
20 Anon. Poem, Box 8, Chapais Collection, APQ
21 Quoted in Jean-Paul Bernard, *Les Rouges: libéralisme nationalisme et anticléricalisme*, 37
22 *Procédés du Comité général du chemin de fer du nord*, Department of Public Works, Ottawa,

Series 3, vol. 473, North Shore Railway file, 8; *Further Correspondence Relative to the Projected Railway from Halifax to Quebec*, 5, 8

23 Ibid.

24 Canada, *Statutes of Canada*, 16 Vic, Cap. 100, 22 April 1853

25 Gerald Tulchinsky, 'Studies of Businessmen in the Development of Transportation and Industry in Montreal, 1837–1853,' (PH D thesis, Toronto, 1971), 459

26 Canada, *Proceedings of the Select Standing Committee on Railroads, Canals and Telegraph Lines*

27 Quebec, *Journals of the Assembly*, Cauchon to E.P. Taché, 29 April 1857

28 Cauchon to E. Colvile, 7 July 1856, Box 28, Chapais Collection

29 Ibid., N. Casault to Langevin, 2 May 1856; F. Evanturel to Langevin, 26 April 1856

30 Ibid., Cauchon to E. Colvile, 22 September 1856

31 Quebec, *Journals of the Assembly*, 16 June 1856

32 Ibid., 24 June 1856

33 Handwritten list of offers, Box 29; tender of François Baby, 1 April 1856, Box 28, Chapais Collection

34 Ibid., Statement of Fact, 31 May 1857; Skelton, *The Railway Builders*, 81; Langevin to F. Baby, 18 April 1856, Box 28, Chapais Collection

35 Cauchon to George Simpson, 4 October 1856, Box 28, Chapais Collection

36 Ibid., F. Baby to the directors of the North Shore Railway, 27 November 1856

37 Ibid., North Shore Railway file, Statement of Facts, 31 May 1857

38 Ibid., Box 28, Cauchon to François Evanturel, 1 September 1856

39 *Le Courrier du Canada*, 20 October 1858

40 Désilets, *Hector-Louis Langevin*, 66

41 For an example of a tirade against modern technology see Father Thomas Hamel to — , 21 January 1854, file no. 65, on Chemin de Fer Québec-Richmond, 12 September 1852, Archives of the Archbishop of Quebec, comte 1831–74, cahier no. 51, 67, ASQ.

42 Hector Langevin to Edmond Langevin, 17 July 1852; Vicar-General Cazeau to religious communities, 22 July 1852, Archives of the Archbishop of Quebec

43 *Le Courrier du Canada*, 21 March 1857; Quebec, *Journals of the Assembly*, Cauchon to Taché, 28 April 1857

44 Ibid., 29 April 1857

45 Ibid.

46 *Le Courrier du Canada*, 5 May 1857

47 Quebec, *Journals of the Assembly*, 2 June 1857

48 Ibid., 8 May 1857

49 Ibid.

50 Canada, *Statutes of Canada*, 20 Vic, Cap. 149, 10 June 1857, 582

51 Cauchon to John Bonner, *Herald* office, New York, 6 December 1856, Chapais Collection; Bernard

Bonin, *L'Investissement étranger à long terme au Canada*, 33

52 Thomas C. Cochran, *Railroad Leaders 1845-1890*, 107

53 Ralph Hidy, *The House of Baring in American Trade and Finance*, 151, 419

54 Roger Fulford, *Glyn's: 1753-1953*, 150-5

55 E. Colvile to Cauchon, 5 December 1855; J.P. Kennard to Colvile, 15 August 1856; Cauchon to Colvile, 1 September 1856, Chapais Collection

56 *Le Courrier du Canada*, 11 July 1857

57 Sir W. Napier to G. Simpson, 2 April 1858, Chapais Collection

58 Ibid., Heywood and Company to G. Simpson, 28 March 1858

59 Ibid., Napier to Simpson, October 1857

60 Ibid., M.W. Baby to Napier, 26 April 1858

61 Ibid., F. Baby to Napier, November 1858

62 Ibid., Report of a Committee of the Executive Council, 6 May 1859; *Le Courrier du Canada*, 12 September 1859

63 J.P. Kennard to Langevin, 10 October 1859, Chapais Collection

64 *Le Courrier du Canada*, 8 January 1860; minutes of meeting of North Shore Railway directors, 23 May 1860, Chapais Collection

65 Canada, *Statutes of Canada*, 24 Vic, Cap. 80, 18 May 1861. Under the terms of its charter the Canada Central could not build from Hawkesbury to Montreal for three years without the consent of the Carillon and Grenville Railway.

CHAPTER 2

1 Rapport du commissaire des chemins de fer, 1881-2, 20

2 G.R. Stevens, *Canadian National Railways*, vol. 1, 124

3 W.E. Greening, 'The Lumber Industry in the Ottawa Valley and the American Market in the Nineteenth Century,' *Ontario History*, vol. 62, no. 2 (June 1970)

4 Montreal *Gazette*, 5 November 1869; while supporting the general principle of railway expansion, the *Gazette* attacked railways that served centres other than Montreal. On 8 July 1871 it described the projected railway between Kingston and Pembroke, Ontario as 'essentially American in its character, and ... designed to direct to American seaports a trade which by every consideration of national interest, should be secured by Canada.'

5 Montreal *Gazette*, 10 December 1870

6 Sydney R. Bellingham Memoirs, 225, PAC

7 Macdonald to Langevin, 28 December 1869, John A. Macdonald Papers, MG 26, LB 13, no. 812, PAC

8 Ibid., Macdonald to Chauveau, 30 November 1869; the letter of M.W. Baby to Langevin, 4 March

1870, confirms that the provincial government could easily be brought to terms. Box 7, Chapais Collection, APQ

9 Langevin to Macdonald, 20 February 1869, Macdonald Papers

10 Chris Massiah, ed., *The Quebec Railway Statutes*, 'Quebec Railway Act,' 32 Vic., Cap. 51, 5 April 1869, 10

11 Ibid., 'Colonization Railway Aid Act,' 32 Vic., Cap. 52, 1869, 59

12 Ibid., 'Act to provide ... certain lands ... in aid of Railway ... ,' 34 Vic., Cap. 21, 1870, 115

13 See, for example, Montreal *Gazette*, 9, 20, 23 November, 4 December 1869.

14 In 1872, C.J. Brydges, general manager of the Grand Trunk, had a subscription of $107,000 in the Montreal and City of Ottawa Junction Railway, Montreal *Gazette*, 4 April 1872

15 Canada, *House of Commons Debates*, 20 April 1870, 380; Montreal *Gazette*, 5 April 1870; Canada: House of Commons *Debates*, 25 April 1870

16 Canada, *Statutes of Canada*, 33 Vic., Cap. 52, 1870; Annual Report of Canada Central Railway Company, Montreal *Gazette*, 15 August 1871

17 Montreal *Gazette*, 4 July 1870, 3 February 1871

18 Montreal *Herald*, 10 February 1871; Report of Louis Beaubien to the shareholders of the Montreal Colonization Railway, *La Minerve*,

29 September 1871; Canada, *Statutes of Canada*, 35 Vic., Cap. 68, 1872

19 Quebec, *Journals of the Assembly*, 1869, vol. 2, 124, 139

20 Engineer's Report, Montreal *Gazette*, 7 October 1869; Charles Legge to Directors of Montreal Colonization Railway, 14 March 1870, Labelle Collection, APQ

21 Massiah, *Quebec Railway Statutes*, 32 Vic., Cap. 54, 5 April 1869, 74

22 Engineer's Report, Montreal *Gazette*, 7 October 1869

23 Elie J. Auclair, *Le Curé Labelle*, 46

24 *La Minerve*, 20 July 1872

25 Archives of the Archbishop of Montreal, no. 730,002, de Bellefeuille to Bishop Bourget, 16 May 1874

26 G. Laviolette to Labelle, 5 April 1871, Labelle Collection

27 Minutes, Montreal City Council, 21 March 1872, 189

28 Montreal *Gazette*, 23 November 1869

29 Quebec, *Journals of the Assembly*, 31 January 1870, 24

30 See, for example, the petition of the Reverend P. Tassé in Quebec, *Journals of the Assembly*, 5 February 1869, 38.

31 Bourget to J.L. Billaudèle, 25 February 1854, RLB 8, Archives of the Archbishop of Montreal

32 Ibid., H. Langevin to Bourget, 15 August 1859; *Le Nouveau Monde*, 5 November 1870; Archives of the Archbishop of Montreal, Corporation Episcopal, RPBB, 9; *Le Journal*

de Québec, 21 May 1873; Gustavus Myers, *History of Canadian Wealth*, makes reference to substantial clerical subscriptions to railways in 1850 including £35,000 from the Hotel Dieu Nunnery and Seminary of Montreal and £223,500 from the Bishop of Montreal. In 1860 George Brown wrote that the Seminary in Montreal held stock worth $100,000 in the Grand Trunk. G. Brown to — Hatch, 16 January 1860, George Brown Papers, PAC

33 Bourget to Labelle, 27 March 1873, Labelle Collection

34 *Le Nouveau Monde*, 20 November 1871; see also Gérard Bouchard, 'Apogée et déclin de l'idéologie ultramontaine à travers le journal *Le Nouveau Monde 1867 1900*,' *Recherches Sociographiques* vol. x, nos. 2-3 (1969), 263

35 *Le Nouveau Monde*, 6 October 1871

36 Montreal *Gazette*, 30 August 1869

37 Ibid., 17 February 1872

38 Curé Labelle to L.H. Huot, 11 May 1873, margin note by Huot, Polygraphic 20, no. 32 R, Labelle Collection

39 Young to Labelle, 8 March 1874, Labelle Collection

40 Ibid., W.H. Vanvliet to Lebelle, 24 September 1874

41 Ibid., de Bellefeuille to Labelle, 27 March 1873

42 Ibid., Labelle to Père Thibeaudeau, 6 May 1872

43 Ibid., Allan to Labelle, 11 November 1872

44 Ibid., J.J.C. Abbott to R. Masson, 6 April 1870; L. Beaubien to Labelle, 16 November 1870; H. Mulholland to Labelle, 26 December 1871

45 *La Minerve*, 18 January 1872; Labelle to Père Thibeaudeau, 14 March 1872, Labelle Collection

46 *La Minerve*, 19 January 1872; see also Hélène Tassé, 'Le Curé Labelle et la Région Labelle, 1879-1891,' (MA thesis, University of Ottawa, 1965), 11, 15, 138.

47 William Ryan, *The Clergy and Economic Growth in Quebec, 1896-1914*, 265

48 F. Catellier to H. Langevin, 24 January 1869, Box 29, Chapais Collection

CHAPTER 3

1 'Municipal Code of the Province of Quebec,' 34 Vic., Cap. 68, 1871, *Statutes and Enactments concerning Railways having Reference to the North Shore Railway*

2 Guy Bourassa, 'Les élites politiques de Montréal: de l'aristocratie à la démocratie,' *Canadian Journal of Economics and Political Science*, vol. 30 (February, 1965)

3 See Michel Brunet, 'The French Canadians' Search for a Fatherland,' Peter Russell, ed., *Nationalism in Canada*, 51; and Brunet, *Québec: Canada Anglais*, 169. An earlier critique by the author of 'The Great Compromise' is included in 'The Defeat of George-Etienne Cartier in Montreal-East in 1872,'

Canadian Historical Review, vol. LI, no. 4 (December, 1970)

4 Montreal *Gazette*, 14 December 1869, 3 November 1871, 13 January 1870

5 Minutes, Montreal City Council, 28 March 1870; *La Minerve*, 3 November 1871

6 *La Minerve*, 25 November 1870

7 *Le Nouveau Monde*, 7 February 1871

8 Montreal *Gazette*, 9 February 1871

9 R.S. Longley, *Sir Francis Hincks*, 411

10 Canada, *Royal Commission on the Canadian Pacific Railway*, 123

11 Pierre Berton, *The National Dream*, 73

12 Anon., *Montreal Northern Colonization Railway: Yea or Nay?*; John Irwin Cooper, *Montreal: A Brief History*, 49

13 Canada, *Royal Commission on the Canadian Pacific Railway*, 158, 174

14 Montreal *Gazette*, 17 February 1872

15 Ibid., 1 May 1872

16 Allan to G.W. McMullen, Canada, *Royal Commission on the Canadian Pacific Railway*, 212

17 C.F. Baillargeon to Allan, Rose and Co., 29 July 1870, quoted in *Le Journal des Trois-Rivières*, 4 August 1870

18 Montreal *Gazette*, 17 February 1872

19 *Le National*, 24 April, 31 May, 13 December, 1872; *Le Nouveau Monde*, 2 November, 23, 28 October, 1871

20 J.J.C. Abbott testimony, in Canada, *Royal Commission on the Canadian Pacific Railway*, 174

21 G.W. McMullen letter to Montreal *Gazette*, 15 July 1873

22 Montreal *Gazette*, 15 November 1871

23 Ibid., 12 November 1870

24 C.J. Brydges to W.J. Patterson, Montreal Corn Exchange and Brydges to Andrew and Hugh Allan, both letters published in the Montreal *Gazette*, 5 January 1874

25 Ibid., 14 December 1872

26 C.J. Brydges to Galt, 13 July 1869, Galt Papers, PAC; C.J. Brydges to Cartier, 5 March 1872, Chapais Collection, APQ

27 Montreal *Gazette*, 17 February 1872; Louis Beaubien, *The Pacific Railway and the Eastern Connection*, 14; J. Young to Labelle, 15 February 1872, Labelle Collection, APQ

28 Toronto *Globe*, 6, 11 October 1871

29 G.R. Stevens, *The Canadian National Railways*, vol. 1, 295

30 Sydney R. Bellingham Memoirs, 219, PAC

31 Letter of John Hamilton to Montreal *Herald*, 13 February 1871; later in 1872 Hamilton reappeared in the Allan forces as a provisional director of the Canadian Pacific Railway.

32 *La Minerve*, 21 March 1873

33 Minutes, Montreal City Council, 21 March 1872, 188

34 A detailed examination of the Interoceanic syndicate is given in

W.T. Easterbrook and Hugh Aitken, *Canadian Economic History*, 416 and Donald Creighton, *The Old Chieftain*, 121.

35 Montreal *Gazette*, 14 February 1872; Minutes, Montreal City Council, 13 March 1872, 171

36 Cartier to H. Langevin, 11 July 1867, Box 8, Chapais Collection

37 According to the *Gazette*, 22 March 1872, Reekie had subscribed $107,000 to the Grand Trunk-oriented Montreal and Ottawa City Junction Railway.

38 Massiah, *Railway Statutes of Quebec*, 36 Vic., Cap. 49, 1872; *Le National*, 14 May 1872

39 Montreal *Gazette*, 1 July 1873

40 Among the petitioners named by the Montreal *Gazette*, 24 March 1873, and *La Minerve*, 26 March 1873, were J.H.R. Molson, Harrison Stephens, Thomas Cramp, Henry Lyman, Henry Munro, Alfred Pinsonneault, Alfred Larocque, Theodore Hart, James Reekie, Theodore Doucet, and David Torrance.

41 H. Langevin to Labelle, 11 March 1873, Labelle Collection; Langevin to J.A. Macdonald, 11 March 1873, 96849, Macdonald Papers, PAC

42 Allan to Labelle, 15 May 1873, Labelle Collection

43 *Le Journal de Québec*, 23 June 1873; Labelle to —, 27 July 1873, Labelle Collection

44 David Macpherson to Macdonald, 21 September 1872, Macdonald Papers, MG 26, vol. 123, 50764

45 Louis Beaubien to Labelle, 5 March 1872, Labelle Collection

46 'The Defeat of George-Etienne Cartier in Montreal-East in 1872,' *Canadian Historical Review*, vol. LI, no. 4 (December, 1970)

47 H. Allan to G.W. McMullen, 12 June 1872, Canada, *Royal Commission on the Canadian Pacific Railway*, 202

48 Alexander Campbell and Francis Hincks, testifying after Cartier's death, insisted that the Cartier-Allan deal had been repudiated immediately by the Macdonald government. Canada, *Royal Commission on the Canadian Pacific Railway*, 17, 94

49 For evidence of these fears see Labelle Papers, Charles S. Borrough to Labelle, 11 October 1871.

50 Massiah, *Quebec Railway Statutes*, 36 Vic., Cap. 49, 1872, 220; Bylaw no. 5 of St. Jerusalem d'Argenteuil, 10 February 1873, no. 9798, Joly de Lotbinière Collection, APQ

51 Montreal *Gazette*, 15 March 1873

52 Ibid., 7 August 1873

CHAPTER 4

1 Langevin to Macdonald, 29 November 1877, 96961, Macdonald Papers, PAC

2 North Shore Railway Company Stock Statement, 3 June 1872, North Shore Railway file, Archives of the City of Quebec

3 J.M. Winchell to Langevin, 20 September 1870, Chapais Collection, APQ; Montreal *Gazette*, 9 November 1870

4 John Young, *The North Shore Railway; A Brief Sketch of Its Commercial Relations and Financial Prospects*, 11

5 Montreal *Gazette*, 8 November 1871

6 Canada, House of Commons, *Debates*, 5 March 1875, 536

7 Montreal *Gazette*, 4 March 1871; for a similar statement see *Le Nouveau Monde*, 16 February 1871.

8 L. Beaubien to Langevin, 18 January 1871, Box 7, Chapais Collection; Montreal *Gazette*, 9 February 1871

9 Montreal *Gazette*, 23 March, 19 April 1871; *Globe*, 11 October 1871

10 Cauchon to Curé Labelle, 2 March 1872, Labelle Collection, APQ

11 Montreal *Gazette*, 7 December 1870

12 Ibid., 17 September 1870

13 *Le Courrier du Canada*, 17 October 1870; *Le Journal de Québec*, 6 October 1870

14 Diary of Abbé Cyrille-Etienne Légaré, 23 September 1870, p. 80; manuscript 677, ASQ; *Le Journal de Québec*, 14 September 1870

15 Adolphe Caron to Langevin, 21 January 1871, Box 8, Chapais Collection

16 Masiah, *Railway Statutes of Quebec*, 126-7, 34 Vic., Cap. 22, article 15, 24 December 1870. If the province substituted provincial bonds for its 2,700,000 acre land grant to the railway, these were to have a value of at least $2 million.

17 *Le Journal des Trois-Rivières*, 4 July, 23 March 1871

18 Montreal *Gazette*, 18 December 1869

19 *Le Journal des Trois-Rivières*, 20 June, 17 October 1870

20 Ibid., 26 September 1870

21 Ibid., 17 October 1870; its enthusiasm for local development can be seen in the editions of 27 December 1867, 17 March 1868, 28 March, 1 August, and 5 September 1870.

22 J.M. Winchell to H. Langevin, 24 September 1870, Chapais Collection

23 In January 1872 Joly resigned as director of the Quebec and Gosford Railway. In his letter of resignation he explained that he wanted the project to succeed but that it was difficult to seek grants from the government while he was a director. H.G. Joly to E. Chinic, 5 January 1872, no. 90, Joly Papers, APQ

24 *Le Journal des Trois-Rivières*, 21 November 1870

25 Sydney Bellingham to Langevin, 25 September 1872, Chapais Collection

26 *Le Nouveau Monde*, 25 November 1870

27 J.M. Winchell to Langevin, 25 September 1870, Chapais Collection; Langevin to Macdonald, 19 May 1874, 96919, Macdonald Papers

28 Andrée Désilets, *Hector-Louis Langevin*, 183; John Hearn to Langevin, 28 February 1872, Box 13, Chapais Collection

29 Montreal *Gazette*, 9 May 1873

30 Archbishop Taschereau to Bishop Laflèche, 19 March 1872, Archives of the Seminaire Saint-Joseph of the Diocese of Trois-Rivières; *Mandements, Lettres Pastorales et Circulaires des Evêques de Québec*, Circular to curés of Portneuf, 21 September 1871, vol. 1, 74

31 *Le Journal de Québec*, 21 May 1873. The Seminary of Quebec had at least $1500 invested in the Quebec and Gosford Railway. North Shore file, 8 May 1871, ASQ

32 Cauchon to Curé Labelle, 6 November 1871, Labelle Collection; Cauchon to George Baby, 16 September 1871, Baby Collection, Archives of the University of Montreal

33 Quoted in *Le Journal des Trois-Rivières*, 18 September 1871

34 *Le Nouveau Monde*, 16 October 1871

35 *Le Journal des Trois-Rivières*, 23 August 1871; according to *l'Evénement*, 7 September 1871, the North Shore Railway was presented to the people 'comme une institution gallicane, comme le pendant de l'Université Laval,' quoted in Hamelin, *Les Premières Années du parlementarisme québécois*, 197.

36 Luc Désilets to A. Noiseux, 29 August 1871, Archives of the Diocese of Trois-Rivières.

37 Ibid., Luc Désilets to Bishop Laflèche, 12 January 1872

38 *Le Journal des Trois-Rivières*, 7 September 1871; the procedure whereby county voters approved the actions of their council was complicated. At public meetings held in every parish the voters were asked by their parish president to approve the bylaw. If six qualified voters disapproved, a poll was immediately held. Although they could remain open from ten until 6:00 PM, polls could be closed if thirty minutes passed without a vote being cast. On 4 September 1871 nine of Champlain's ten parishes voted against the subsidy.

39 *Le Journal des Trois-Rivières*, 12 September, 4, 8 February 1870

40 Quebec, *Documents of the Session*, no. 17, 33 Vic., 1869–70. P.J.O. Chauveau to J.M. Winchell (ND); Winchell to Chauveau, 24 January 1870

41 J.M. Winchell to H. Langevin, 24 December 1870, Box 24, Chapais Collection

42 *La Minerve*, 30 April 1873

43 Silas Seymour, *Report of the North Shore Railway of Canada*, 9-15

44 Montreal *Gazette* 13, 19 July 1872

45 *Le Journal de Québec*, 15 November 1873

46 Montreal *Gazette*, 5 October 1872; *La Minerve*, 26 May 1873

47 *Le Journal de Québec*, 30 May 1873

48 John Rose to H. Langevin, 27 March 1873, Chapais Collection

49 Telegram of Curé Labelle to L.H. Huot, 11 May 1873, Polygraphic 20, no. 32 R, ASQ

50 *La Minerve*, 30 April 1873

51 *La Minerve*, 16 May 1873; Montreal *Gazette*, 14 May 1873; *Le Journal de Québec*, 3 February 1874 stated that Attorney-General Irvine was behind the invasion of the company's offices.

52 *Le Journal des Trois-Rivières*, 26 May 1873

53 *Le Journal de Québec*, 28, 30 May, 9 June 1873

54 Translated in Montreal *Gazette*, 28 May 1873

CHAPTER 5

1 The Tanneries scandal and resulting change of government are effectively treated in Hamelin's, *Les Premières Années du parlementarisme québécois*, 119.

2 The settlement with Ottawa and Ontario of the division of Canada's pre-Confederation debts made Robertson amenable to provincial loans to railways, ibid., 160, 200; Masiah, *Railway Statutes of Quebec*, 260, 265, Quebec Railway Aid Act of 1874,' 37 Vic., Cap. 2, 28 January 1874.

3 *Le Journal de Québec*, quoted in *Le Nouveau Monde*, 4 February 1874

4 *Le Journal de Québec*, 18 February 1874; Montreal *Gazette*, 19 February 1874; North Shore Railway Factum, 31 May 1875, 1, Chapais Collection, APQ

5 Langevin to Macdonald, 19 May 1874, 96919, Macdonald Papers, PAC

6 Montreal *Gazette*, 7 December 1875

7 *Le Journal de Québec*, 30 June 1874; Quebec *Morning Chronicle*, 21 July 1874; Montreal *Gazette*, 14 December 1874; *L'Evénement*, 18 August 1875

8 Montreal *Gazette*, 7 December 1875

9 Ottawa *Times*, 5 February 1875; Montreal *Gazette*, 22 February 1875; *Le Nouveau Monde*, 23 February 1875

10 Quebec, *Sessional Papers*, 1875, Vol. 9, no. 11, 111, Colonel W. Rhodes to Boucherville, 9 February 1875

11 *Le Nouveau Monde*, 19 August 1874

12 *Le Journal de Québec*, 31 July 1875; North Shore Railway Factum, Colonel W. Rhodes to Boucherville, 31 May 1875, Chapais Collection; *Sessional Papers of Quebec*, 1875, Vol. 9, no. 11, 114

13 *L'Evénement*, 21 August 1875

14 *Le Courrier du Canada*, 28 July 1875; Montreal *Gazette*, 31 August 1875; *Sessional Papers of Quebec*, 1875, Vol. 9, no. 11, 112

15 *Le Nouveau Monde*, 14 August 1874; *Le Journal de Québec*, 31 January 1874; J.E.L. de Bellefeuille to Labelle, 3 May 1874; H. Allan to Labelle, 30 January 1875, Labelle Collection;

16 C. Legge to Labelle, 21 May 1875, Labelle Collection; Montreal *Gazette*, 13 July 1875

17 Ottawa *Times*, 17 December 1874

18 Pierre Berton, *The National Dream*, 87; Montreal *Gazette*, 2 November 1874

19 *Le Nouveau Monde*, 5 February 1874, 28 November 1874; Montreal *Gazette*, 17 June 1874, 8 April 1875

20 L.F.R. Masson to Labelle, 6 October 1872, Labelle Collection

21 Montreal *Gazette*, 12 January 1874

22 C.J. Brydges to Langevin, 10 February 1869, Box 29, Chapais Collection

23 Cauchon to Labelle, 24 March 1875, Labelle Collection

24 Montreal *Gazette*, 18 September 1874; *Le Nouveau Monde*, 12 June 1875

25 Ottawa *Times*, 17 December 1874

26 Montreal *Gazette*, 19 December 1874; *Le Nouveau Monde*, 20 February 1875; Asa Foster's career is described in Donald Swainson's biography of the entrepreneur in the *Dictionary of Canadian Biography*, vol. x. In favouring the Canada Central, the Liberals may have been rewarding Foster for his role in supplying evidence in the Pacific scandal. See Gustavus Myers, *A History of Canadian Wealth*, 235.

27 *Le Nouveau Monde*, 13 March 1875; Montreal *Gazette*, 9 November 1875

28 *L'Evénement*, 15 March 1875

29 J.E.L. de Bellefeuille to Labelle, 23 March 1875, Labelle Collection

30 *Le Nouveau Monde*, 19, 24, 25 March, 2 April 1875; Ruggles

Church to Labelle, 27 March 1875, Labelle Collection

31 Montreal *Gazette*, 26 January, 23 May, 26 June, 14 July 1874

32 Report of Montreal Colonization Engineer, 19 January 1872 in *Quelques Notes sur la vente du chemin de fer*, 9

33 Montreal *Gazette*, 17, 19 March, 6 April 1875; *Le Nouveau Monde*, 10 March, 14, 15 May 1875; Young's role in the bridge affair and commercial life of Montreal is explained more fully in G. Tulchinsky and B. Young's article on John Young in the *Dictionary of Canadian Biography*, Vol. x.

34 Montreal *Gazette*, 24 June 1875

35 *Le Nouveau Monde*, 17 March, 19 April 1875

36 H. Abbott to Labelle, 22 September 1874, Labelle Collection

37 Quebec, *Journals of the Assembly*, 18 February 1875, 274; Hamelin, *Les Premières Années du parlementarisme québécois* 139-55

38 G. Laviolette to J.E.L. de Bellefeuille, 30 March 1875, Labelle Collection

39 Montreal *Gazette*, 24 July 1874; A.W. Currie, *The Grand Trunk Railway of Canada*, 145

40 H. Allan to Labelle, 15 April 1875, Labelle Collection

41 London *Times*, 29 March, 3, 15, 23 April 1875

42 Montreal *Gazette*, 30 July 1875, 10 June 1875

43 *Le Nouveau Monde*, 15, 31 July 1875

44 *Royal Commission concerning the Quebec, Montreal, Ottawa and Occidental Railway* (hereafter cited as the *Routhier Commission*), testimony of Arthur Dansereau, 670.

45 Quebec, *Sessional Papers*, 1875, Vol. 9, no. 11, 119; Montreal *Gazette*, 13, 30 July 1875

46 Masiah, *Quebec Railway Statutes*, 259; 'Railway Subsidy Act of 1875,' 38 Vic., Cap. 40, 23 February 1875

47 *Le Journal de Québec*, 23 August 1875; *Le Nouveau Monde*, 20 August 1875

48 Quebec, *Documents of the Session*, 40 Vic., no. 19, 1876, 77-80

49 Speech by provincial Treasurer Ruggles Church in Legislative Assembly, 1 December 1876, quoted in Montreal *Gazette*, 2 December 1876

50 J.G. Robertson to H. Langevin, 12 June 1875, Chapais Collection

51 Quebec, *Rapport du commissaire des chemins de fer*, 1881-1882, 28

52 Quebec, *Sessional Papers*, 1875, Vol. 9, no. 11. 122, 130, 146. It is not clear why there was a discrepancy between the figure of $24,801 and the $18,881 announced earlier as the total private investment in the Montreal Colonization Railway; Quebec, *Documents of the Session*, no. 19, 1876, 111.

53 Montreal *Gazette*, 23 November 1875

54 Quebec, *Journals of the Assembly*, 8 November 1875, 7

55 *L'Evénement*, 23 December 1875; *Le Canadien*, 9, 10 November 1875; *La Minerve* (ND), quoted in *Le Canadien*, 23 November 1875

56 Montreal *Gazette*, 15, 9 December 1875

57 *L'Evénement*, 10 December 1875

58 Montreal *Gazette*, 15 December 1875

59 *L'Evénement*, 16 November 1875

60 Montreal *Gazette*, 15 December 1875

61 Ibid., 6 December 1875

62 Masiah, *Quebec Railway Statutes*, 311-24, 'Statute of Quebec,' 39 Vic., Cap. 2, 24 December 1875; see also the *Rapport du commissaire des chemins de fer, 1882-3*, 16-27

63 *Le Nouveau Monde*, 23 September 1875; Walter Shanly, *Rapport au sujet de l'affaire Duncan Macdonald*, 7

64 Montreal *Gazette*, 18 September 1875; *Sessional Papers of Quebec*, vol. 9, no. 11, 127. Montreal City Council accepted the terms by a vote of nineteen to five.

65 Masiah, *Quebec Railway Statutes*, 311-24, 'Statute of Quebec,' 39 Vic., Cap. 2, 24 December 1875

66 Quebec, *Debates of the Legislative Assembly*, 24 July 1879, 212; Montreal *Gazette*, 7 December 1875

67 Quebec, *Documents of the Session*, no. 2, 97, 1876; Montreal *Gazette*, 7 December 1875

CHAPTER 6

1 *L'Evénement*, 29 January 1876
2 Labelle Papers, de Bellefeuille to Labelle, 7 January 1876, Labelle Collection, APQ; *L'Evénement*, 13, 29 January 1876; Quebec, *Documents of the Session*, 40 Vic., no. 19, 1876, 96
3 *Le Canadien*, 2 March 1876; Masiah, *Quebec Railway Statutes*, 311, 'An Act respecting ... the Quebec, Montreal, Ottawa and Occidental Railway,' 39 Vic., Cap. 2, 24 December 1875; Quebec, *Documents of the Session*, 40 Vic., no. 19, 1876, 146
4 J.G. Robertson quoted in Montreal *Gazette*, 23 March 1883; Quebec, *Routhier Commission*, testimony of A.L. Light, vol. 3, 147-8
5 Quebec, *Documents of the Session*, 42 Vic., no. 9, 1878, 617-52, 746, 749; *Documents of the Session*, 40 Vic., no. 19, 1876, 123, 126
6 Godefroy Laviolette to Labelle, 7 December 1876; H.G. Malhiot to Labelle, 26 December 1876, Labelle Collection; Quebec, *Documents of the Session*, 42 Vic., no. 9, 1878, 689
7 Montreal *Gazette*, 6 February 1878; H.G. Malhiot to Langevin, 18 July 1878, Box 18, Chapais Collection; *L'Evénement*, 18 December 1876

8 Quebec, *Documents of the Session*, 40 Vic., no. 19, 1876, 137, 134
9 *L'Evénement*, 12, 19 July 1876
10 Joseph Reynar to Joly, 30 November 1878, Joly Papers, APQ
11 Ibid., no. 1027, Peter Mason to Joly, 19 November 1879
12 Montreal *Gazette*, 6 July 1878
13 Ibid., 27 December 1876
14 R. Thibaudeau to F. Langelier, 4 July 1879, no. 1867, Joly Papers
15 Ibid., Walter Shanly to Joly, 15 October 1878
16 *Routhier Commission*, vol. 3, 392-7, testimony of T. McGreevy
17 Quebec, *Documents of the Session*, 40 Vic., no. 19, 1876, 56-8, 91. In April 1877 the federal government ratified the reorganization of the Jacques Cartier Bank voted by the shareholders in March 1876. The capital of the bank was reduced from $2,000,000 to $1,000,000 and the value of individual shares halved to $25. *Statutes of Canada*, 40 Vic., Cap. 55, 1877, 4.
18 Report of Walter Shanly to Joly, 5 August 1878; L.O. Loranger to De Boucherville, 27 September 1877, Joly Papers, APQ; Montreal *Gazette*, 23 June 1876
19 Robert Rumilly, *Histoire de la Province de Québec* vol. 2, 106; Montreal *Gazette*, 15 January 1878
20 Quebec, *Documents of the Session*, 1877-8, no. 11, 4; *Le Canadien*, 4 December 1875; Quebec, *Journals of the Legislative Assembly*, 29 November 1876, 67
21 Montreal *Gazette*, 23 August 1877

22 *Routhier Commission*, vol. 3, 149, testimony of A.L. Light

23 Ibid., 618, testimony of Walter Shanly

24 *L'Evénement*, 4 June 1877

25 Montreal *Gazette*, 21 December 1876; Quebec, *Documents of the Session*, no. 11, 1877-8, 10; *Routhier Commission*, vol. 3, 515, testimony of H.G. Malhiot

26 Montreal *Gazette*, 21 December 1876

27 Ibid., 6 April 1876

28 *L'Evénement*, 5 June 1877; De Boucherville to Labelle, 18 February 1877, Labelle Collection; *Routhier Commission*, vol. 3, 541, testimony of De Boucherville

29 Ibid., vol. 3, 671, testimony of C.A. Dansereau; vol. 3, 45, testimony of F.X. Trudel

30 Montreal *Gazette*, 22 December 1877

31 *L'Evénement*, 4, 13 June 1872; Minutes, Montreal City Council, 30 May 1877

32 *Le Canadien*, 10 January 1876; Quebec, *Documents of the Session*, 41 Vic., no. 11, 1877-8, 6

33 R. Masson to Labelle, 15 March 1877, Labelle Collection

34 Quebec, *Documents of the Session*, 40 Vic., no. 19, 1876, 27, 47, 26; speech of J.G. Robertson quoted in Montreal *Gazette*, 5 December 1876

35 The London *Times* (ND), quoted in Montreal *Gazette*, 11 August 1876

36 Montreal *Gazette*, 22 June 1877, 1 February 1878; Quebec, *Docu-ments of the Session*, 40 Vic., no. 19, 1876, 2; G. Hagar to J. Mc-Lennan 24 October, 7 November 1877, McLennan Papers, PAC

37 M. Denison, *Canada's First Bank* (Toronto, 1967), vol. 2, 185; Montreal *Gazette*, 21, 22 December 1877, 1 February 1878

38 Budget speech as reported in Montreal *Gazette*, 1 February 1878

39 Quebec, *Debates of the Legislative Assembly*, 24 July 1879, 212

40 Rumilly, *Histoire de la Province de Québec*, vol. 2, 183-9

41 F. Ouellet, ed., *Rapport de l'Archiviste de Québec*, 1959-60, 'Lettres de Chapleau,' 50, Chapleau to H. Langevin, 23 November 1877

42 *L'Evénement*, 24 January 1878; Chapleau to Labelle, 19 March 1878, Labelle Collection

43 Langevin to Macdonald, 28 January 1878, no. 96964, Macdonald Papers, PAC; Adolphe Caron to Macdonald, 26 January 1878, Macdonald Papers, quoted in J. Saywell, *The Office of Lieutenant-Governor*, 117

44 Montreal *Gazette*, 30 January 1878

45 *La Minerve*, 1 February 1878; Montreal *Gazette*, 28 January 1878

46 *La Minerve*, 1 February 1878; Montreal *Gazette*, 6 February 1878; *Le Nouveau Monde*, 8 January 1878

47 *L'Evénement*, 21 January 1878

48 Quebec *Morning Chronicle*, 29 January, 14 February 1878; *Le Canadien*, 16 February 1878; De Boucherville to Weston Hunt (ND)

quoted in *La Minerve*, 12 February 1878

49 Quebec *Morning Chronicle*, 9 February 1878

50 Ibid., despite his harsh condemnation of life in Quebec, Rhodes did not leave the province permanently and continued to lobby for his railway interests.

51 R. Rumilly, *Histoire de la Province de Québec*, vol. 2, 189; *Le Canadien*, 31 January, 6, 13 February 1878; Quebec, *Journals of the Assembly*, 6, 12 February 1878

52 Letellier's notes of conversations with Boucherville (ND), published in Quebec *Morning Chronicle*, 28 March 1878. Other aspects of the dismissal are described in J. Saywell, *The Office of Lieutenant-Governor*, 117; R. Rumilly, *Histoire de la Province de Québec*, vol. 2, 193; and Hamelin, *Les Premières Années du parlementarisme québécois*, 274.

53 Quebec *Morning Chronicle*, 9 March 1878; Montreal *Herald*, 13 April 1878; *La Minerve*, 11 April 1878; Montreal *Gazette*, 25 March 1878

54 R. Laflamme to F.G. Marchand, 10 March 1878, Joly Papers

55 Chapleau to Macdonald, 8 July 1879, 86512, Macdonald Papers

56 *Routhier Commission*, vol. 3, testimony of Joly, 96; Montreal *Gazette*, 27 June, 10 July 1878

57 *Routhier Commission*, vol. 3, testimony of Joly, 108; Fonds Nicolet, Six Month Report ending 28 February 1879 of Quebec,

Montreal, Ottawa and Occidental Railway, 9, Archives of the Université de Québec à Trois-Rivières

58 Quebec *Morning Chronicle*, 10 February 1879

59 Montreal *Gazette*, 20 May 1878; S. Haycock to Joly, 19 October 1878, no. 952; W. Shanly to Joly, April 7, 1879, no. 1402, Joly Papers

60 Canada, *House of Commons Debates*, 7 May 1878, 2500-1

61 J. Chapleau to Macdonald, 19 September 1878, quoted in Laurier Lapierre, 'Politics, Race and Religion in French Canada: Joseph Israel Tarte,' (PH D, University of Toronto, 1962), 96

62 Canada, *House of Commons Debates*, 11 March 1879, 252; 12 March 1879, 325; Canada, *Statutes of Canada*, 42 Vic., Cap. 56, 15 May 1879

63 *Routhier Commission*, testimony of G. Malhiot, vol. 3, 516; F. Langelier, vol. 3, 31; E. Pacaud, vol. 1, 313

64 Ibid., G. Irvine testimony, vol. 3, 1199; G. Malhiot, vol. 3, 520

65 Ibid., Henri Beautey testimony, vol. 3, 163; Charles Langelier, vol. 3, 232; A.R. Macdonald, superintendent of Intercolonial Railway, vol. 3, 584

66 Ibid., G. Starnes testimony, vol. 3, 525; C.W. Carrier, vol. 3, 93

67 Ibid., A.R. Macdonald testimony, vol. 3, 585; C. Langelier, vol. 3, 233; Chapleau's censure of the Liberals was defeated 25 to 22.

Quebec, *Debates of the Assembly*, 21 August 1879, 337

68 *Routhier Commission*, John Mac-Kay testimony, vol. 3, 20; C.A. Dansereau, vol. 3, 672

69 Ibid., G. Malhiot testimony, vol. 3, 518; W. Shanly to Joly, 18 October 1878, 948, Joly Papers; *Routhier Commission*, Joly testimony, vol. 3, 106

70 Montreal *Gazette*, 24 November 1881

71 *Routhier Commission*, testimony of Joly, vol. 3, 105; vol. 4, 37

72 W. Shanly to Joly, 23 July 1878, no. 645, Joly Papers; no. 435 A.L. Light to Railway Commissioners, 20 April 1878, no. 435; Quebec, *Documents of the Session*, no. 9, 1878, 419, 581

73 Clippings (ND) from Montreal *Herald* and Montreal *True Witness*, nos. 398-9, Joly Papers

74 Ibid., D. Macdonald to Joly, 13 April 1878, no. 400; E. Theodore Paquet to Joly, 17 August 1878, no. 756

75 Montreal *Gazette*, 2 September 1878; *Le Canadien*, 6 September 1878; Quebec *Morning Chronicle*, 31 August 1878

76 Fonds Nicolet, Six Month Report ending 28 February 1879 of Quebec, Montreal, Ottawa and Occidental Railway, 1-9, Archives of the Université de Québec à Trois-Rivières

77 Montreal *Gazette*, 14 September 1878; 31 May, 15 June 1881.

78 Pierre Bachand, 13 December 1875, quoted in Hamelin, *Les Premières Années du parlementarisme québécois*, 259

79 Ibid., 5 February, 5 April, 1 November 1878; Quebec *Morning Chronicle*, 8 December 1878; W. Shanly to Joly, 8 February 1879, no. 1236, Joly Papers

80 Quebec *Morning Chronicle*, 22 May 1878

81 Quebec, *Debates of the Assembly*, 11 August 1879, 300; 16 August 1879, 309, 335, 16 June 1880, 467

82 Ibid., 16 June 1880, 452-4

83 M.W. Baby to D.A. Ross, 17 May 1878, no. 495, Joly Papers; 1878; Baby was even more interested in the Quebec and Lake St. John Railway which he described as a 'national and catholic' railway and the 'essentially colonization Railway of the Province.' M.W. Baby to George Baby, 25 September 1879, Box 3, Baby Collection, Archives of Université de Montréal

84 Montreal *Gazette*, 10, 1 June 1878

85 Quebec, *Debates of the Assembly*, 27 August 1879, 368; 29 October 1879, 388

CHAPTER 7

1 Quebec, *Rapport du commissaire des chemins de fer, 1881-2*, 28-9

2 *Routhier Commission*, report of cabinet committee, 28 February 1880, vol. 2, 188-9; Walter Shanly to Chapleau, 24 May 1880, vol. 2, 341

3 *Routhier Commission*, report of

cabinet committee, 28 February 1880, vol. 2, 190; statement of A. Louthood, vol. 2, 232

4 Quebec, *Documents of the Session*, 1880, no. 2, 9; Montreal *Gazette*, 4 March 1882

5 *Routhier Commission*, vol. 2, 230, 329; Montreal *Gazette*, 24 August 1880, 27 July 1880

6 Montreal *Gazette*, 12, 24 August 1880; R. Rumilly, *Histoire de la Province de Québec*, vol. 3, 81

7 *Routhier Commission*, vol. 4, 28; vol. 2, 199; Quebec, *Debates of the Assembly*, 23, 28 March 1882, 568, 650; Quebec, *Rapport du commissaire des chemins de fer*, 1885-6, 19

8 Montreal *Gazette*, 22 June, 16 March 1881; Quebec, *Documents of the Session*, 1880 no. 2, 38

9 Andrew Robertson, quoted in Montreal *Gazette*, 21 April 1881

10 Ibid., 2 August 1880

11 Quebec, *Debates of the Assembly*, 3 July, 11 June 1880, 561, 558; Quebec *Morning Chronicle*, ND, quoted in Montreal *Gazette*, 22 April 1881

12 *Routhier Commission*, vol. 3, 573, testimony of W.E. Blumhart. Despite his protests of innocence Blumhart was described by Liberal critics as 'une belle fleur' who operated from a special railway car equipped with champagne and fine cigars. Quebec, *Debates of the Assembly*, 31 March 1882, 736

13 *Routhier Commission*, testimony of Adolphe Davis, vol. 3, 169

14 M.W. Baby to George Baby, 12 January 1880, Box 111, Baby Papers, Archives of Université de Montréal; Chapleau to Macdonald, 13 January 1880, no. 86517, Macdonald Papers, PAC

15 P.A. Peterson to Joly, 4 July 1879, no. 1870, Joly Papers; Montreal *Gazette*, 31 May 1881; Quebec, *Documents of the Session*, 1880, no. 2, 2, report of A. Light, 10 June 1880

16 R. Rumilly, *Histoire de la Province de Québec*, vol. 3, 70; M.W. Baby to George Baby, 12 January 1880, Baby Collection, Archives of the Université de Montréal

17 Quebec, *Debates of the Assembly*, 24 March 1882, 96; Montreal *Gazette*, 12 November 1881; Rumilly, *Histoire de la Province de Québec*, vol. 3, 65

18 Quebec, *Debates of the Assembly*, 27, 30 March 1882, 576, 711-27

19 Montreal *Gazette*, 23 June, 20, 21, 24 July 1880

20 *Routhier Commission*, vol. 3, 491

21 Ibid., testimony of Ludger Roberge, vol. 3, 292

22 Ibid., W. Shanly to Sénécal, 24 June 1880, vol. 2, 359

23 Ibid., copy of sale of Joliette Railway to the Queen, 25 August 1881, vol. 2, 82

24 Ibid., vol. 2, 181; vol. 3, 120. Lacoste and Benjamin Globensky acted as Sénécal's Montreal law firm.

25 Ibid., vol. 2, 300; vol. 3, 418, 497; vol. 4, 46. Roberge was paid

$10,078 for the Joliette extension.

26 Ibid., Bradley Barlow to Sénécal, 27 May 1880, vol. 2, 346; testimony of Sénécal, vol. 3, 511

27 Ibid., vol. 2, 349, Sénécal to Chapleau, 28 May 1880; Quebec, *Sessional Papers of 1885*, no. 75; Montreal *Gazette*, 22 June 1881. J.B. Renaud again appeared as a stockholder but testified that he had invested nothing.

28 *Routhier Commission*, testimony of Chapleau, vol. 3, 645; Montreal *Gazette*, 2 May 1881

29 Ibid., 25 January 1878; *L'Evénement*, 25, 26 January 1878; Quebec, *Debates of the Assembly*, 21 February 1878, 1612

30 *Routhier Commission*, testimony of Charles King, vol. 3, 626

31 Chapleau to Macdonald, 31 October 1880, no. 86535, Macdonald Papers; Montreal *Gazette*, 17 May 1880, 16 May 1882

32 Montreal *Gazette*, 7 December 1880; Quebec, *Debates of the Assembly*, 9 June 1880, 406

33 Minutes, Quebec City Board of Trade, APQ, 638, 657; Annual Report of Quebec City Board of Trade, 1880, 57-8 APQ; see also Fernand Ouellet, *Histoire de la Chambre de Commerce de Québec*, 49-52.

34 Chapleau to H. Langevin, 6 March 1881, quoted in F. Ouellet, 'Lettres de Joseph-Adolphe Chapleau (1870-1896),' *Rapport de l'Archiviste de la Province de Québec:*

1959-60, 73; Montreal *Gazette*, 21 March 1882

35 Chapleau to Macdonald, 5 March 1882, no. 86648, Macdonald Papers

36 J. Hickson to Joly, 1 October 1878, no. 890, Joly Papers

37 Quebec, *Debates of the Assembly*, 9 June 1880; Masiah, ed., *Quebec Railway Statutes*, 44-45 Vic., Cap. 2, 30 June 1881, 485

38 Canada, *Statutes of Canada*, 43 Vic., Cap. 55, 1880; Masiah, ed., *Quebec Railway Statutes*, 43-44 Vic., Cap. 44, 1880, 444; Quebec, *Debates of the Assembly*, 9 June 1880, 428

39 Quebec, *Debates of the Assembly*, 28 March 1882, 655; Quebec, *Documents of the Session*, 43 Vic., no. 39, 1879, 28-9; *Routhier Commission*, vol. 4, 22-3

40 Copy of cabinet committee report, 14 June 1879, quoted in *Routhier Commission*, vol. 4, 25-6

41 W. Shanly to Chapleau, 27 December 1881, quoted in appendix of Quebec, *Debates of Assembly*, 1883, 1407

42 Quoted by Chapleau in Canada, *House of Commons Debates*, 12 April 1884, 1533

43 Chapleau to Macdonald, 15 October 1880, no. 86519, Macdonald Papers

44 Quebec, *Debates of the Assembly*, 27 March 1882, 597

45 *Routhier Commission*, vol. 3, 244, testimony of William Van Horne; vol. 4, 96; A.W. Currie, *The Grand*

Trunk Railway Company of Canada, 240

46 R.B. Angus to Chapleau, 8 February 1881, no. 86556; Angus to Chapleau, 14 January 1881, no. 86563, Macdonald Papers

47 Ibid., Chapleau to Angus, 10 February 1881, no. 86558; Chapleau to Langevin, 15 February 1881, quoted in F. Ouellet, 'Lettres de Joseph-Adolphe Chapleau (1870–1896),' *Rapport de l'Archiviste de la Province de Québec; 1959-60;* Chapleau to Macdonald, 26 January 1881, no. 86547; Chapleau to Macdonald, 11 February 1881, no. 86561, Macdonald Papers

48 Ibid., Macdonald to Chapleau, 19 January 1881, no. 86570

49 Pierre Berton, *The Last Spike*, 41; Fred Williams, 'The Story of an Early Railway,' *Globe and Mail*, 19 July 1937; Montreal *Gazette*, 13 October, 4 November 1881; in 1880 the premier was one of the incorporators of the Quebec and Ontario Railway which would join Toronto and Ottawa, Montreal *Gazette*, 26 February 1881.

50 Quoted by Chapleau in Quebec, *Debates of the Assembly*, 27 March 1882, 599

CHAPTER 8

1 In exploring the possibility of a liberal-conservative coalition, Chapleau was simply reviving the idea begun as early as 1875 by Rodrigue Masson and Joseph

Cauchon; see Andrée Désilets, *Hector-Louis Langevin*, 305.

2 A. Desjardins to R. Masson, 23 November 1881, quoted in Désilets, *Hector-Louis Langevin*, 359. In the election the Conservatives won 56 per cent of the popular vote and 50 seats to 15 for the Liberals.

3 Tarte to H. Langevin, 20 December 1881, Chapais Collection, I, APQ

4 *Routhier Commission*, testimony of Louis Beaubien, vol. 3, 225

5 Ibid., testimony of T. McGreevy, vol. 3, 400

6 J. Aldéric Ouimet was a Montreal lawyer, director of the Montreal and City District Savings Bank and the Montreal Park Railway and Elevator Company, 1881, and MP for Laval, 1873-96; Alphonse Desjardins was president of the Jacques Cartier Bank, the Terra Cotta Lumber Company, and the Crédit Foncier, editor of *Le Nouveau Monde*, MP for Hochelaga, 1874-6, and close political associate of Chapleau; James G. Ross was president of the Quebec Bank and director of the Guarantee Company; Pierre Valin was a Quebec City ship-builder, chairman of the Quebec Harbour Board, member of the Quebec City Council, 1872-4, and MP for Montmorency, 1878-96; Nazaire Turcotte was a Quebec City importer; William Carrier was a prominent manufacturer in Lévis; Jean-Baptiste Renaud was a director of the Union Bank, 1872, the Lévis and Kennebec Railway, 1872,

la Compagnie d'Assurance de Québec, 1862, the South Shore Railway and Tunnel Company, 1880, president of the St. Eustache Railway and Stadacona Assurance Company, 1874, and vice-president of the Joliette Railway. Victor Hudon owned a cotton mill in Hochelaga and was director of the Richelieu Company, 1851, the Montreal Terminus Company, 1861, and the Jacques Cartier Bank, 1871; J.O. Villeneuve was a Montreal merchant and a director of the Jacques Cartier Bank and Dominion Cotton Mills; Jean-Baptiste Mongenais was a merchant in Rigaud and Montreal, director of the Vaudreuil Railway, 1853, and MP for Vaudreuil, 1878-82; Bradley Barlow was president of the South-Eastern Railway.

7 *Routhier Commission*, vol. 2, 87-107; vol. 3, 600, testimony of C.A. Dansereau

8 Ibid., vol. 2, 115-21

9 Ibid., vol. 2, 107-14

10 Ibid., testimony of C.A. Dansereau, vol. 3, 225; testimony of Louis Beaubien, vol. 3, 656

11 Ibid., vol. 2, 126-9, H. Allan and S. Rivard to Chapleau, 21 February 1882; L.H. Massue was president of the Quebec Council of Agriculture, director of the Provident Mutual Association and MP for Richelieu, 1878-87; Hugh McLellan was president of the Montreal Board of Trade, 1872; Jacques Grenier was president of the

Montreal St. Jean-Baptiste Society, 1875, city councillor, 1872, Justice of the Peace, 1875, first vice-president of the Board of Trade, 1888, and mayor of Montreal, 1889-1890; F.X. St. Charles was a city councillor, 1870; Gustave Drolet was a Montreal lawyer.

12 Ibid., testimony of S. Rivard, vol. 3, 210

13 Ibid., testimony of C.A. Dansereau, vol. 3, 676; testimony of Curé Labelle; vol. 3, 203; testimony of John Jones Ross; vol. 3, 332; testimony of Chapleau, vol. 3, 658

14 Ibid., G. Stephen to Chapleau, 6, 9 January 1882, vol. 3, 655; Quebec, *Debates of the Assembly*, 27 March 1882, 599

15 *Routhier Commission*, testimony of Curé Labelle, vol. 3, 704

16 Ibid., testimony of William Van Horne, vol. 3, 248

17 Quebec, *Debates of the Assembly*, 27 March 1882; Chapleau to Macdonald, 19 February 1882, no. 86641, Macdonald Papers

18 Masiah, ed., *Quebec Railway Statutes*, 45 Vic., Cap. 19, 1882, 534, 'Sale of the Western Section of the Quebec, Montreal, Ottawa and Occidental ... '

19 *Routhier Commission*, vol. 4, 90, 305; Chapleau denied any wrongdoing in his testimony to the Commission, vol. 3, 661.

20 Ibid., vol. 3, 600, testimony of C.A. Dansereau

21 Ibid., vol. 2, 131-5

22 Ibid., vol. 2, 142

23 Ibid., vol. 3, 555, testimony of J.E.L. de Bellefeuille

24 Quebec, *Debates of the Assembly*, 28 March 1882, 661

25 Ibid., 29 March 1882, 695-6

26 *Routhier Commission*, testimony of John Hearn, vol. 4, 15; vol. 3, 163; Quebec, *Debates of the Assembly*, 28 March 1882, 626; Rumilly, *Histoire de la Province de Québec*, vol. 3, 169

27 *Le Monde*, 1, 7 March 1882; Montreal *Gazette*, 13, 31 March 1882; *Le Constitutionel*, 6 April 1882

28 Désilets, *Hector-Louis Langevin*, 358; Quebec, *Debates of the Assembly*, 28 March 1882; *Routhier Commission*, testimony of Israel Tarte, vol. 3, 37

29 Quebec, *Debates of the Assembly*, 13 March 1882

30 Quebec, *Debates of the Council*, 15 March 1882, 534; 28 March 1882, 663; Montreal *Gazette*, 14 April 1882

31 *Routhier Commission*, testimony of Boucherville, vol. 3, 545; Montreal *Gazette*, 10 May 1882

32 Macdonald Papers, no. 86656, Chapleau to Macdonald, 26 March 1882; according to the Montreal *Gazette* of 28 March 1882, the following federal MPs signed a telegram wishing Chapleau 'health and success' in his railway policy: J.G. Blanchet, Ernest Cimon, F. Dugas, R.P. Vallée, G. Amyot, A. Pinsonnault, F. Routhier, Joseph Bolduc, Simon X. Cimon, P.E. Grandbois, Désire Girouard,

J.G.H. Bergeron, Joseph Tassé, C.J. Coursol, G.A. Girouard, P.C. Beauchesne, Michael P. Ryan, G.A. Gigault, J.B. Mongenais, Louis Tellier, D.A. Manson, W.B. Ives, Alonzo Wright, J.J. Gauthier, E.F. Brooks, François Rouleau, E.C. Cuthbert, J. Poupore, Fabien Vanasse, A.C.P. Landry, Hilaire Hurteau, J.B. Daoust.

33 Montreal *Gazette*, 28 March 1882; Quebec, *Debates of the Assembly*, 28 March 1882, 676, 664

34 Ibid., 29 March 1882, 634; Montreal *Gazette*, 14 April 1882

35 Ibid., 25 April 1882

36 *Routhier Commission*, testimony of John McDougall, vol. 2, 184, 185; vol. 3, 353

37 G.R. Stevens, *The Grand Trunk Railway*, vol. 1, 352

38 See the resolutions of the Quebec City Board of Trade in the Macdonald Papers, no. 53850.

39 Désilets, *Hector-Louis Langevin*, 360; see also, Blair Neatby and John Saywell, 'Chapleau and the Conservative Party in Quebec,' *Canadian Historical Review*, vol. 37 (March, 1956).

40 Chapleau is quoted in Désilets, *Hector-Louis Langevin*, 372

41 Marginal note on letter of Hector Langevin to L.H. Huot, 9 March 1884, Lettres P, no. 202, ASQ

42 Rumilly, *Histoire de la Province de Québec*, vol. 4, 132

43 J.A. Maxwell, *Federal Subsidies to the Provincial Governments in*

Canada, 59; A.W. Currie, *The Grand Trunk Railway of Canada*, 314

44 23 September 1884, no. 53877, Macdonald Papers

45 Ibid., G. Stephen to Langevin, 5 April 1884, no. 53846

46 Wilfrid Laurier mentioned Stephen's Portland speech in Canada, *House of Commons Debates*, 5 February 1885, 42; G. Stephen to Macdonald, 5 April 1884; 21 March 1885, no. 53971, Macdonald Papers

47 Montreal *Gazette*, 20 January 1885

48 No. 54043, 13 May 1885, Macdonald Papers; Tyler was quoted in the Montreal *Gazette*, 1 June 1885.

49 Langevin to Macdonald, 6 November 1884, no. 97452; Chapleau to Macdonald, 6 May 1885, no. 86804, Macdonald Papers;

50 Montreal *Gazette*, 23 March 1885; resolution of Quebec City Board of Trade, 5 May 1885, resolution of Quebec City Board of Trade, 16 June 1885, no. 54113, Macdonald Papers

51 The Riel crisis and the Canadian Pacific's needs for an increased subsidy are treated in Pierre Berton, *The Last Spike* 328-418; G. Stephen to Macdonald, September 14, 17, 1885, no. 54202; Stephen to Macdonald, 12 May 1885, no. 54005; J. Hickson to Macdonald, 4 July 1885, no. 54126, Macdonald Papers

52 *Routhier Commission*, 'Agreement between the Grand Trunk Railway ... and Her Majesty,' 19 September 1885, vol. 2, 383-7

53 Ibid., 'Agreement between Her Majesty ... and the Canadian Pacific Railway,' 19 September 1885, vol. 2, 394-7

CHAPTER 9

1 See, for example, Gerald Tulchinsky, *The River Barons: Montreal Businessmen and the Growth of Industry and Transportation, 1837-53*

2 Canada, *Royal Commission on the the Canadian Pacific Railway*, 1873, 212

3 London *Times*, 3 April 1875, quoted in Montreal *Gazette*, 23 April 1875

4 J. Hickson to Joly, 1 October 1878, no. 890, Joly Papers, APQ

. 5 J.G. Robertson to H. Langevin, 12 June 1875; Chapais Collection, APQ

6 Appendix to Quebec, *Debates of the Assembly*, 1883, 1393, speech of Chapleau to voters of St. Laurent, 6 September 1883

7 Montreal *Gazette*, 7 December 1875

8 Ibid., 1 February 1878; Quebec, *Report of the Railway Commissioners, 1881-2*, 28

9 S. Bates, *A Financial History of Canadian Governments*, 148

10 Ontario, *Sessional Papers*, 1880, no. 1, 221; 1882, no. 1, 236

11 See, for example, Désilets, *Hector-Louis Langevin*

12 H. Blair Neatby and John T. Saywell, 'Chapleau and the Conservative Party in Quebec,' *Canadian Historical Review*, vol. 37 (March, 1956), 5

13 M. Hamelin, *Les Premières Années du parlementarisme québécois*, 253

14 Quebec City's attitudes are explained more fully in F. Ouellet, *Histoire de la Chambre de Commerce de Québec*; Montreal *Gazette*, 30 July 1880

15 *L'Evénement*, 21 January 1878

16 Montreal *Gazette*, 15 December 1875

17 William Ryan, *The Clergy and Economic Growth in Quebec (1896-1914)*, 265

Bibliography

PRIMARY SOURCES

Manuscript collections

ARCHIVES OF THE ARCHBISHOP OF MONTREAL
  Letterbooks and financial records
ARCHIVES OF THE ARCHBISHOP OF QUEBEC
  Assorted correspondence and financial records
ARCHIVES OF THE CITY OF MONTREAL
  Map collection
  Minutes of Montreal City Council, 1870-2
ARCHIVES OF THE CITY OF QUEBEC
  North Shore Railway file
ARCHIVES OF THE DIOCESE OF TROIS-RIVIÈRES
  Assorted correspondence
ARCHIVES OF THE HISTORICAL SOCIETY OF MAINE
  John Alfred Poor Papers
ARCHIVES OF THE PROVINCE OF QUEBEC (APQ)
  Chapais Collection
  Joly de Lotbinière Collection
  Curé Labelle Collection
  Annual Reports of Quebec City Board of Trade, 1867-85
  Minutes of Quebec City Board of Trade, 1858-82
ARCHIVES OF THE SEMINARY OF QUEBEC (ASQ)
  Assorted correspondence
ARCHIVES OF THE UNIVERSITY OF QUEBEC AT TROIS-RIVIÈRES
  Nicolet Seminary Collection

ARCHIVES OF THE UNIVERSITY OF MONTREAL
Baby Collection
PUBLIC ARCHIVES OF CANADA (PAC)
Sydney R. Bellingham Memoirs
George Brown Papers
Department of Public Works, unnumbered correspondence, 1859-79, RG II, Series III, vol. 473, file on North Shore Railway, 1852
Alexander T. Galt Papers
John A. Macdonald Papers
Alexander Mackenzie Papers
John McLennan Papers
Gédéon Ouimet Papers

Newspapers

Le Canadien. October 1875-March 1876; June 1877-April 1879
Le Courrier du Canada. February 1857-December 1864; November 1867-December 1868; January 1870-January 1871; February 1875-January 1876
Ottawa *Daily Citizen.* January-February 1874
L'Evénement. May 1874-January 1878
Montreal *Gazette.* August 1869-July 1885
Toronto *Globe.* August 1851; September-October 1871
Montreal *Herald.* January 1871-May 1872
Le Journal de Québec. May-July 1869; September 1870-October 1875
Le Journal des Trois-Rivières. May 1867-October 1873
La Minerve. September 1850-December 1873; January-July 1878
Quebec *Morning Chronicle.* January 1878-February 1879
Le National. April-December 1872
Le Nouveau Monde. October-December 1871; *Le Monde.* November 1881-April 1882
Ottawa *Times.* October 1874-February 1875
True Witness. December 1871-June 1872

Government documents

CANADA, DOMINION OF. *Canada Year Book for 1872* (Ottawa)
- *House of Commons Debates,* 1867-72, 1877-85 (Ottawa)

- *Procédés du Comité Général du chemin de fer du Nord*, Department of Public Works, Series 3, vol. 473, North Shore Railway file (Ottawa, ND)
- *Rapports: statistiques des chemins de fer du Canada*, 1875-6, 1877-8, 1879-80, 1880-1, 1882-3, 1884-5 (Ottawa)
- *Report of the Select Committee on the Affairs of the Northern Railway and the Northern Extension Railway* (Ottawa, 1877)
- *Royal Commission on the Canadian Pacific Railway* (Ottawa, 1873)
- *Statutes of Canada*, 1874-85 (Ottawa)

CANADA, PROVINCE OF. *Census of Canada*, 1851 (Quebec, 1855)
- *Census of Canada*, 1861 (Quebec, 1863)
- *Debates of the Legislative Assembly and Legislative Council of Canada*, 1846, 1854-60
- *Proceedings of the Select Standing Committee on Railroads, Canals and Telegraph Lines* (Toronto, 1856)
- *Rapport du comité nommé pour s'enquérir des transactions de la compagnie du chemin de fer de Montréal et Bytown* (Toronto, 1856)
- *Sessional Papers of the Legislative Council*, 1852, Appendix z: Chemin de Fer de Québec et Halifax; 1853, Appendix xxx: Railway Suspension Bridge, Quebec; 1857, Appendix xii: Returns of the Banks of Canada; 1858, Appendix xv: Report of Survey on Canals, Montreal to Lake Huron
- *Statutes of Canada*, 1853-8

ONTARIO, PROVINCE OF. *Sessional Papers*, 1880, no. 1; 1882, no. 1

QUEBEC, PROVINCE OF. *Documents of the Session*, 1876, no. 1, 2, 19; 1877-8, no. 11; 1878, no. 9; 1880, no. 2; 1885, no. 27, 80; 1889, no. 13; 1893, no. 51
- *Journals of the Legislative Assembly of Quebec*, 1867-85
- *Journals of the Legislative Council of Quebec*, 1867-75
- *Rapport du commissaire des chemins de fer*, 1881-2, 1885-6
- *Revised Statutes of the Province of Quebec* (1888)
- *Royal Commission concerning the Quebec, Montreal, Ottawa and Occidental Railway* (1887)
- *Sessional Papers*, 1875, vol. 9, no. 11
- *Supplement to the Revised Statutes of the Province of Quebec* (1889)

OTHER SOURCES

ADLER, DOROTHY R. *British Investment in American Railways, 1834-1898.* Charlottesville: University Press of Virginia, 1970

ALLAN, HUGH. *The 'Times' and its Correspondents on Canadian Railways: The Montreal Northern Colonization Railway Company*. London: Whitehead, Morris and Lowe, 1875

ANGERS, A.R. *Discours de l'Hon. Solliciteur-Général Angers exposant la politique du gouvernement relative à la construction d'un chemin de fer provincial sur la rive nord du Saint-Laurent*. Quebec: Le Canadien, 1875

ATHERTON, WILLIAM H. *Montreal from 1535 to 1914*, vols. II and III. Montreal: S.J. Clarke Publishing, 1914

AUCLAIR, ELIE J. *Le Curé Labelle: sa vie et son oeuvre*. Montreal: Librairie Beauchemin, 1930

BAKER, GEORGE PIERCE. *The Formation of the New England Railroad Systems*. New York: Greenwood Press, 1968 (1937)

BATES, S. *A Financial History of Canadian Governments*. Ottawa: Kings Printer, 1939

BEAUBIEN, LOUIS. *The Pacific Railway and its Eastern Connection*. Montreal: Gazette Printing House, 1875

BENSON, LEE. *Merchants, Farmers, and Railroads: Railroad Regulation and New York Politics, 1850-1867*. New York: Russell and Russell, 1955

BERNARD, JEAN-PAUL. *Les Rouges, libéralisme, nationalisme et anticléricalisme au milieu du XIXe siècle*. Montreal: Les Presses de l'université du Québec, 1971

BERTON, PIERRE. *The National Dream*. Toronto: McClelland and Stewart, 1971

BOND, C.C.J. 'Tracks into Ottawa: The Construction of Railways into Canada's Capital,' *Ontario History*, LVII (September, 1965)

BONIN, BERNARD. *L'Investissement étranger à long terme au Canada*. Montreal: Les Presses de l'Ecole des Hautes Etudes Commerciales de Montréal, 1967

BORTHWICK, REV. J. DOUGLAS. *History of Montreal including the Streets of Montreal*. Montreal: D. Gallagher, 1897

BOUCHARD, GÉRARD. 'Apogée et déclin de l'idéologie ultramontaine à travers le journal *le Nouveau Monde* 1867-1900,' *Recherches Sociographiques*, X, no. 2-3 (1969)

BOURASSA, GUY. 'Les élites politiques de Montréal: de l'aristocratie à la démocratie,' *Canadian Journal of Economics and Political Science* (February, 1965)

BRUNET, MICHEL. *Québec: Canada Anglais*. Montreal: HMH, 1968

CALLOW, ALEXANDER B. (ed.). *American Urban History: An Interpretative Reader with Commentaries*. New York: Oxford University Press, 1969

CARELESS, J.M.S. *The Union of the Canadas*. Toronto: McClelland and Stewart, 1967

CHANDLER, ALFRED D. *The Railroads: The Nation's First Big Business*. New York: Harcourt, Brace, 1965

Charter for the Construction of the Pacific Railway with Papers and Correspondence. Ottawa: I.B. Taylor, 1873

Chemin de fer de Québec, Montréal, Ottawa et Occidental: clauses générales. Quebec: NP, 1879

Chemin de fer Transcontinental National: ressources du pays de Québec à Winnipeg le long de la ligne du Grand Trunk Pacific Railway. Ottawa: S.E. Dawson, 1903

COCHRAN, T.C., and WILLIAM MILLER. *The Age of Enterprise.* New York: Harper Torchbooks, 1942

COCHRAN, THOMAS C. *Railroad Leaders 1845-1890: The Business Mind in Action.* New York: Russell and Russell, 1965

COMEAU, R. (ed.). *Economie québécoise.* Montreal: Les presses de l'université du Québec, 1969

COOPER, JOHN I. 'French-Canadian Conservatism in Principle and in Practice: 1873-1891' (PH D Thesis, McGill University, 1938)

– *Montreal: A Brief History.* Montreal: McGill-Queen's University Press, 1969

COOTNER, PAUL. 'The Economic Impact of the Railroad Innovation,' in B. Mazlish, ed., *The Railroad and Space Program: An Explanation in Historical Analogy.* Cambridge, Mass.: MIT Press (1963)

CREIGHTON, DONALD. *The Empire of the St. Lawrence.* Toronto: Macmillan, 1956

– *John A. Macdonald: The Young Politician.* Toronto: Macmillan, 1952

– *John A. Macdonald: The Old Chieftain.* Toronto: Macmillan, 1955

CURRIE, A.W. 'British Attitudes toward Investment in North American Railroads,' *Business History Review,* XXXIV, no. 2 (1961)

– *The Grand Trunk Railway of Canada.* Toronto: University of Toronto Press, 1957

DAWSON, S.E. *Semi-Centennial Report of the Montreal Board of Trade.* Montreal: Gazette Printing Company, 1893

DECHÊNE, LOUISE. 'Les entreprises de William Price,' *Social History,* I (April, 1968)

DENISON, MERRILL. *Canada's First Bank,* vols. 1-2. Toronto: McClelland and Stewart, 1967

DÉSILETS, ANDRÉE. *Hector-Louis Langevin: un père de la confédération canadienne.* Quebec: Laval University Press, 1969

– 'La Succession de Cartier, 1873-1891,' *Historical Papers of the Canadian Historical Association* (1968)

DESLISLE, A.M. *Railroad Between Quebec, Montreal, Bytown and Georgian Bay: Great Public Demonstration.* Montreal: W. Salter and Co., 1853

DORMAN, ROBERT (ed.). *A Statutory History of the Steam and Electric Railways of Canada, 1836–1937*. Ottawa: King's Printer, 1938

EADIE, JAMES. 'Edward Wilkes Rathbun and the Napanee Tamworth and Quebec Railway,' *Ontario History*, LXIII, no. 2 (June, 1971)

EASTERBROOK, W.T., and HUGH G.J. AITKEN. *Canadian Economic History*. Toronto: Macmillan, 1956

EVANS, D.M. *The History of the Commercial Crisis 1857–1858, and the Stock Exchange Panic of 1859*. London: Groombridge and Sons, 1859

FAUCHER, ALBERT. *Histoire économique et unité canadienne*. Montreal: Fides, 1970

– 'Le fonds d'emprunt municipal dans le Haut-Canada 1852–1867,' *Recherches Sociographiques*, I, no. 1 (January-March, 1960)

– *Québec en Amérique au XIXe siècle*. Montreal: Fides, 1973

FIELD, FRED W. *Capital Investments in Canada*. Montreal: Monetary Times of Canada, 1911

FISHLOW, ALBERT. *American Railroads and the Transformation of the Ante-Bellum Economy*. Cambridge, Mass.: Harvard University Press, 1965

FOGEL, ROBERT WILLIAM. *Railroads and American Economic Growth: Essays in Economic History*. Baltimore: Johns Hopkins Press, 1964

FULFORD, ROGER. *Glyn's: 1753–1953*. London: Macmillan, 1953

Further Correspondence Relative to the Projected Railway from Halifax to Quebec. London: NP, 1852

GILMOUR, JAMES M. 'Structural and Spatial Change in Manufacturing Industry: South Ontario, 1850–1890,' (PHD Thesis, University of Toronto, 1970)

GLAZEBROOK, G.P. DE T. *A History of Transportation in Canada*. Toronto: Ryerson, 1938

GOLDBERG, SIMON A. 'The French-Canadians and the Industrialization of Quebec' (MA Thesis, McGill University, 1940)

Grand Trunk Railway: Correspondence between the Company and the Dominion Government respecting advances to the Canadian Pacific Railway Company. NP, ND

GREENING, W.E. 'The Lumber Industry in the Ottawa Valley and the American Market in the Nineteenth Century,' *Ontario History*, vol. 62, no. 2 (June, 1970)

GREGORY, FRANCES W., and IRENE D. NEU. 'The American Industrial Elite in the 1870's: Their Social Origins,' in W. Miller, ed., *Men in Business*. New York: Harper Torchbook, 1952

GRESSLEY, GENE M. *Bankers and Gentlemen*. New York: Knopf, 1966

GRODINSKY, JULIUS. *Transcontinental Railway Strategy, 1869–83: A Study of Businessmen*. London: University of Pennsylvania Press, 1961

HALPENNY, FRANCESS G. (ed.). *Dictionary of Canadian Biography*, vols. 9, 10. Toronto: University of Toronto Press, 1972, 1976

HAMELIN, J., and Y. ROBY. *Histoire économique du Québec: 1851–1896*. Montreal: Fides, 1971

HAMELIN, MARCEL. *Les Premières Années du parlementarisme québécois (1867 1878)*. Quebec: Les Presses de l'Université Laval, 1974

HIDY, RALPH W. *The House of Baring in American Trade and Finance*. Cambridge: Harvard University Press, 1949

INNIS, HAROLD A. *A History of the Canadian Pacific Railway*. Toronto: University of Toronto Press, 1971 (1923)

IRWIN, LEONARD B. *Pacific Railways and Nationalism in the Canadian-American Northwest, 1845–1873*. Philadelphia: University of Pennsylvania, 1939

JENKS, LELAND H. *The Migration of British Capital to 1875*. New York: Knopf, 1927

KEEFER, THOMAS. *Philosophy of Railroads*. Ottawa: Bell and Woodburn, 1871 (1849); (reprint ed., Toronto: University of Toronto Press, 1972)

KIRKLAND, EDWARD CHASE. *Dream and Thought in the American Business Community*. Chicago: Quadrangle, 1964 (1956)

– *Industry Comes of Age: Business, Labor and Public Policy, 1860–1897*, Chicago: Quadrangle, 1961

KLASSEN, HENRY C. 'L.H. Holton: Montreal Businessman and Politician 1817–1867' (PHD Thesis, University of Toronto, 1970)

KLEINER, GEORGE. 'Capital Accumulation in Canada since Confederation' (MA Thesis, McGill University, 1937)

KOLKO, GABRIEL. 'Brahmins and Business, 1870–1914: A Hypothesis on the Social Basis of Success in American History,' in K.H. Wolff and B. Moore, ed., *The Critical Spirit*. Boston: Beacon, 1967

– *Railroads and Regulation 1877–1916*. New York: Norton, 1965

LANGELIER, J.C. *La nécessité et la possibilité d'un chemin de fer au Lac St-Jean*. Quebec: L.H. Huot, 1873

LAPIERRE, LAURIER. 'Politics, Race and Religion in French Canada: Joseph Israel Tarte' (PHD Thesis, University of Toronto, 1962)

LEGGE, CHARLES. *Report on Proposed Railway Bridge over the River St. Lawrence, Coteau to Valleyfield and Rail Connection of the Ottawa Valley with the New England States*. Montreal: Herald Steam Press, 1873

LEVITT, JOSEPH. 'The Social Program of the Nationalists of Quebec, 1900–1914' (PHD Thesis, University of Toronto, 1967)

LONGLEY, R.S. *Sir Francis Hincks: A Study of Canadian Politics, Railways and Finance in the Nineteenth Century*. Toronto: 1943

LOWER, A.R.M. *Settlement and the Forest Frontier in Eastern Canada.* Toronto: Macmillan, 1936

- 'The Trade in Square Timber,' in W.T. Easterbrook and M.H. Watkins, ed., *Approaches to Canadian Economic History*, Carleton Library ed. Toronto: McClelland and Stewart

Mandements, lettres pastorales, circulaires et autres documents, vol. III, IV, and V. Montreal: J.A. Plinguet, 1887

Mandements, lettres pastorales et circulaires des évêques de Québec, vol. I, IV, and V. Quebec: NP, 1889

MARX, LEO. *The Machine in the Garden.* New York: Oxford, 1964

MASSIAH, CHRIS (ed.). *The Quebec Railway Statutes.* Quebec: A. Coté, 1883

MASSON, HENRI. *Joseph Masson: dernier seigneur de Terrebonne.* Montreal: published by author, 1972

MAXWELL, J.A. *Federal Subsidies to the Provincial Governments in Canada.* Cambridge: Harvard University Press, 1937

MCLEAN, SIMON J. 'The Railway Policy of Canada, 1849–1867,' *Journal of Political Economy*, IX, no. 2 (March, 1901)

MCLOSKEY, ROBERT G. *American Conservatism in the Age of Enterprise: 1865–1910.* New York: Harper Torchbook, 1951

MEMMI, ALBERT. *The Colonizer and the Colonized.* Boston: Bacon Press, 1967 (1957)

On the Military and Commercial Importance of Completing the Line of Railway from Halifax to Quebec. London: William Penny, 1862

MONTIGNY, B.A.T. DE. *La Colonisation: le nord de Montréal ou la région Labelle.* Montreal: Beauchemin, 1895

Montreal Directory. Montreal: John Lovell, 1870–1, 1872, 1875

Montreal: Northern Colonization Railway – Yea or Nay? NP, 1873

MORTON, ARTHUR S. *Sir George Simpson: Overseas Governor of the Hudson's Bay Company.* Toronto: J.M. Dent, 1944

MYERS, GUSTAVUS. *History of Canadian Wealth.* Chicago: Charles H. Keer, 1914

NAYLOR, TOM. *The History of Canadian Business, 1867–1914*, vols. 1, 2. Toronto: James Lorimer, 1975

NEATBY, BLAIR H., and JOHN T. SAYWELL. 'Chapleau and the Conservative Party in Quebec,' *Canadian Historical Review*, 37 (March, 1956)

NELLES, H.V. *The Politics of Development: Forests, Mines and Hydro-Electric Power in Ontario, 1849–1941.* Toronto: Macmillan, 1974

NERVA (pseud. for SAMUEL GALE). *Railways and Repudiation.* Montreal: Montreal Herald, 1855

The North Shore Railway: Its Legal and Financial Basis. Quebec: Leger Brousseau, 1870

The Ogilvies of Montreal with a Geneological Account of the Descendants of their Grandfather, Archibald Ogilvie. Montreal: Gazette Printers, 1904

OUELLET, FERNAND. *Histoire de la Chambre de Commerce de Québec.* Quebec: Laval University Press, 1959

- *Histoire économique et sociale du Québec,* 1760-1850. Montreal: Fides, 1966
- 'Lettres de Joseph-Adolphe Chapleau (1870-1896),' *Rapport de l'Archiviste de la Province de Québec (1959-1960)*

PENTLAND, H.C. 'The Role of Capital in Canadian Economic Development before 1875,' *Canadian Journal of Economics and Political Science,* XVI, no. 4 (November, 1950)

Petition and Other Documents Showing the Nullity of the By-Law of the City of Montreal, No. 59, authorizing Subscription for $1,000,000 Stock, and of the Act of the Quebec Legislature ... Montreal: Herald Steam Press, 1873

POULIOT, LÉON. *Monseigneur Bourget et son Temps,* vol. 3. Montreal: Bellarmin, 1972

The Province of Quebec and European Immigration. Quebec: L'Evénement, 1870

Procédés du Comité général du chemin de fer national. Quebec: Augustin Côté 1882

Quelques notes sur la vente du chemin de fer. Quebec: NP, 1882

Une Question de véracité: correspondance entre Sir Hector Langevin, M. George Stephen, président du Pacifique et M.L.A. Sénécal, président du Chemin de Fer du Nord, sur l'achat du Chemin de Fer du Nord. NP, ND

The Railway Interests of the City of Montreal: submitted for the Consideration of the Merchants of this City. Montreal: Gazette Printing House, 1872

Rapport concernant le Chemin de Fer de Québec, Montréal, Ottawa et Occidental. Quebec: Langlois, 1881

Reports of the Chief Engineer on the Survey of the North Shore Railway of the Directors on the Proper Resources of the Same. Quebec: Augustin Côté, 1854

RICH, E.E. *Hudson's Bay Company: 1670-1870,* vol. 3. Toronto: McClelland and Stewart, 1960

ROGERS, JOHN S. 'The Philosophical and Literary Background of French-Canadian Nationalism (Garneau to Groulx)' (MA Thesis, University of Western Ontario, 1958)

RUMILLY, ROBERT. *L'Histoire de la Province de Québec,* vols. I, II, III, IV. Montreal: Fides, 1940

RUSSELL, PETER. *Nationalism in Canada.* Toronto: McGraw Hill, 1966

RYAN, WILLIAM F. *The Clergy and Economic Growth in Quebec (1896-1914).* Quebec: Laval University Press, 1966

SANDWELL, B.K. *The Molson Family.* Montreal: privately published, 1933

178 Bibliography

SAYWELL, JOHN T. *The Office of Lieutenant-Governor*. Toronto: University of Toronto Press, 1957

SCHULL, JOSEPH. *100 Years of Banking in Canada: The Toronto Dominion Bank*. Toronto: Copp Clark, 1958

SEYMOUR, SILAS. *The Railway Policy of the Government of Quebec*. Boston: NP, 1878

- *Report in Relation to the Past History, Present Condition and Future Prospects of the North Shore Railway of Canada*. Quebec: Augustin Côté, 1872

SHANLY, WALTER. *Rapport au sujet de l'affaire Duncan Macdonald entrepreneur de la section ouest du Chemin Q.M.O. et O. et le gouvernement de la province de Québec*. Quebec: NP, 1879

SHARKEY, ROBERT P. *Money, Class, and Party: An Economic Study of the Civil War and Reconstruction*. Baltimore: Johns Hopkins Press, 1959

SHEA, PHILIP E. 'Electoral Practices in Quebec, 1867–1882,' (MA Thesis, McGill University, 1968)

SKELTON, O.D. *Life and Times of Sir Alexander Tilloch Galt*. Toronto: McClelland and Stewart, 1966 (1920)

- *The Railway Builders*. Toronto and Glasgow: Brook and Co., 1916

SMITH, HENRY NASH. *Virgin Land: The American West as Symbol and Myth*. New York: Vintage, 1950

Statements, Reports and Accounts of the Grand Trunk Railway in Canada. Toronto: NP, 1857

Statutes and Enactments Concerning Railways Having Reference to the North Shore Railway of the Province of Quebec. Quebec: A. Côté, 1872

STEVENS, G.R. *The Canadian National Railways*, vol. 1. Toronto: Clarke, Irwin and Co., 1960

The St. Maurice Territory: Being Extracts from the Montreal Commercial Advertiser and Three Rivers Enquirer. Montreal: Salter and Ross, 1858

TASSÉ, HÉLÈNE. 'Le Curé Labelle et la région Labelle, 1879–1891' (MA Thesis, University of Ottawa, 1965)

THOMAS, DALE. *Alexander Mackenzie: Clear Grit*. Toronto: Macmillan, 1960

TROUT, J.M. and EDWARD. *The Railways of Canada for 1870–1871 showing the progress ... of the Railways of the Dominion*. Toronto: Monetary Times, 1871

TULCHINSKY, GERALD. *The River Barons: Montreal Businessmen and the Growth of Industry and Transportation, 1837–1853*. Toronto: University of Toronto Press, 1977

WAITE, P.B. *Arduous Destiny*. Toronto: McClelland and Stewart, 1971

WATKIN, E.W. *Canada and the States: Recollections 1851 to 1886*. London: Ward, Lock and Col., 1887

WHITE, THOMAS. *The Protestant Minority in Quebec in its Political Relations with the Roman Catholic Majority.* Montreal: Dawson Bros., 1876

WILLIAMS, FRED. 'The Story of an Early Railway,' *Globe and Mail,* 19 July 1937

YOUNG, BRIAN J. 'The Defeat of George-Etienne Cartier in Montreal-East in 1872,' *Canadian Historical Review,* vol. LI, no. 4 (December, 1970)

YOUNG, JOHN. *The North Shore Railway: A Brief Sketch of its Commercial Relations and Financial Prospects.* Montreal: NP, 1872

Index

Quebec Notre Dame Savings Bank 56
Quebec, provincial government
- finances of xi, 86-7, 90, 97-9, 110,
  112-13, 120, 135, 140
- and municipalities 38, 86-7 (see
  also Montreal, municipal subsidies,
  Quebec City)
- provincial treasurer 78, 82, 88 (see
  also Ruggles Church,
  J.G. Robertson)
- and railway commission 89-90, 103
- railway legislation 60-2, 70, 72,
  83, 141 (see also Montreal Colonization Railway, North Shore
  Railway, QMO&O)
- subservient to Ottawa 25, 60, 76
Quebec Railway Act, 1869 25
Quebec Warehousing Company 56
Le Quotidien 131

reciprocity treaty 6
Redpath, Peter 78
Reekie, Robert J. 30, 48, 151n
Renaud, Jean-Baptiste 18, 55, 56, 58,
  68, 118, 162n, 163n
repatriation of French Canadians (see
  colonization)
Rhodes, Colonel William 8, 16, 55,
  56, 58, 68, 72, 102
Richelieu, Drummond and Arthabasca
  Railway 113
Richelieu Navigation Company 47, 48
Richelieu and Ontario Navigation
  Company 42, 126, 132
Richmond, Quebec 7
Ridley, J.J. 127
Ridout, Thomas Gibbs 19
Rimouski and Gaspé Railway 36
Rivard, Sévère 122, 128, 130
Rivière du Loup 7

Rivière des Mille-Isles 49
Rivière des Prairies 49, 104
Roberge, Ludger 117, 118, 119
Robertson, Andrew 143
Robertson, Joseph Gibb 70, 72, 103,
  116, 154n
- allied to ultramontanes 115, 125,
  132, 142
- attacks contractors and labourers
  90, 92
- provincial treasurer and railway
  executive 73
- resignation of 82-5, 89
Robitaille, Olivier 18
Rodden, William 28, 40, 44
Rodier, Charles-Séraphin 51, 82
Roman Catholic Church xii, 11, 16,
  31-7, 62-3, 65, 97, 143 (see also
  archbishop of Quebec, Bishop
  Bourget, Castors, colonization,
  Labelle, ultramontanism,
  programme catholique)
Rose, John 68
Ross, James Gibb 68, 127, 163n
Ross, John Jones 19, 25, 55, 63, 125,
  127, 132, 135, 142
Rouges xiii (see also Liberal Party in
  Quebec)
Routhier Commission 117
Royal Albert Bridge 78, 85, 96
Russell county 28, 36
Russell's Hotel 56
Russell, Willis 55, 58, 63, 68
Ryan, Michael 40, 79
Ryan, Thomas 40
Ryan, William 35

Saguenay and Lake St. John Railway
  36
Ste. Adèle 28, 29